AMERICA IN LITERATURE

The Northeast

AMERICA IN LITERATURE

General Editor, Max Bogart

The Northeast, James Lape, editor
The South, Sara Marshall, editor
The West, Peter Monahan, editor
The Midwest, Ronald Szymanski, editor
The Small Town, Flory Jones Schultheiss, editor
The City, Adele Stern, editor

AMERICA IN LITERATURE

The Northeast

EDITED BY

James Lape

Head of Secondary English (Retired, 1977)
Lexington Schools
Lexington, Massachusetts

CHARLES SCRIBNER'S SONS · NEW YORK

To Elizabeth Lape,
without whose help in every step of the process,
this book could not have been completed.

Library of Congress Cataloging in Publication Data
Main entry under title:
America in literature: the Northeast.
  Includes index.
  1. American literature—New England.
I. Lape, James T.
PS541.A64   809' .9'74   78-25617
ISBN 0-684-16063-3

1 3 5 7 9 11 13 15 17 19   V/P   20 18 16 14 12 10 8 6 4 2

Printed in the United States of America

Cover Illustration: "Breezing Up" by Winslow Homer. Courtesy of the National Gallery of Art, Washington. Gift of the W. L. and May T. Mellon Foundation.

Picture Research: Yvonne Freund

ACKNOWLEDGMENTS

MAUREEN HOWARD, "Sweet Memories." Copyright © 1975, 1978 by Maureen Howard. From *Facts of Life* by Maureen Howard, by permission of Little, Brown and Co.
RICHARD EBERHART, "Orchard." From *Collected Poems 1930–1976* by Richard Eberhart.
  Acknowledgments continue on page 276, an extension of the copyright page.

CONTENTS

AMERICA IN LITERATURE

The Northeast

Introduction

Literature of the Northeast, for the purposes of this anthology, includes writing that is inspired by the culture and environment of New England. The works of three kinds of authors have been included: (1) writers born in New England who have made it their residence; (2) natives who have lived elsewhere but returned; (3) writers born elsewhere who have made New England home long enough to be influenced by the experience.

THE VARIETY OF NEW ENGLAND

What qualifies and distinguishes New England writing? One can begin to answer this fundamental question by considering the immense variety of the New England area, geographically, industrially, and culturally. Mountains, gentle hills, lakes, ponds, forest, cleared land, salt marshes, bays, the sand dunes on Cape Cod, and the great rocks of the Maine coast—all are within a short distance of each other. The weather also exhibits extremes of violence, temperature, and rapid change. As Charles Dudley Warner (New England writer and editor of the late 1800s) observed, "If you don't like the weather, wait a minute." Emerson's vision of nature in his essay *Nature,* May Sarton's "All Day I Was with Trees," E. B. White's reflections on Walden Pond, and Wallace Stevens' thoughts on "The River of Rivers in Connecticut" express views of the diverse New England scene.

Another evidence of variety within this small area is the multiple activities by which New Englanders earn their livelihood. Shipping, fishing, farming, industries of all kinds (from the now diminishing textile mills and shoe factories to the twentieth-century growth of electronic, plastic, and solar ventures), publishing, lumbering, and tourism are some of the important sources of employment. Gerald Brace's "Boats" and Donald Hall's "Blueberry Picking" reflect aspects of this diversity in New England life, both past and present.

From 1636 onward, universities and colleges have extended the educational opportunities of natives and have drawn increasing numbers of stu-

1

dents from other regions of the United States. With the schools have come museums, libraries, laboratories, concert halls, and theaters. Artists in all fields either have been nurtured or oppressed, according to their temperaments, by the New England experience. Emily Dickinson's life as a recluse (1830–1886), for example, may be attributed, at least in part, to the pressures of her Puritan inheritance as well as to the rejection of her poems by critics doubtful of untraditional writing. On the other hand, Ralph Waldo Emerson and Margaret Fuller, to mention only two, found in *The Dial* magazine (1840–1844) a medium for freely developing ideas about literature, philosophy, and religion.

From the vantage point of the late twentieth century, one can discover a common ground for these tremendous differences in the ideas and life styles of New Englanders. This common ground was a shared heritage. When New England was settled in the seventeenth century, the variety in landscape existed. But the Puritans traveled here (in the 1620s and 1630s) with one unswerving purpose: they believed that they were God's chosen few, put here to challenge the authority of the Established Church of England. They were not fighting the cause of all oppressed people, but rather they wanted to lead the whole Christian world to accept their one true faith. When they were unable to reform the Established Church in England, they sought in this new land a fresh beginning, an opportunity to form communities to fulfill God's will.

Despite limitations on their creative energies, as they cleared the land and erected houses and planted crops, New Englanders produced the greatest literary output of any of the American colonists. Puritanism acted as a stimulus for writing in New England. The Puritan colonist often possessed lofty intellectual ambitions, a true desire for knowledge, and an available store of learning. By 1639 a printing press was established in Cambridge, Massachusetts. Governor Bradstreet (Massachusetts Bay Colony, in office 1679–1692) spoke several foreign languages and was well grounded in classical literature. John Winthrop (governor of Massachusetts in 1631) was a university man of learning and distinction. Later, Cotton Mather (1663–1728, scholar and minister) displayed his learning by writing nearly five hundred books and pamphlets. The Puritan clergymen were highly educated individuals who promoted the cause of learning in the wilderness. Before the middle of the century, Harvard College had been founded and free grammar schools had been established. The Harvard charter decreed that students should master a thorough knowledge of the classics, the Bible, medieval philosophy and art, as well as Renaissance studies. Like Bradford, Winthrop, and Mather, many had brought their precious Greek and Latin volumes with them; with every ship came more books for the colonists.

Besides such studies, the Puritan clergy needed a knowledge of law and government to make their contributions to the colony. They firmly believed that political ideals had their origin in the Bible and that the church and state must act as one. To further God's will in suppressing the human tendency toward wickedness, the Puritans felt that a firm control of congregations, towns, and communities was a necessity. As ideas of democratic government took shape, questions of the relationship between church and state became increasingly crucial. To advance their positions, the writers advocating unity of church and state and those championing separation used satire and logic to try to win support.

As time went on, other additions were made to this early Puritan literature in the form of arguments against absolute Puritan authority, glowing accounts of the New World (emigration tracts that were forerunners of modern travel agency propaganda), journals mirroring daily happenings and inner tensions of spirit, complete historical records, meditations, and sermons. Poetry, too, influenced by English and French writers, appeared. Two excellent poets, only recently recognized for the quality of their work, were Anne Bradstreet and Edward Taylor. From many points of view, the Puritan tradition gave American literature a sound and well-rounded beginning.

NEW ENGLAND PURITANISM

The Puritan heritage, however, involved more issues than the beginnings of an American literature. Certain "massive" traits of character formed an integral part of the Puritan heritage. The Puritans were the rebels of their century, true radicals who turned against the Establishment in religious practice. When they first came to New England, they believed that their stay would be only temporary; they would remain only until they had proved to the world the importance of their way of life. When Oliver Cromwell became Lord Protector of the Commonwealth of England in 1653, the Puritans fully expected to be welcomed again in England. They were largely ignored. When the Loyalists (the king's supporters) overthrew the Commonwealth and Charles II reigned, these colonists found themselves isolated. Then in the highest heroic tradition, they determined to set their independent course against all odds.

3

Introduction

From this historic turnabout New Englanders can trace their reliance upon their own inner resources. In the middle of the seventeenth century, Puritanism in Massachusetts was a way of life in which each person was charged with the responsibility of living in the world without being actually a part of it. The life of this world was corruptible, but the life of the spirit was regarded as incorruptible and enduring. The individual lived in time and place, and yet realized that these will not last. The Puritans had to strive daily to achieve a delicate balance between this world and the next. Often they faced an insoluble dilemma. Men and women were directed to seek salvation but remained helpless to do anything that was not evil. Each must place his or her entire faith in Christ; yet all knew that Christ would not receive them unless God had willed their salvation before they were born. People must refrain from sin; yet they must sin because they were human. Thus life for the Puritan became a series of irresolvable conflicts. How could anyone be himself in the face of predestination, as God's decision was called? Sensitive people like Edward Taylor and Anne Bradstreet struggled uneasily with the problem; in their poems today's readers can hear the repressed voices of the Puritan age.

The Puritan's dilemma may be compared to that of the hero of Greek tragedy. For the Greek hero, life consisted of a constant effort to live without disobeying the will of the gods. Fate could not be opposed without bringing harm upon oneself and one's family. Like the Greek, the Puritan felt helpless; yet each person had to struggle to make the best of life. The Puritans were aware of the supreme effort that must be expended in living. Their ideals were as great as their spirit. Since the individual could not be sure whether or not he was in God's favor or totally damned, each person acknowledged the obligation to be personally and socially pure, to oppose injustice, greed, political and religious corruption, lewdness, and any other kind of debasement of God's gifts. From this tension between the ideal and the real, between the demands of the spirit and the weakness of the flesh, the Puritan faced life with dignity and courage, as the Greek hero had.

The zeal of the early Puritans began to wane when various groups questioned the concept of God's absolute control over people. Ann Hutchinson (1591–1643) was one of the first to disagree, and others followed. At the same time in England, during the Commonwealth, innumerable dissenting sects arose as the pressure to conform to Puritanism in its more rigid form diminished. During the eighteenth century the autocratic hold of the church on the state likewise began to weaken. Jonathan Edwards

4

(1703–1758), renowned preacher and one of the most brilliant of the Puritans, perceived what was happening to the ancient relationship of church and state, but he could not stem the tide of dissent. Ultimately, he gave up his church.

Other influences encroached upon the Puritans' absolute faith in God. The eighteenth century, like our own, spawned revolution in religious, social, and political thought. As a whole new culture began to evolve, many attacks on traditional institutions weakened their influence. Interest in things of the spirit gave way to concern with affairs of the world. The study of how the world and nature function replaced the study of God. Since the Universe and God were one, the universe was now viewed as a harmonious whole. The notion of progress (that people would continue to improve themselves and the world) and of human happiness depended, it now seemed, upon the laws that govern the way nature operates and what makes people perform as they do. What a contrast to the old Puritan image of the miserable sinner unable to govern his own destiny was this new vision! This scientific approach to understanding life led to a recognition of people's inalienable rights, such as life and liberty. No government could take away these rights because government was created by the people and derived its powers from them. In these views, one can see the seeds of the ideas for our Declaration of Independence and our Constitution. But another scientific view caused some to think of the universe as a machine and people as merely a cog in it. One can readily imagine how greatly all these conflicting views diminished the influence of Puritanism.

The Puritans' shift in attitude toward the land brought about a change in their system of values. Originally, the Puritans valued the land as God's gift to use, improve, and return ultimately to its Maker. This view permitted the Puritans to seize land from the Indians who made little use of its potential. The Indians fought the usurpers and were driven westward or were contained in small areas. As the original purity of intention toward the land became tainted by greed, the Puritans frequently ignored the steps needed to preserve the fertility of the land. Exploitation replaced improvement. Although New England originally had adequate arable lands, many farms and pastures became exhausted. People abandoned the poverty they had created in the soil and sought the richer lands to the west. Today, throughout New England, one can see many cellar holes and stone walls, gaunt reminders of a forsaken heritage.

Other qualities of character also began to change. People gradually rejected the idea that they were hopeless sinners, for as individuals they perceived that they could conquer themselves and win redemption. They no longer believed that every disaster, whether personal or natural, was God's punishment for sin. They still felt a sense of guilt for their shortcomings, but they did not see themselves as sinful. They were still given to self-questioning, but increasingly this act became an effort to understand one's own true nature. They accepted the need to feel deeply and were not suspicious of staunchly held religious beliefs. Nature they could appreciate as a manifestation of God or as a part of human existence. In many ways, the individual's own world became of highest importance.

NEW ENGLAND TRAITS OF CHARACTER

This emphasis upon individualism prompted the development of a number of character traits often admired in the personalities of New Englanders. Among these traits was the inclination to be one's own person, to face unflinchingly the trials inflicted by the severities of nature and the exacting demands of life (such as facing life and death). Mary E. Wilkins Freeman's "A Churchmouse," in this anthology reflects aspects of this self-reliance. Other significant traits include a sense of integrity that leads people to trust the word of others, and an intense concern for the rights of everyone. Thoreau in "A Plea for Captain John Brown" shows this concern. There also exists a compassion that assures a human regard for the troubles of one's neighbor as seen in "Going to Shrewsbury" by Sarah Orne Jewett. Most particularly there appears an ability to make practical, sound judgments about life and business, as in Melville's "The Lightning-Rod Man." Some people had insights into the contradictions and absurdities of existence, as in Edwin Arlington Robinson's "Mr. Flood's Party" and Louise Bogan's "Women." Others possessed a sense of life's mission that persuades a few to make heroic efforts to realize an idea, as for example, in Nathaniel Hawthorne's "The Gray Champion." There were those also who displayed a cynicism that prompted doubts that ideals were worth the effort. Many questioned the value of experience as in Richard Wilbur's "The Writer" and Robert Lowell's "Grandparents." In varying degrees, all these dominant New England traits stem from Puritan origins.

Not least among these characteristics was the New Englander's preoccupation—one might almost say, obsession—with nature. Of course this trait does not belong exclusively to New Englanders. It has, however, a unique manifestation in New England, one that arises because one could find religious faith by appreciating the wonders of nature. Recall that to the Puritan, anything in nature, good or bad, might be God's way of making evident His will. A drought would be interpreted as punishment for sin. The beauty of a sunset, on the other hand, praised His glory. As faith diminished and new points of view gained strength, awareness of nature assumed a changed role. The poets William Jennings Bryant (1794–1878) and Ralph Waldo Emerson (1803–1882) for example, could appreciate nature's beauties without fear of being sinful in enjoying physical sensations. They could continue to view natural phenomena as evidences of God's presence while still enjoying the color of leaves, the sound of a stream, or the odor of flowers. Henry David Thoreau (1817–1862) could rely on his observation of nature as a guide to important principles of living. The varieties of landscape and the extremes of climate still fascinate writers as purely sensual experience, as in John Updike's story, "Man and Daughter in the Cold." Others find an indication of a force that transcends the splendor of the sea, the forest, the lakes, or the mountains; for example, look at Henry Beston's evocative description, "Night on the Great Beach."

The landscape also was instrumental in establishing the quality of life in New England. The early Puritans, natives of England's temperate climate and cultivated fields, confronted forests, gigantic boulders and rocks, untilled soil, and unplumbed water supplies. They faced the many challenges of "wrenching their living from a grudging soil" as well as those provided by a climate marked by drastic extremes. The effect on traits of character was significant. Under pioneer conditions, life in New England demanded physical work, practicality, shrewdness, and stamina. The facts of life transformed the most idealistic into strong realists. People were forced to lead frugal lives; they even became sparing of their speech, except for lengthy discussions of religious doctrines. This economy of speech characterizes Emily Dickinson's poetry. They became noted for a pithy, ironic sense of humor, a quality still apparent among the natives in many regions of Vermont, New Hampshire, and Maine. Edith Wharton's eerie story "Bewitched" exhibits traces of this concise speech and understated humor.

REBELLION AND REFORM

Even when Puritan authority waned, Puritan influences exerted an almost hypnotic force. Rebellion against social, literary, or religious views marked the work of Thoreau, Dickinson, and Melville. Austerity, denial of the demands of the body, self-renunciation, introspection, preoccupation

Edward Hopper, *Lighthouse at Two Lights*

with the power of evil—all these traits, in varying forms and in different degrees of intensity, show up in the literature and art of New England.

Meanwhile other forces were reinterpreting and redirecting New England's heritage of Puritan concepts. In the late eighteenth century, a movement now known as Unitarianism developed the idea that people and the environment could be perfected. This new emphasis upon human perfectibility made reform movements morally necessary, for it pointed to a direction that all religious groups could accept. From the Unitarian movement resulted such programs as more liberal land policies and currency reforms. Women's rights found advocates among liberal thinkers who acknowledged Margaret Fuller (notably in her tract, "Woman in the Nineteenth Century," 1845) as spokesperson. Also by 1845, an organized temperance movement had begun. But the reform that exerted the deepest influence was the Abolitionist Movement (1831–1860), as antislavery leaders described it. The purpose of the movement was to abolish slavery by one means or another. Among New England writers John Greenleaf Whittier and James Russell Lowell, to mention only two, used their writing skill and energies to forward the antislavery cause.

Unfortunately, the Puritan tradition in New England developed a seamy as well as an admirable side. As the intensity of belief declined before the close of the eighteenth century, certain negative aspects of Puritanism, such as pettiness, hypocrisy, and a narrowness of moral outlook increased. These negative aspects also concerned New England writers. Constance Carrier's poem about her Salem ancestor, "Martha Carrier, 1669–1692," although concerned with an earlier manifestation of Puritanism, the terrible witch hunts of the seventeenth century, also reveals the power of blind dogmatism. Other writers, as early as Nathaniel Hawthorne or as contemporary as Robert Frost, reacted strongly to the tensions created by the contrasting qualities of breadth of vision and narrowness of outlook in the New England character.

THE DEVELOPMENT OF A LITERATURE

Jonathan Edwards' strenuous contributions to literature ended in 1758. An interval of relative inactivity in writing followed. As Puritan concepts diminished in authority, other important ideas influenced New England writers. One of these ideas, rationalism, taught that people can reason their way to faith and knowledge. Another, mysticism, stressed that people can understand the world through intuition. A third idea, humanitarianism, expressed concern for the well being of all people. Concepts such as these made thinkers and writers in Concord, Cambridge, and Boston open to experiment, reform, and concern for humanity. James Russell Lowell (1819–1891), a noted Abolitionist and scholar, wrote poetry, criticism, and essays. He attempted in his witty poems and essays to destroy generally accepted nineteenth-century illusions about self-cures, and he attacked such Calvinistic ideas as predestination. For many years Henry Wadsworth Longfellow's (1807–1882) poetry attracted the largest audience of any American poet. Historians, too, enriched the Boston literary scene with their vivid re-creations of the past—Francis Parkman (1823–1893), John Lothrop Motley (1814–1877), and William Hickling Prescott (1796–1859). In Salem, Nathaniel Hawthorne (1804–1864), the greatest American artist of Puritan ancestry, wrote with the strong ethical sense of his ancestors, but reacted against the negativism of the Puritan. Only a writer engrained in the Puritan tradition could have probed so deeply the nature of evil. In Concord, both Ralph Waldo Emerson and Henry David Thoreau distinguished themselves as authors. Interested in Oriental literature and in nature, they found many areas of common ground in their thinking and writing. So far-reaching was the influence of these writers upon American letters that the period became known as the "New England Renaissance" or the "Golden Age in Literature."

An important development in the thinking of some New England writers became known as transcendentalism. Definition of this so-called movement is difficult because the term took on different meanings for different groups. Many sources of transcendentalism contributed to its usefulness for writers, particularly Emerson and Thoreau. German philosophers and authors, English writers of the Romantic period, ancient Greek philosophers, Chinese, Mohammedans, and Buddhists gave the transcendentalist ideas. Essentially, transcendentalism stressed peoples' ability to receive divine inspiration or insight into God's being directly from the whole of nature, referred to as the *oversoul*, because the individual was connected to the soul of the universe. In other words, a person's insight went beyond the limits of, or *transcended*, what his senses told him because intuition and feelings were more accurate than any other means of acquiring spiritual insight. Emerson maintained that every person is a poet, whose inner vision must stem from his feelings. From this concentration on the reliability of the individual's inner sense arose such Emersonian views as self-reliance and the importance of nature in stimulating intuition. Thoreau's stress upon human independence and inborn nobility also was derived from this concept. Thus, in ways perhaps not foreseen by Bronson Alcott and the other idealists who set up Fruitlands, Brook Farm, and other utopias, the New England traits of independence, reliance on self, and a deep regard for nature were fostered.

When the Civil War ended in 1865, people tended to leave off their ideals and act with a diminished moral sense. Corruption spread. Business and industry expanded rapidly. Speculation was rampant, and the exploitation of the West continued. The Gold Rush emphasized that an age of materialism had arrived. Much of the literature of the post-Civil War period reflected moral indignation and exposed corrupt practices: *The Gilded Age, A Tale of Today,* by Mark Twain and Charles Dudley Warner, is an example. Labor disputes became more frequent, and farmers were beset by depression. Yet through all this gloom shone the light of a hopeful and growing nation. In New England the theater and music attracted widespread support; schools and colleges increased in number; under Carnegie grants, libraries flourished. New England writers turned toward realism (an attitude of telling it as it is), yet without forsaking romance and sentiment. The interest in the West encouraged descriptions of particular regions in America and became known as the local color movement. Mary E. Wilkins Freeman and Sarah Orne Jewett focused upon life in New England. Winston Churchill (of New Hampshire, not the British leader) wrote fiction of escape which dealt with the Revolutionary War in terms of historical or "costume" romance.

Discoveries in science, like Darwin's *On the Origins of the Species by Means of Natural Selection* (1859), emphasized the powerful forces of inheritance and environment. This concept, linked with democratic views, tended to dethrone the heroes of old. Writing had never focused more closely on life. William Dean Howells dealt with divorce in *A Modern Instance* when the word was almost unmentionable; he also studied the character of the modern businessman in *The Rise of Silas Lapham.* Henry James, too, pointed out the contrasting virtues and vices in American and European society. Although her voice was not heard by her contemporaries, Emily Dickinson's poetry cut through whatever was hypocritical and pretentious.

After the turn of the twentieth century, the literature of New England responded to the dynamic forces at work in the world at large. Two catastrophic world wars and several devastating minor ones, uneasy peace in the intervals between, threats of new wars and nuclear annihilation, and the variety of realignments between people and state (as in communism, fascism, and democracy) have afforded writers almost too much action. The twentieth century has also provided extensive data for the study of the subconscious—peoples' motives and dreams have yielded, through the insights of modern day psychiatrists such as Freud, Jung, and their disciples, tremendous areas of the mind hitherto unexplored except intuitively by gifted writers such as Shakespeare.

RECURRING THEMES

From this consideration of the influences at work on New England writers, one can perceive certain themes that help classify their experiences. One of these themes is *Root Images*. The selections grouped under this heading focus upon the character of the people, the land and climate, or the pressures of circumstances. There is also an examination of the impact of experiences that influence a person to become or act or that reveal why he wants to remember times and places of the past.

In *Civilization Versus Wilderness* the selections concentrate on expressing the possibilities of the wilderness for restoring one's self, for getting away from the press of affairs, for absorbing nature's beauties, and for communing with whatever life force one believes in. Yet conversely, people may become savages if they remain isolated too long. People often want the benefits of both society and the wilderness, but as soon as they arrive in a wilderness, they begin to tame it to their needs. Early in the history of our country, many talked of "a civilized wilderness." Tensions arise in determining where civilization should cease and the wilderness begin. The authors in this section, even those of today, try to find answers to this riddle.

A third theme is that of *Appearance Versus Reality*. The question of the individual's relationship to the world has preoccupied people from earliest Puritan times. In many situations one needs to grapple with the question of what is real and what only seems to be. As Anne Bradstreet pondered, how could one be sure what was true admiration of God's creation and what was delight in one's physical pleasures. Very simply, a thing may appear one way at one moment and quite different the next. Writers become fascinated with the shadowline distinctions between illusions and realities.

Finally, a theme inherent in the New England experience is that of *The Undiminished Hero*. It takes true courage to face the situation of the Puritans who believed themselves so completely at the mercy of God that they had no choice in their salvation. Then, too, there was the high resolve of the Puritans to bring their true insight to all the world. High, noble purposes, nearly impossible to fulfill, were also a part of heroism. To what extent were those who stood against the witch hunts, whether in Salem in 1692 or in the United States Senate in the 1950's, heroes? Were people staunchly facing the hardships of existence, heroes? Are miserable people struggling to find themselves, diminished heroes? The values readers place on their own and others' actions will suggest how they interpret the selections gathered in this section.

By examining these themes as authors illustrate them, one may discover that the six New England states in their diversity of geography, government, and culture, provide a fertile ground in which creativity can thrive. Integrity, individualism, industry, frugality, practicality, stamina, awareness of nature, heroic vision, depth of feeling, self-questioning, a sense of guilt, ironic insight, and rebelliousness—traits of character demonstrated by New Englanders in varying degrees—make rich material for authors. Counter qualities of pettiness, hypocrisy, and narrowness have set up tensions conducive to effective writing. The writers working in the New England scene continue to respond to these many stimuli.

Root Images

Those vividly remembered people, events, and places of one's past are the result of indelible images gained when one's life is lived to its fullest. Since writers penetrate more deeply the meaning of moments drawn from their early environment, sensitive writers find the remembrance of things past of vital importance in understanding themselves. They seek answers to such questions as, "Why do I remain here? Why do I look back on the experience? What do these recollections do to help me now?"

For many authors included in this section, recollections of experiences with people, with boats, with places, with legends, with sudden flashes of insight have engendered clearer understanding into the course of their existence. In other selections, it is the voice speaking that recollects the incident and comprehends the meaning. Root images, those recollections of great events or little, nameless things, can assume significance in the life and writing of an author. Recalling past experiences may well be one of life's richest pleasures. New England is a land fertile for roots.

Sweet Memories

MAUREEN HOWARD

"Ah, did you once see Shelley plain," one of my mother's beloved lines, delivered on this occasion with some irony as we watched Jasper McLevy, the famed socialist mayor of Bridgeport, climb down from his Model A Ford. "Laugh where we must, be candid where we can," was another of her lines, a truncated couplet, one of the scraps of poems, stories, jingles that she pronounced throughout the day. Like station breaks on WICC, her quotations punctuated the hours. Vacuum off: "One thing done and that done well / is a very good thing as many can tell." Out on the back stoop to take in the thick chipped bottles of unhomogenized milk, she would study the sky over Parrott Avenue—"Trust me Clara Vere de Vere from yon blue heavens above us bent . . ." George and mother and me, pressed against the sun-parlor doors watching a September hurricane play itself out. Ash cans rattling down the drive, gutters clotted with leaves, shingles flying, the rambler rose torn from its trellis whipping the cellar door. Her gentle, inappropriate crooning: "Who has seen the wind/ Neither you nor I: / But when the trees bow down their heads, . . ."

My mother was a lady, soft-spoken, refined; alas, she was fey, fragmented. I do not know if it was always so, but when we were growing up, broken off bits of art is what we got, a touch here and there. A Lehmbruck nude clipped out of *Art News* tacked in the pantry, a green pop-eyed Sienese Madonna folded in the Fannie Farmer cookbook. She was sturdy when we were children, with high cheekbones and red hair, like a chunky Katherine Hepburn, so the fragility, the impression of fragility was all in her manner, her voice. Her attitude toward anything as specific as a pile of laundry was detached, amused. It might not be our dirty socks and underwear that she dealt with at all, but one of our picture books or a plate of cinnamon toast. As she grew older her fine red hair faded to yellow, then to white, but it was still drawn back from her face and pinned at the neck as she wore it in college. Her clothes were old but very good. And my mother—the least independent of women—always used her maiden name,

17

her married name tacked on as though she was listing herself in her *Smith Alumnae Quarterly*. Loretta Burns Kearns. Somewhat wistful. You do remember me? Loretta Burns.

I sensed that my mother was a misfit from the first days when, dressed in a linen hat and pearls, she walked me out around the block. She was too fine for the working-class neighborhood that surrounded us. "Flower in the crannied wall/ I pluck you out of the crannies." Down Parrott Avenue around to French Street we marched, taking the air—"As I was going down the stair/ I met a man who wasn't there./ He wasn't there again today. . . ." I never knew when I was growing up whether my mother didn't have time to finish the poems what with the constant cooking, cleaning, washing, or whether this was all there was, these remnants left in her head.

To the crowded A & P we charged on a Saturday morning—ours not to make reply, ours not to reason why, ours but to do and die. If she gave us a ride back to school after lunch and the scent of spring was heavy over the schoolyard fence as the nuns filed in from the convent, my mother would sing out to us, triumphant behind the wheel of the old brown Auburn: "Come down to Kew in lilac-time . . . And there they say, when dawn is high and all the world's a blaze of sky. . . . Come down to Kew in lilac-time (it isn't far from London!)"

"There once was a molicepan who met a bumblestum. . . ." A witless ditty—it must have been hilarious in her public-speaking class at college and never failed to please at lunch or dinner. But it wasn't mere nonsense or chestnuts from the laureates she quoted. My mother had studied German and I believe been quite a serious student before life caught up with her. "*So long man strebt, er ist erlost*," she said. As long as man strives he is saved. "*Wer reitet so spät durch Nacht und Wind?*" We were treated to disjointed lines, lots of *Faust*, some Schiller and Heine, the final watery gurglings of the Rhine maidens and, of course, "*Freude, schöner Götterfunken . . .*"

It sounded beautiful gibberish to me as did the Latin verbs she conjugated to the remote pluperfect tense, but for my mother it was to prove that she could still do it, could reel it off with ease—as naturally as an athlete doing push-ups before the flab sets in. "*Amāveram, amāveras, amāverat.*" That was the trick my mother could do and other mothers couldn't, as well as smock my dresses by hand and overcook the meat to

18

please my father and not speak to George when he was rotten, but be elegantly wounded, disappointed in her son, a grieving queen.

She kept a plain brown copybook to mark down all our childhood diseases and achievements. This chronicle is of no general interest: while it is gratifying for me to know that I went to the World's Fair in 1939 with the last scabs of my chicken pox and still had a wonderful time, it is terrifying to read my first poem (age seven) about the Baby Jesus and George's loathsome moral verse (age six)—both efforts already corrupted by the worst literary traditions. "Thus should a little child be merry/ In snowy, blowy January."

We were dressed in our Sunday best and taken to the concert series at Klein Memorial Hall. My father wouldn't go near the stuff. Helen Traubel stomped onto the stage in a black tent and something like gym shoes. The Budapest Quartet, all young and buoyant, stunned us with the knowledge of their own brilliance. The Connecticut Symphony ground out their Debussy and Ravel, their sloppy Beethoven, their inevitable Gershwin jolly-up. Me and my mother and George, proud and rather excited by the grandeur we could pull off in Bridgeport. The audience—a sprinkling of local music teachers, a solid core of middle-class Jewish shopkeepers and professionals who were more sophisticated than the Irish in town, and that set of rich old ladies who stumble into concert halls all over the world, canes and diamonds, hearing aids, rumpled velvet evening capes from long ago.

We never made it to Kew where all the world's a blaze of sky, but to the first little temple of civic culture, the Klein Memorial out near Bassick High School beyond the Cadillac showroom. On those special nights we were there. The price of the tickets was something awful, but my mother wanted this for us. I ran off pictures in my head, beautiful scenery, lakes and rills, mountains and fens. I called upon the great myth that one *must* be moved. I strained, while the violins soared, for deeper finer thoughts, but it was beyond my childish endurance. I tap, tap, tapped my patent-leather pump into my brother's ankle until it drove him mad, found that I had to cough, begged to go to the water fountain and was kept in my seat by a Smith Brothers' cough drop from my mother's purse.

What did it mean to her? Was my mother full of a passionate yearning like those starved women of taste who carted their pianos across the prairie? God knows, Bridgeport was raw land in the thirties. Before my

19

father died, she sat in perfect harmony with him in front of the Lawrence Welk show. She was lost in the old sappy songs, lost. Walled in by her vagueness, all the fragments of herself floating like the million orange, green and purple dots that formed the absurd image, the bobbing head of the lisping bandmaster. My parents took my anger as a joke. Disgust swelled from me: at the time I was not ready for compassion.

Or did Loretta Burns know that her chance was gone and only want those ineffable finer things for me and George? Well, we sure got them. We got the whole culture kit beyond her wildest dreams. There came a day when George knew who was dancing what role in which ballet that very evening up at City Center. For the pure clean line of a particular Apollo he would leave his gray basement on St. Mark's Place—burnt-out pots, ravioli eaten cold from the can, grit in the typewriter keys. His coffee-stained translations from the Spanish and Greek littered the floor. No closets. No bathtub. Now, as an adult, my brother takes with him wherever he lives an intentional chaos that is impressive, a mock poverty. Orange crates and real Picassos. Thousands of records and books but no dishes, no curtains. Money handled like trash. Twenty-dollar bills crumpled in ash-trays, checks left to age, income tax ignored. He is quite successful really. Her boy has become a strange man, but not to himself and he is not unhappy. My brother, a middle-aged man, can come to visit (filthy jeans and Brooks Brothers blazer), take William Carlos Williams off the shelf and read a passage, rediscovered: "At our age the imagination across the sorry facts"—then tell me why it is so fine, and it *is* fine. As we talk beneath my Greenwich Village skylight, he threads his speech with lines—like our mother, of course.

While I'm split, split right down the middle, all sensibility one day, raging at the vulgarities that are packaged as art, the self-promotion everywhere, the inflated reputations. In such a mood I am unable to sit in a theater or pick up a recently written book. I am quite crazy as I begin to read in stupefying rotation—*Anna Karenina, Bleak House, Persuasion, Dubliners, St. Mawr, Tender is the Night, The Wings of the Dove.* I play the Chopin Mazurkas until the needle wears out. Drawings are the only works I can bear to look at. The atmosphere I demand is so rarified it is stale and I know it.

Then again, everything is acceptable to me. In an orgy I can ogle the slickest movie or love story on TV, suck in the transistor music and thrill to the glossy photographs of sumptuous salads and stews, the magnificent bedrooms and marble baths in *House and Garden*. Our great living junk art. The Golden Arches of McDonald's rise, glorious, across the landscape, contempo-monolithic, simple in concept as Stonehenge if we could but see it. Then the nausea overtakes me in Bloomingdale's "art gallery" or as I listen to all that Limey Drah-ma on Public Television. Sick. I am often sick of art.

It would never have occurred to my mother that the finer things might be complicated for us, less than sheer delight. She simply stopped after her children left home. There were no more disembodied lines, not even the favorite "Little Orphant Annie's come to our house to stay," or "Where are you going young fellow my lad/ On this glittering morning in May?/ I'm going to join the colors, Dad . . ." No. She settled into Lawrence Welk, "Double Jeopardy," Dean Martin no less, and she had all her life been such a lady. She read the *Bridgeport Post* and clipped the columns of some quack who had many an uplift remedy for arthritis and heart disease. She followed the news of the Kennedys in *McCall's* magazine, until the last terrible years when she was widowed, when the blood circulated fitfully to her cold fingers and her brain. Then, from a corner of her dwindling world, she resurrected Ibsen's *Rosmersholm* in a German translation and underlined in a new ballpoint pen the proclamations of Rebecca West, all that heroic bunkum about the future and her festering spiritual love.

Mother would sit on the brown velvet couch day after day, rejecting tapioca and Jell-O, smiling at the pictures in her art books like a child . . . such pretty flowers . . . all the colors . . . by some Dutchman . . . in a bouquet. The fat ladies she laughed at were Renoir's, bare bottoms by a hazy stream. Her mind skipped the shallow waters of her past like a stone. George and her father were one man. My father was "that fellow" and there was a picture she found of Loretta Burns with a whole band of robust Smith girls, each one warmly recalled, who'd gone hiking up Mt. Tom on a fine autumn day in her sophomore year. Sometimes she could not place me and so she entertained me graciously, gave me pieces of crust and cake. She was tiny now, nestled in the big couch. Her thoughts fluttered away from her. "By the shores of Gitche Gumee,/ By the shining Big-Sea-Water," she said. Gaily she'd recite her most cherished lines of Heine:

> *Ich weiss nicht was soll es bedeuten*
> *Das ich so traurig bin?*

What does it mean that I am so sad? She seemed happy to remember the words at all.

Orchard

RICHARD EBERHART

I

Lovely were the fruit trees in the evening.
We sat in the automobile all five of us,
Full of the silence of deep grieving,
For tragedy stalked among the fruit trees.

Strongest was the father, of solid years,
Who set his jaw against the coming winter,
Pure, hard, strong, and infinitely gentle
For the worst that evil brings can only kill us.

Most glorious was the mother, beautiful
Who in the middle course of life was stalked
By the stark shape of malignant disease,
And her face was holy white like all desire.

And we three, in our benumbing youngness,
Half afraid to guess at the danger there,
Looked in stillness at the glowing fruit trees,
While tumultuous passions raged in the air.

II

And the first, the father, with indomitable will
Strove in iron decision, in all human strength
With a powerful complete contempt of defeat,
Six feet of manhood and not a mark of fear.

And the next, the mother, wonderfully mild,
Wise with the wisdom that never changes,
Poured forth her love divinely magnified
We knew not by what imminent despair.

While the older brother and the younger,
Separate, yet placed in the first light
Of brutal recognition, held a trembling sister
Who knew not the trial of fortitude to come.

And in the evening, among the warm fruit trees
All of life and all of death were there,
Of pain unto death, of struggle to endure,
And the strong right of human love was there.

Winslow Homer, *Gathering Autumn Leaves*

The Blueberry Picking

DONALD HALL

One day in late July 1945, I woke at six when my grandmother brought the black coffee into my bedroom. I sat on the edge of the bed and gulped it down. It was made in an old drip coffee pot on the iron stove, where a kettle was always simmering, and it was nearly as thick as Turkish. The shades were still down, and the morning light showed in a thousand pinpricks through the worn green cloth. I crossed the room and opened the shades, and heard a rooster crow in the hen yard across the road. A big automobile blew past, making an early start for the White Mountains. I always looked out to see what kind of day it would be. Rain? A scorcher? It looked fine and sunny today. I walked back to the bed, where my coffee cup sat on the table between my typewriter and a vase of flowers which my grandmother had picked. I sat on the bright quilt and finished the coffee.

This was the start of a day we had planned for weeks. In the years past, before I was born, my grandfather had made an annual excursion to pick blueberries. I had heard about those days in many of his stories. The blueberries were the low, wild kind, and they grew among the ledges of blue rock at the top of Ragged Mountain. They were a three-mile walk from the farmhouse, and the walk was mostly up. When my grandfather was younger, he and a hired man would pick for one long day, and my grandmother and her daughters would wash, sort, and can them for two days. A shelf of cold-packed quarts of blueberries would wait in the cellar for the piecrusts of winter. It was one of the many ways in which a farmer compensated for his lack of cash—like the eggs from the laying season stored in waterglass, and like the salted meat from the slaughtering.

My grandfather had talked about it so much that it seemed as much past as the Lyceum and the two-hour sermons. But a few weeks earlier, this past had strangely seemed present to us. Paul Whittier had been chasing a bear which had tramped down his peas, and had followed him all the way to the top of Ragged. (It was not only a lust for revenge which drove him; the anachronistic bounty on bears was $50.) He had lost his bear among the rocks on the other side of the mountain, but among the blue ledges of the top he had found the blueberries thicker than ever. They were green then, or he said he would have been up there eating them still.

No one, as far as my grandfather knew, had picked there for twenty years. The berries were higher up than the forests which had been cut of their soft wood ten years before, or the lumberjacks would have stripped them. No one else in the neighborhood would have cared to make the climb. The thought of all those blueberry pies growing, maturing, and dropping every year—unappreciated except by the birds—troubled my grandfather's sense of propriety. We decided we would go blueberry picking that year.

My grandmother fretted a little: it was a long trip; the rocks were hard to climb; the blueberries would be too heavy for us to carry; my grandfather was too old. But the thought of her rows of blueberries, cold-packed in their quart jars, overcame her opposition. She made us promise to stop and rest when we were tired, and my grandfather fixed the time when he thought the blueberries would be ripe.

This morning I took my second cup of coffee in the kitchen, and ate breakfast in the old chair beside the window, under the canary named Christopher. I was impatient to be started. I heard a strange noise outside, a high-pitched hoot from behind the sheep barn, where railroad tracks of the Boston and Maine cut through the soft dirt. It was the time for the morning Peanut, the train that went up to White River Junction in the evening and came back in the morning, but the whistle of the Peanut was the long, throaty lament of the steam engine. I stared at the gap in the ensilage corn through which I would be able to see the train flash. When it came it looked like a trolley car, short and self-propelled, and it hooted again its ridiculous horn. "I suppose that's one of these new Diesels," my grandmother said. "Somebody said they'd seen one this summer."

When I had finished my eggs, I walked up to the tie-up where my grandfather was doing the morning chores. The cows were moving out to pasture, and behind them my grandfather was clapping his hands and shouting. In the spring they would gallop out like young horses, but by this time of year they acted like cows again, and my grandfather was in a hurry to shut the gates behind them. I went into the tie-up to start cleaning it. With the edge of a hoe I lifted up the hinged floorboard over the manure pit, and splattered the cowflops onto their cousins below. My grandfather came in. "How did you like the new whistle?" he said.

"Not so much," I told him. "I like the old kind."

"I suppose there's a reason for it," he said. He picked up the other hoe and scraped along with me. "You should be resting," he said, "for what's ahead of you." He sang one of his tuneless songs, and seemed as excited as I was.

When we walked into the kitchen, my grandmother was packing pie and sandwiches into an enormous paper bag. "You'll need your strength," she said. "Now, Wesley, you eat a good breakfast." He ate his oatmeal and bread and coffee, sitting at one of the set-tubs which was covered with oilcloth. My grandmother finished packing the paper bag and disappeared into the shed. A moment later I heard her pumping at the deep well in the back, and I followed her out to relieve her. I pumped and we filled three milk bottles with cold well water, and she put cardboard tops on the bottles.

We left them inside the shed, and brought the paper bag out with us when my grandfather had finished eating. Two huge pails, shaped wider at the bottom than at the top, lay waiting for us. We put the food in one and the water in the other. Then my grandfather found a wooden yoke which went over the back of his neck, from which the two great pails hung down like enormous earrings. It was the apparatus he used when he made maple sugar in the winter, pouring the sap from the little buckets at each sugar maple into the big pails. I carried two sap buckets in which we would pick the berries, and we started off.

It was seven o'clock. The air was cool and the grass was soaking wet under our feet. Low light from the east came through the trees, which were full and dark green. My grandmother called after us from the end of the porch, warning us to be careful. We turned into New Canada Road and started to climb. "It'll be heavy coming back," said my grandfather, "but at least it will be downhill." He paused, the light buckets swinging easily from the ends of the yoke. Then he laughed. "The only man I ever knew," he said, "who could walk all day and not be tired was your Great-Grampa Keneston. He must have touched every inch of this mountain. Days when he couldn't do much else he would walk around his pasture looking at the fencing. My, he was sprightly. You heard your mother tell about how, the day before he died, he walked clear down to West Andover to buy some Canada Mints. He was eighty-seven then. When he had his seventieth birthday, he stood up on the horse's back and galloped up the hill to the barn. Bethuel Peasley told how when he was seventy-five or so he set off on a walk with a two-year-old dog following him, and he came back four hours later with the dog slung along the back of his neck like a lamb. All tired out."

In the shade of the gray birch, and of the maples that met over New Canada Road, it was almost cold that morning, but I was already sweating because of the climb. I took off the sweater which my grandmother had asked me to wear and tied it around my waist. "That's the last you'll use your sweater today," my grandfather said.

After a mile of New Canada Road, we climbed over some bars into a pasture. I thought I felt ruts underneath the old leaves where we were walking. "Is this a lumber road?" I asked.

"Yes," said my grandfather. "It's Paul Whittier's pasture, though he only keeps a few head now. He took the lumber off about ten years ago." The only old trees were twisted ones which the lumberers had scorned. Young fir was growing thickly everywhere but the road, which the spring waters had eroded into cliffs and islands of rock. I fell and scraped my knee. We climbed most of the time, but the road avoided the steepest parts. Sometimes we passed through a clearing, flatter than the rest of the land, which the cows patronized. Squashed bushes grew there among the cowflops: new and steaming, old and gray.

At a little after eight, we paused in one of those clearings and sat on rocks to catch our breath. My grandfather's shirt was wet through. I already felt as tired as if I had hayed for a whole afternoon. We said nothing for a while. Then I said, "I'm thirsty."

My grandfather shook his head. "You'll be thirstier," he said. "It's thirsty work. You'll do better to wait."

In a moment we set out again. The road failed us and we climbed a stone wall out of Paul Whittier's pasture. "I reckon this is part of our land you've never seen," said my grandfather. "Took the timber off nearly twenty years ago." Pine grew tall around us. "It won't be long before we take it off again."

We walked parallel to the stone wall until we came to a dry creek bed, and we used it as our road up the mountain. It was very rocky and I found myself using my hands to climb with. "How will we get down," I asked, "when we're carrying blueberries?"

"There are other ways," said my grandfather. We stood still for a moment in order to talk. "Or there used to be. One way is steeper than most of

28

this but it's steadier. Not that this creek used to be so dug out. I suppose you can't know what you will find." We both wiped our faces with our handkerchiefs. I looked at my watch and it was only eight-thirty. "We'd better move on," my grandfather said.

After fifteen minutes of climbing, we left the creek and came to more level land. A surprising plain of heavy grass made easy walking for a moment. "Too bad we can't get the hayrack up here," I said. My grandfather nodded and smiled. He was looking ahead at the fringe of trees on the edge of the clearing. When we came up to them, he motioned to me to go first. I stepped through and stopped still. The land in front of me sloped slightly, and I saw that it raised again two hundred yards further, making a little saucer of a valley high up on the mountain. In the bowl, flat down and rust red, and all pointing in the same direction, lay a forest of dead trees.

It could not have been larger than ten acres, but it seemed vast as I looked at it, like a crater of the dead. Desolation made it look immense. There seemed to be no growth under the dead branches of the huge trees. The soil had fallen away from the exposed roots, and the roots looked like bunches of dead nerves. We were so high, beyond paths and people, that it seemed as if we were the first to know. I felt as if I had been walking on the shore and found a drowned submarine rolled up by the tide.

My grandfather was looking over my shoulder. "The hurricane?" I asked. I meant the storm of September 1938.

"Yes," said my grandfather. "Do you know what kind of trees they were?"

I shook my head.

"This was the stand of rock maple," he said. "It must have taken a hundred and fifty years to grow so big. They would have been worth hauling from here, being rock maple." The chopping block in the woodshed was rock maple, I knew. It was about the hardest wood which grew in New England. "We were planning to sell them in 1940 but after everything blew down nobody would come up here for them. They were too busy with the trees low down."

I had nothing to say. I just stared. It was so huge and so wasted.

"Dead but not buried," my grandfather went on. "I hadn't seen it since the time I climbed up here after the hurricane. Pine a few rods away wasn't touched. The roots aren't deep here; that's why I feared and climbed up. There's ledge down a few feet. It looked different then. You couldn't see the trunks for all the leaves, and of course you couldn't walk through it. I could see that everything was pointing the same way. A lumber man from the government told me one gust probably did it."

A moment later my grandfather stepped past me and we began to pick our way through the dead trees. The branches made a continuous dry hedge which snapped at the touch and scratched our faces and arms. My watch was nearly torn from my wrist. I put it in my pocket. We climbed over and under the great trunks, and weaved back and forth as if we were lost in a maze. Finally we rose at the other side of the lot, and looked back again. "We won't be coming through here on the way back," said my grandfather. "Lucky thing." He took one last look at his trees and then turned up the hill.

We were beginning to climb the blue ledges which made the top of Ragged. It was only four hundred yards to the blueberries, but they were hard going. "I can see the bushes," said my grandfather. My feet felt lighter and I climbed more rapidly. Only my throat remained tight and dry, and I looked forward to water as much as to sitting down. Soon the dome of Ragged flattened out, and the rocks which had seemed to lie closely together turned into islands in a sea of blueberries.

They were as low as grass, hardly taller than the flat rock they surrounded. The blue of the berries seemed more prominent than the green of the leaves, so that the earth looked blue everywhere—from blue stone to blue fruit. Only the texture varied. The berries were ripe and full. Some of them had burst and oozed a blue liquid. Most of them were small, and as sweet as I had ever tasted.

We squatted on a rock. My grandfather delved into his pails. "Now's when the work starts," he said, "so I reckon you'll want some strength." He opened the paper bag and handed me a sandwich. I looked at my watch and it was nine o'clock. "Have yourself some water," he said.

The milk bottle of well water was already warm. I pried the top off and tilted my head back and swallowed luxuriously. When I took it away, I had drunk nearly half the bottle. My grandfather looked over. "Careful," he said. "It's a hot day and a long way to water."

I nodded but I didn't really care. I took another sip before I put it back. Then I ate my egg sandwich while the sun rose higher and warmed the back of my neck. There was no wind this morning, or we would have been open to it. I realized that we had left trees behind at the level of the dead forest. I looked down at it now, a red-brown patch among the green. Elsewhere, as far as I could see, there was only the green of the trees and the blue-silver of small lakes. Here and there in the distance I saw the white of a farmhouse. Suddenly something occured to me. "I should think that rock maple might catch on fire," I said.

My grandfather nodded. "Lightning might do it," he said. "Of course nobody walks up here to throw a cigarette away. I've thought of it. It would blaze down the whole mountain if it started, and we're on the mountain."

I stood up and walked a little way toward the other side of Ragged. I felt as solitary as an explorer. A low cloud stopped another peak a few miles off, and in between I saw the same green, and the same white specks of the farms.

I heard my grandfather call, "Want any more to eat now?" He was packing up the lunch.

"I guess not," I said, and walked back next to him. He put the bag and the bottles in a crack in the rock, and stood up.

"All set?" he said. He handed me one of the sap buckets. The two big pails were standing on a flat piece of rock. "These berries are mighty low," he said. "You may prefer to sit on the rock and pick them. A sore back is a sore back."

We each took a pail and set out in different directions. I had never picked low-bush berries before, and there were tricks I didn't know. When I tried to scoop off a handful at once, I crushed some of the berries and pulled a leaf or a bit of stem along with them. My pail was full of foreign matter, which would make for a lot of picking over back at the farm. Yet when I tried to be careful I went so slowly that it would have taken all morning to pick one bucket. The trouble with sitting was that I had to slide myself over the bumpy rock, and I began to feel paralyzed where I sat. The heaviest stems of berries were always slightly out of reach. I tried kneeling, but my knees gave out. I tried standing, and it felt all right until I unbent, when I thought I would crack apart. Finally I sat again, as the least evil.

My grandfather stood and bent. Whenever he straightened up he grimaced. "Why don't *you* sit down?" I asked.

"I'd never stand up again!" he said. He pointed to the calves of his legs without breaking the rhythm of his fast picking. "Cramps," he said. "From climbing up here."

I picked and picked. I switched from the right hand to the left and back again and picked two-handed, and still my pail was only a quarter full. I realized that even when I had filled it, it would barely cover the bottom of one of the big pails. I thought we would never fill even one of them. Then I heard my grandfather grunt as he straightened up, and saw him empty his full bucket into one of the big pails. "There's one," he said.

"Look at all I've done," I said, lifting my pail to show it to him.

"You don't know how to pick them yet." He walked over to me and leaned down. He took hold of a stem heavy with blueberries and stripped it clean between his index and middle fingers, without crushing a berry or tearing off a leaf. "Do you see?" he said. "You have to be gentle and let your hand feel them coming. You'll learn it."

In the whole morning I only filled my pail twice, while his pail emptied itself five times into our storage bins on the flat rock. My hands felt twisted out of shape and nervous with their continual darting. My back felt welded in a leaning curve. Worst of all, my throat parched with the thirst, and parched more and more as the sun rose in the sky and the sweat dried on my body. A hundred times I almost complained, or almost rose to have a drink of the water without saying anything, but each time the sight of my grandfather—picking steadily and humming to himself, and seventy-two years old—shamed me into silence. He worked with utter delight in the growing pile of berries. He talked of the number of blueberry pies which we had already gathered, and all I could think of was the dampness of them. When I ate a handful of blueberries, my mouth felt better for a moment, but then felt unutterably worse: so thick that its sides would stick together, and my tongue clung to the roof of my mouth. I knew that we would break for lunch, but I had put my watch in my pocket. I kept squinting up at the sun to guess the time. Finally, when I didn't even know I was going to say it, I heard my dry voice squeaking, "I think I'll have a drink."

My grandfather pulled his gold watch from the pocket of his trousers. "My, my," he said. "It's past lunch time. Twelve-fifteen." He put his watch away and stretched carefully. "I guess we'd better do some eating."

I rose gratefully and walked toward our cache of food and water. I lifted the bottle I had started before and, though I knew I was foolish, drained it dry. A minute after I had set it back on the rock, my thirst returned. I reached for a second quart, which stood propped against rock in the crack, and when I lifted it out my stiff fingers slipped, and the bottle fell and rolled from me, and the water poured out over the blue rocks and drained among the blueberry plants. "Look!" I said. I was exhausted and angry to the point of tears. I could say nothing more.

32

My grandfather shook his head and smiled at me. "I suspect you'll wish you had that quart of water," he said. I dipped my finger in a small puddle in the rock and sucked it. The third quart had to do for both of us now, and my grandfather hadn't drunk anything yet.

"You handle the other quart," I said.

"We'll be careful with that one."

As I ate, I felt a little better. The custard pie, the pickles, and the butter in the chicken sandwiches were all damp. I ate as slowly as I could, pushing away the moment when the picking began again. When we had finished the whole bag, my grandfather tucked it tidily—waxed paper and hard-boiled-egg shells inside—into a crevice of the stone.

"Now let's have a bit of that water," said my grandfather. He lifted the remaining bottle and took a mouthful, keeping it in his mouth a long time, and letting it go down in slow sips, luxuriously. "That's good," he said, and handed it to me. I tried to do the same trick, and choked.

He stood up and stretched again. "I could relish a few minutes on the sofa just now," he said. "Don't see any sofas hereabouts." He walked to where he had left his pail, and began to pick again.

I looked at my watch. It was nearly one o'clock. On my way to my bucket, I looked in the big pails. One was nearly full, and the other was barely covered with berries on the bottom. When I sat down on the hard rock again, my old bruises of the morning felt worse than before, and I suppose I felt more tired than I did three hours later.

During the afternoon I filled my bucket more rapidly, and every time I emptied it I took a sip of water. It was my reward for being quick. I saw my grandfather wet his lips once, and stand staring across the valley below us at the hills on the other side. I stood up and watched with him, and for a moment forgot blueberries and sore backs, fatigue and thirst. But in a moment my throat contracted with its drought again, and I raced to fill up another pail.

My grandfather seemed to pick more slowly than he had picked in the morning, and when he stood up to carry the bucket to the big pail, he usually paused for a minute before walking. In the middle of the afternoon I calculated that two more bucketfuls would fill the last big pail, and I raced to fill my bucket and be done. My grandfather and I met at the big pails at the same time, and poured our blueberries to the very top. I took another sip of water, unable to speak with the dryness of my throat. About an inch

33

was left in the bottom of the bottle. I was already thinking of the well water at home, after our walk down the mountain, but then I saw my grandfather walk back to the berries.

"What are you doing?" I said. "We filled the pails."

"Not these," he said, waving the sap bucket. "Are you tired?" He set the bucket down and walked back to where I was standing. "I didn't think of that."

"No," I said.

"We could go home," he said. "We have plenty of berries."

"No, no," I said. "I don't want to."

I would have been ecstatic if he had overruled me, but he didn't. He said, "You really sure?" and when I nodded he walked back to his berries. When he turned away, I was filled with anger and frustration, and I lifted the milk bottle and drained the last of the water.

We each filled our buckets. My grandfather was finished a moment before me, and he gathered a few handfuls to top off mine. We carried the sap buckets to the high rock where the two big pails stood. We looked all around us once more. It was only three-thirty, but a wind was rising and I began to feel a little cool. My grandfather put the milk bottles in the pockets of his overalls. He fastened the ends of the wooden yoke to the two big pails and lifted them. His face looked red, and veins stood out on his temples. "It must be very heavy," I said. I lifted the sap buckets and they were heavy enough to suit me.

"They're tolerably heavy," he said, and started along the stones.

"Let me carry them," I said rather feebly. I didn't even hear his answer, and he kept walking straight on.

As I walked my thirst seemed to grow and grow, until I found it utterly intolerable. We were going slowly down a steep grassy slope. If there had been a cliff handy, I would have been tempted to jump from it. I felt as if my throat were being stung by red ants. My lips felt as if they were cracking open, and my tongue felt as dry as old newspaper. "Is there any water on the way?" I asked when I came abreast of my grandfather.

We had been walking for ten minutes. When my grandfather turned to me, his face was dead white. I was shocked. He knelt until the pails touched the ground and then shrugged from under the yoke. He sat on the ground and I thought he was going to be sick. "Might be," he said.

"Are you all right?" I asked.

34

"Don't worry," he said. "Don't worry." His face gradually relaxed and color returned to his cheeks.

"It's my turn to carry the yoke," I said. "My hands hurt from the wire handles of these buckets, and anyway, I want to learn how to carry the yoke."

He looked at me. "It's a longer walk if we go by water. Are you that thirsty?"

"I am thirsty, but I want to carry."

"All right," he said, "you young bull." I didn't feel much like a bull. "I guess I shouldn't be surprised. See if you like it."

The novelty of the yoke took my mind off my thirst. When I crouched under it and stood up, I nearly lost my balance. I swayed with the pails dangling clumsily at my sides. Then I hunched forward and they settled. My grandfather picked up the sap buckets and looked at me. "All right?" he said.

"I guess so," I said. "Go slowly."

We doubled back a few yards and then started to walk north on the same level, moving away from the farmhouse. At first I had to walk very cautiously, because the rhythm of the swinging pails threatened my balance, but soon I learned to use the swing of the weight to help me keep moving, and I shrugged until the yoke felt comfortable on the back of my neck. When I felt secure in the walking, the thirst came back upon me.

After a few minutes my grandfather felt able to talk again. I realized that today had been the most silent day we had ever spent together, and I decided that he must have been more tired than I had suspected all along. "I had that pain in my side," he said, "which comes when I run sometimes. I'd rather you didn't say much about it back home. Katie frets so much." I said I wouldn't. "I'm glad to show you the pool where we'll find the water, if it's still there. It was there six years ago. No, eight years. It was there about eighty years ago, for that matter. But on the way I'm going to show you something else."

"What is it?"

"You wait," he said. "Seeing will be good enough for you." Then he snorted and remembered an anecdote about a man from Concord who was curious about how Lucas Blount had lost his leg, and how Lucas Blount left him more curious than ever. He seemed himself again.

We had passed the forest of dead rock maples, going slightly below it, and then we had followed a steep path downhill for several hundred yards. Now we came on to a part of Ragged which was entirely new to me. It seemed to be a high plain, quite level and thick with fir trees. Ragged could hardly be called a mountain, or even a hill, any longer. Then we descended a few feet into what looked like a narrow, flat road. I saw that banks rose on either side of it, perhaps twelve feet apart. It was too level for one of the makeshift lumber roads. Branches leaned together over it, but only goldenrod and small bushes were growing in its narrow path. "What's this?" I asked, as I paused when I had scrambled down to it.

"Look," said my grandfather, and pointed to the ground. First I was aware that the path seemed made of ridges going from side to side, like a corduroy road except that the ridges were a foot apart. Then I saw what looked like long streaks of orange, running parallel across the ends of the ridges.

"It's a railroad!" I said.

"It used to be," he said. "I remember when they closed it down. It's narrow gauge, see? One of your Foster cousins was a brakeman here. It was just a little branch line, built for hauling timber to the freight depots. They took the mail and some passengers too, when there were any, when there were more people here."

We walked on the rotted ties. Except that we had to duck overhanging branches, it was the easiest walking of the day. Here and there one of the banks had caved in, and dirt had fallen onto the old track, but most of it seemed nearly intact. It was like Pompeii, and the close foliage of the heavy trees around us closed us in, as if we were sealed off in an alley separate from the world of Diesels.

"Where did it go?" I asked.

"It stopped just back there, at no place. They called it Ragged Station. Nothing's there now but I'll show you where it was sometime. Wash used the wood from the old station when he built his lean-to. Up here is where your Great-Grampa Keneston came from, you know."

I had the pails working well now, and took giant steps, two ties at a time. We walked in silence for a way. I was watching the ties as I walked and seldom looked up. To slip and fall would have meant blueberry picking all over again, and the very thought of it made the fire in my throat sizzle. Then I heard my grandfather say, "Hold on there, boy. Look ahead."

He stood out of my way. Ahead was something dark and covered with

36

vines. It obstructed the tracks we walked on. My grandfather stopped. I set down the yoke and the blueberries and walked past him. Under the wooden hulk of the coal car the red wheels fitted the red tracks. I could see fungi growing on the rotten sides where the vines were thinnest. Then I looked beyond the coal car to the red, pitted hulk of the locomotive. As I started to edge my way toward it, I looked back and saw my grandfather follow, grinning in his delight at my excitement.

Branches leaned in the cab, where the throttle, corroded with rust, stood out from the rusted instruments. The coal shovel lay in the bottom of the cab, and, though leaves had drifted into every opening, I could see that there was still a heap of coal in the coal car. I walked around the engine. It was intact, down to the rope which led to the bell dangling in front. The smokestack was tall, and the unbroken glass of the headlight covered an oil lamp. The apparatus of wheels and pistons was fixed in a red trance, yet it looked as perfect as if it had just moved to a stop. Nothing had come loose or fallen. I had a momentary vision that my grandfather and I would clean the boiler, carry water, light a fire, heap on coal, blow the whistle, and gradually pull the throttle toward us; I saw the old pistons groan and start to move, flecks of rust fall like red snow from the whole machine, and the wheels turn on the red tracks as we plunged ahead on the dead railway, going nowhere on an errand among the farms of the past.

"Why did they leave it here?" I said.

"Nobody ever said. I suppose because of the gauge. It would be hard work moving it anywhere anybody could use it, even for scrap." He was grinning at me. "Now I bet you feel like an explorer," he said.

I didn't want to tell him what I had been thinking. I came back to the cab with the idea of getting up into it, but when I set my foot on the rung outside, it broke off.

"I wonder how long it will stay here," I said.

"Shouldn't wonder if it kept up a hundred years," he said. "It's been here for fifty now."

We walked back along the coal car. I knocked off some of the fungi and saw the black paint blistered underneath. My grandfather walked ahead of me, and lifted the yoke and straightened his shoulders under it. "You ready?" he said. "You've got more to see before you're home again."

"You let me do that," I said.

"I'll carry it to the water," he said. "You fetch the buckets." He started off. I walked after him, edging past the locomotive, and my neck began to straighten itself from the posture it had learned under the yoke. But as soon as we were well past the engine, my thirst returned.

We continued on the track for only two hundred yards. Then my grandfather turned and squatted so that the big pails rested on the ground and relieved him of their weight. "Here's where we go off," he said. "First you walk up ahead fifty yards and take a look. Leave your buckets. Be careful when you get up there."

My thirst had returned so badly that any delay was agony, but I did what he said. The foliage leaned over the track thickly and I couldn't see far ahead. I trotted lightly in order to be done quicker. Then suddenly the foliage thinned and I saw the track go on ahead of me in mid-air. Below was a ravine, cut by the tiny stream I could see at the bottom. It was spanned by a rotting trestle which had mostly fallen away, but across which the red rails narrowly tottered still. I took one long look. This is where my grandfather and I would have driven my imagined train. Then I turned and trotted back to my grandfather.

When he saw me coming, he stood up under the yoke again. I saw the veins stand out at his temples. I picked up my buckets. "Is it standing?" he said. I told him. "When they built it," he said, "they said it would last. Washington helped to keep it up, when he was a young man."

We turned from the track into the forest and immediately started to go downhill. The growth was thick and my grandfather moved slowly with the yoke.

"Are you all right, carrying that?" I asked.

"We're pretty close," he said. Soon we came into a pine forest. The trees were tall and as straight as the masts of ships. It was like walking under water, the way the light moved down through the green needles. Only a few low branches bothered our walking, and they snapped off when we brushed them. The needles felt as soft as air underneath my hot feet. I would have enjoyed it if the thirst had not throbbed in my mouth and throat.

I wanted to talk just to forget the hurt. "Is this virgin pine?" I asked. The moment I asked it, I knew it was a stupid question.

My grandfather laughed. He started to say something, but he was out of breath. "I'll tell you later," he said in gasps.

In a few minutes we left the pine and entered a clearing where I could see only a few ancient maples and some bushes. He set the pails on the ground and ducked out of the yoke. I could see by his face that he had the pain again. I set my buckets beside the pails. "It's my turn now," I said.

He gestured down a slope at one side of the clearing. "Water down there," he said.

I jogged down the slope and found a pool at the bottom. I dropped to my knees and cupped the water in my hands and splashed it into my mouth. The first water seemed painful because it was so meager. I brought more and more upward to my mouth and covered my shirt with the drips from my fingers. Finally I sat back panting to wait for a second wind. Then my grandfather came walking down the slope beside me, and took a quart bottle from his pocket and filled it and drank from it.

I borrowed it for my second round of drinking, and in a few minutes stood up, my stomach cramped full of water. My grandfather filled the quart again and put the cardboard stopper on it. "For the trip home," he said. He looked better now.

I looked at the pool for the first time. It was small and perfectly round. It looked utterly still, yet the water was clear and cool, with no scum on top and only a few lily pads to vary the surface.

My grandfather saw me looking at it. "God's pool," he said. "Uncle Luther used to walk up here, summers when he took a vacation from Connecticut, back when he was young enough, back before he retired. I believe he used to read books here, or write sermons maybe. I was afraid it might not be here any more. You never can be sure. A stream can shift underground. It comes from the stream which you saw under the trestle, and it goes out beneath that tree. I suppose it's one of the streams which fills up our lake down below."

"It's good water," I said. "I remember Uncle Luther telling me about it."

"In the old days, before they had a well, lots of your ancestors drew all their water here. Come back up and I'll show you something."

"How do you feel?" I asked.

"Better," he said. "Come along."

I followed him back to the clearing with the maples. He pointed with his foot to a flat stone. "Many people of your blood stepped on that stone," he said. "That's the doorstep, and there's the cellar hole." I looked behind the stone and saw the depression in the ground, a small cellar hole walled with dry stone, where the potatoes and apples and carrots and turnips and cabbages and parsnips and salted meat and fish had been stored for decades of winter. "Is this . . .?" I began.

"The Kenestons," he said. "Uncle Luther grew up here, and your Great-Grampa Benjamin, and the others before him. The well they dug is over that way, so mind your feet when you look around. They tapped the stream that flowed from the pool when they got tired of hauling it up that slope in buckets."

I wandered in the old dooryard. A maple above me stretched out a great branch which must have suspended a swing for the children. I stubbed my toe on an old piece of metal that stuck up through the ground. It was the wheel of a cultivator.

My grandfather sat on the doorstep. "I'm sorry to stop," he said. "I know you'd like some coffee and pie. I didn't reckon I'd get so tired." He paused a moment, looking at his hands. "You know the timber you asked about? You thought it might be virgin pine?" he said. "Your great-grand-father cut the virgin timber there, in the fifties, before the war. He stumped it with oxen and planted it with potatoes and hired a crew to dig them in the fall and he hauled them to the old railroad and sold them to a man who took them clear down to Boston, to sell them in the big vegetable market down there. But when the war came he couldn't hire a crew, and the fields grew up with bush, and after the war he just couldn't get started again. He lived so long he sold the pine twice, from the land he cleared and stumped himself. I reckon to sell it the third time, come next spring."

I wandered to the other side of the clearing, into a bushy meadow which slanted steeply downward. Under my feet I felt the earth wave like the sea, and I suddenly realized that I was walking on land which retained the ridges which my great-grandfather had plowed into it. I came back to my grandfa-ther. He was examining his hands again and did not hear me coming. I saw how old his hands looked. Then he looked over at the yoke. "Do you really feel like carrying that?" he asked.

"Sure I do," I said. I took a swallow of water and then lifted the yoke again, and settled it where I liked it on my neck. My grandfather lifted the sap buckets and led the way. We descended the bushy meadow into a strip of forest, and then climbed an old stone wall to a road.

My grandfather laughed. "You know where we are?" he asked. "New Canada?" I said hopefully.

"Almost," he said. "Two hundred yards down we come to New Canada. This is what they called New Road, and the town keeps it up though I don't know as anybody's living on it now."

We turned into New Canada and walked downhill all the way home. It was four miles, and my back was sore, but my strength revived when I imagined coffee and pie waiting on the oilcloth of the set-tubs. We walked quietly past Washington Woodward's camp, for fear he could discover us and want to chat for an hour or two; he was too lame to walk with us any more.

At last we turned onto the macadam of the main road, and in a moment I saw the white smoke of our chimney. "Well," I said with sudden gaiety, "we've brought the berries."

"Yes," said my grandfather, "and I don't know when we'll make the trip again. I'm glad I could show you some things to remember."

Grandparents

ROBERT LOWELL

They're altogether otherworldly now,
those adults champing for their ritual Friday spin
to pharmacist and five-and-ten in Brockton.
Back in my throw-away and shaggy span
of adolescence, Grandpa still waves his stick
like a policeman;
Grandmother, like a Mohammedan, still wears her thick
lavender mourning and touring veil;
the Pierce Arrow clears its throat in a horse stall.
Then the dry road dust rises to whiten
the fatigued elm leaves—
the nineteenth century, tired of children, is gone.
They're all gone into a world of light; the farm's my own.

The farm's my own!
Back there alone,
I keep indoors, and spoil another season.
I hear the rattly little country gramophone
racking its five foot horn:
"O Summer Time!"
Even at noon here the formidable
Ancien Régime still keeps nature at a distance. Five
green shaded light bulbs spider the billiards-table;
no field is greener than its cloth,
where Grandpa, dipping sugar for us both,
once spilled his demitasse.

His favorite ball, the number three,
still hides the coffee stain.
Never again
to walk there, chalk our cues,
insist on shooting for us both.
Grandpa! Have me, hold me, cherish me!
Tears smut my fingers. There
half my life-lease later,
I hold an *Illustrated London News*—;
disloyal still,
I doodle handlebar
mustaches on the last Russian Czar.

Boats

GERALD WARNER BRACE

Of all fabricks a ship is the most excellent, requiring more art in building, rigging, sayling, trimming, defending, and moaring, with such a number of several termes and names in continual motion, not understood of any landsman, as none would thinke of, but some few that knew them.
—CAPTAIN JOHN SMITH

Men look at great ships and little ships with the same sort of appraisal. The sheer of a liner can seem spiritual—or beautiful in some unexplained way; so also can a dory be beautiful. Whether ten feet or a thousand, a ship is a ship. The great schooners and the smallest sloops used to be timbered, caulked, rigged, equipped, and even handled exactly the same. When you see a yacht under sail at a little distance with no scale, nothing to measure her by, you can't tell if she's an ocean cruiser or a day sailer manned by ten-year-olds. Nothing made by man comes closer to animation. Every ship acquires what we call character. We like her, dislike her—we can love her, hate her, we are moved with admiration or disgust. Men marry ships as legally as they marry women, and suffer the same trials, feel the same kind of fidelity and responsibility, have the same pride and patience, and the same dream of a beauty and perfection just beyond mortal reach.

Since the first logs and bundles of reeds were manned the form of the hull has evolved and responded to need and function. It should by now be final. But I think every designer of a skiff or a cup defender begins with a vision of such elegance and performance as the world has never yet seen. Perfection is always ahead, beckoning. Hull form may have attained a classic finality here and there—in a Viking long ship, say, or a Baltimore clipper, or a Maine peapod—but he hardly admits it, and he knows that new materials lead to new perfections. If he is working with power and great speed he is in the midst of innovation.

But Maine ships were the wooden ones, and achieved ideal form from the little double-enders called peapods, like small domesticated whale boats, to the great full-rigged downeasters, the last and most splendid of the age of sail. The big schooners were native to Maine: I remember them lying in every port waiting with infinite patience for wind and tide, five-masters, six-masters, with their long, long sheer line sweeping forward to the great bowsprit and jib boom with all the heavy rigging of chains, stays, martingale, knightheads. In the fresh northwesters they kited off, out of the bays and harbors, running free on the starboard tack, topsails, staysails, flying jibs all set and molded to the wind, twelve knots—maybe fifteen, steady and grand in the bright sunlight. At all times of day you saw schooners in the offing, two masters working through the channels and reaches, bucking tides, tacking among ledges, sluggish and slow, cargoes of stone, lumber, bales of hay; or you saw the big ones offshore, beating westward, long and short hitches, hull down over the edge, all topsails set and showing against the white of the horizon sky. Hard-working ships, weathered, moldy, coal-blackened, patched, fighting a losing battle in a changing world, but part of the old age of the sea and backed by a host of trained workers, builders, smiths, riggers, caulkers, sailmakers, and seamen. A whole world and life, all gone.

Every deep cove on the coast once had its resident sloop lying at mooring or grounded beside a wharf. If you came as a stranger, groping in through foggy or dusky channels, you expected her; you at once looked for her as the local guardian or divinity, and even in gathering darkness you saw the distinctive profile that has remained one of the classic strokes of boat design. How many times in my youth has the white form taken shape against a dusky shore, the low freeboard aft sweeping upward in a noble curve toward the clipper bow and then subtly reversing itself and running out to the long bowsprit—a line of beauty, as old Hogarth would have called it, so delicate that sketchers and painters never quite get it: the Maine sloop, the Friendship sloop (not always built in Friendship), came as near sharing man's spirit as anything ever built of oak and pine and galvanized nails. She gave a new character to the loneliest waters. She was always a reassurance, a message that a good man had conceived and made her, a triumph of function and elegance in a world of rock and fog and storm. She is still vivid in my old dreams, her silhouette in a remote cove, the white-topped mast way forward, stayed forward, the lone white boom cocked over the stern, moving a little on its topping lift, the gray canvas loosely gath-

45

ered, and the beautiful sweep of the sheer, mounting and mysteriously curving. She was the emblem of the old coast life.

With all that look of grace she could be a brutal boat. Heavy gear, long spar, long sprit, harsh weather helm, slow to windward—but always reliable—or nearly always: I remember a day of gusty northwest wind when the *Linnie Belle* swamped and sank and drowned many people—and no doubt she was over-sailed and badly handled. They used to say a Friendship sloop could "go anywhere," and some have, and now they preserve and build them as yachts, and there is a kind of fervor about the process that makes me think once more of that old touch of divinity the sloops once had as though somehow they carried some spiritual mystery within their timbers.

It is romantic to say it this way, but without romance we are better dead. I lived as a child in a dream of boats, I drew them, whittled them, sailed them in tide pools, watched them near and far, listened to talk about them. I hoarded pictures. I knew the names and the look of the great yachts: the *Reliance*, fastest of all Cup defenders, the *Defender* herself, "with her crew of Deer Islers," as the caption said—a detail I've never forgotten because in a small way I was a Deer Isler too. And the splendid schooners, *Enchantress, Irolita, Elena, Queen Mab*, and the *Atlantic*, three-masted, breaking all records for an eastward crossing to England—the picture of her charging to windward under full sail, all topsails set, is still as dramatic as anything I can remember. They had nothing to do with earthly life, those boats; they were pure visions, and reflected a romance not of mortal people and their concerns but rather of triumphant speed and grace and mastery of wind and sea. Herreshoff the designer was like a god and in the ancient Olympian hierarchy would have sat at the right hand of Poseidon; even now he seems more myth than man.

They were long-ended and low, with deep lead keels and huge spreads of sail. They were more beautiful, more mysteriously graceful, and probably faster than anything under sail today, but they represented a more fantastic extravagance—it is hard to believe that the old *Reliance*, for example, could have been anything but a dream. But all yachts are dreams, and I grew up among them—I grew old among them. I filled countless margins and notebooks with sketches, mostly abortive. The lovely long sheer and overhangs of a William Gardner sloop, like the *Vanitie*, say—could I ever quite get it on paper? Or the subtle reversing curves of a Friendship? Or a Banks dory? If you want to put a sketcher to the test, set him to draw a

46

dory. There's something in such craft beyond the lines themselves; there's an animation as though the thing had breath and soul. My everlasting sketching never quite succeeded: the beauty and truth I sought always eluded—just barely eluded me by the smallest of margins.

Summer Remembered

ISABELLA GARDNER

Sounds sum and summon the remembering of summers.
The humming of the sun
The mumbling in the honey-suckle vine
The whirring in the clovered grass
The pizzicato plinkle of ice in an auburn
uncle's amber glass.
The whing of father's racquet and the whack
of brother's bat on cousin's ball
and calling voices call-
ing voices spilling voices . . .

The munching of saltwater at the splintered dock
The slap and slop of waves on little sloops
The quarreling of oarlocks hours across the bay
The canvas sails that bleat as they
are blown. The heaving buoy bell-
ing HERE I am
HERE you are HEAR HEAR

listen listen listen
The gramophone is wound
the music goes round and around
BYE BYE BLUES LINDY'S COMING
voices calling calling calling
"Children! Children! Time's Up
Time's Up"

Merrily sturdily wantonly the familial voices
cheerily chidingly call to the children TIME'S UP
and the mute children's unvoiced clamor sacks the summer air
crying Mother Mother are you there?

Going to Shrewsbury

SARAH ORNE JEWETT

The train stopped at a way station with apparent unwillingness, and there was barely time for one elderly passenger to be hurried on board before a sudden jerk threw her almost off her unsteady old feet and we moved on. At my first glance I saw only a perturbed old countrywoman, laden with a large basket and a heavy bundle tied up in an old-fashioned bundle-handkerchief; then I discovered that she was a friend of mine, Mrs. Peet, who lived on a small farm, several miles from the village. She used to be renowned for good butter and fresh eggs and the earliest cowslip greens; in fact, she always made the most of her farm's slender resources; but it was some time since I had seen her drive by from market in her ancient thorough-braced wagon.

The brakeman followed her into the crowded car, also carrying a number of packages. I leaned forward and asked Mrs. Peet to sit by me; it was a great pleasure to see her again. The brakeman seemed relieved, and smiled as he tried to put part of his burden into the rack overhead; but even the flowered carpet-bag was much too large, and he explained that he would take care of everything at the end of the car. Mrs. Peet was not large herself but with the big basket, and the bundle-handkerchief, and some possessions of my own we had very little spare room.

"So this 'ere is what you call ridin' in the cars! Well, I do declare!" said my friend, as soon as she had recovered herself a little. She looked pale and as if she had been in tears, but there was the familiar gleam of good humor in her tired old eyes.

"Where in the world are you going, Mrs. Peet?" I asked.

"Can't be you ain't heared about me, dear?" said she. "Well, the world's bigger than I used to think 't was. I've broke up,—'t was the only thing *to* do,—and I'm a-movin' to Shrewsbury."

"To Shrewsbury? Have you sold the farm?" I exclaimed, with sorrow and surprise. Mrs. Peet was too old and too characteristic to be suddenly transplanted from her native soil.

50

" 'T wa'n't mine, the place wa'n't." Her pleasant face hardened slightly. "He was coaxed an' over-persuaded into signin' off before he was taken away. Is'iah, son of his sister that married old Josh Peet, come it over him about his bein' past work and how he 'd do for him like an own son, an' we owed him a little somethin'. I 'd paid off everythin' but that, an' was fool enough to leave it till the last, on account o' Is'iah's bein' a relation and not needin' his pay much as some others did. It's hurt me to have the place fall into other hands. Some wanted me to go right to law; but 't would n't be no use. Is'iah's smarter 'n I be about them matters. You see he's got my name on the paper, too; he said 't was somethin' 'bout bein' responsible for the taxes. We was scant o' money, an' I was wore out with watchin' an' being broke o' my rest. After my tryin' hard for risin' forty-five year to provide for bein' past work, here I be, dear, here I be! I used to drive things smart, you remember. But we was fools enough in '72 to put about everythin' we had safe in the bank into that spool factory that come to nothin'. But I tell ye I could ha' kept myself long's I lived, if I could ha' held the place. I'd parted with most o' the woodland, if Is'iah 'd coveted it. He was welcome to that, 'cept what might keep me in ovenwood. I 've always desired to travel an' see somethin' o' the world, but I 've got the chance now when I don't value it no great."

"Shrewsbury is a busy, pleasant place," I ventured to say by way of comfort, though my heart was filled with rage at the trickery of Isaiah Peet, who had always looked like a fox and behaved like one.

"Shrewsbury's be'n hold up consid'able for me to smile at," said the poor old soul, "but I tell ye, dear, it's hard to go an' live twenty-two miles from where you've always had your home and friends. It may divert me, but it won't be home. You might as well set out one o' my old apple-trees on the beach, so 't could see the waves come in,—there would n't be no please to it."

"Where are you going to live in Shrewsbury?" I asked presently.

"I don't expect to stop long, dear creatur'. I'm 'most seventy-six year old," and Mrs. Peet turned to look at me with pathetic amusement in her honest wrinkled face. "I said right out to Is'iah, before a roomful o' the neighbors, that I expected it of him to git me home an' bury me when my time come, and do it respectable; but I wanted to airn my livin', if 't was so I could, till then. He 'd made sly talk, you see, about my electin' to leave the farm and go 'long some o' my own folks; but"—and she whispered this carefully—"he did n't give me no chance to stay there without hurtin' my pride and dependin' on him. I ain't said that to many folks, but all must have suspected. A good sight on 'em 's had money of Is'iah, though, and they don't like to do nothin' but take his part an' be pretty soft spoken, fear it 'll git to his ears. Well, well, dear, we 'll let it be bygones, and not think of it no more;" but I saw the great tears roll slowly down her cheeks, and she pulled her bonnet forward impatiently, and looked the other way.

"There looks to be plenty o' good farmin' land in this part o' the country," she said, a minute later. "Where be we now? See them handsome farm buildin's; he must be a well-off man." But I had to tell my companion that we were still within the borders of the old town where we had both been born. Mrs. Peet gave a pleased little laugh, like a girl. "I'm expectin' Shrewsbury to pop up any minute. I'm feared to be kerried right by. I wa'n't never aboard of the cars before, but I 've so often thought about em' I don't know but it seems natural. Ain't it jest like flyin' through the air? I can't catch holt to see nothin'. Land! and here's my old cat goin' too, and never mistrustin'. I ain't told you that I 'd fetched her."

"Is she in that basket?" I inquired with interest.

"Yis, dear. Truth was, I calc'lated to have her put out o' the misery o' movin', an spoke to one o' the Barnes boys, an' he promised me all fair; but he wa'n't there in season, an' I kind o' made excuse to myself to fetch her along. She 's an' old creatur', like me, an' I can make shift to keep her some way or 'nuther; there 's probably mice where we 're goin', an' she 's a proper mouser that can about keep herself if there 's any sort o' chance. 'T will be somethin' o' home to see her goin' an comin', but I expect we 're both on us goin' to miss our old haunts. I'd love to know what kind o' mousin' there 's goin' to be for me."

"You must n't worry," I answered, with all the bravery and assurance that I could muster. "Your niece will be thankful to have you with her. Is she one of Mrs. Winn's daughters?"

"Oh, no, they ain't able; it 's Sister Wayland's darter Isabella, that married the overseer of the gre't carriage-shop. I ain't seen her since just after she was married; but I turned to her first because I knew she was best able to have me, and then I can see just how the other girls is situated and make me some kind of a plot. I wrote to Isabella, though she *is* ambitious, and said 't was so I'd got to ask to come an' make her a visit, an' she wrote back she would be glad to have me; but she did n't write right off, and her letter was scented up dreadful strong with some sort o' essence, and I don't feel heartened about no great of a welcome. But there, I've got eyes, an' I can

see *how* 't is when I git *where* 't is. Sister Winn's gals ain't married, an'
they've always boarded, an' worked in the shop on trimmin's. Isabella's well
off; she had some means from her father's sister. I thought it all over by
night an' day, an' I recalled that our folks kept Sister Wayland's folks all one
winter, when he'd failed up and got into trouble. I 'm reckonin' on sendin'
over to-night an' gittin' the Winn gals to come and see me and advise.
Perhaps some on 'em may know of somebody that'll take me for what help I
can give about house, or some clever folks that have been lookin' for a smart
cat, any ways; no, I don't know 's I could let her go to strangers."

"There was two or three o' the folks round home that acted real warm-
hearted towards me, an' urged me to come an' winter with 'em," continued
the exile; "an' this mornin' I wished I'd agreed to, 't was so hard to break
away. But now it's done I feel more 'n ever it's best. I could n't bear to live
right in sight o' the old place, and come spring I should n't 'prove of nothing
Is'iah ondertakes to do with the land. Oh, dear sakes! now it comes hard
with me not to have had no child'n. When I was young an' workin' hard and
into everything, I felt kind of free an' superior to them that was so blessed,
an' their houses cluttered up from mornin' till night, but I tell ye it comes
home to me now. I'd be most willin' to own to even Is'iah, mean 's he is; but
I tell ye I'd took it out of him 'fore he was a grown man, if there 'd be'n any
virtue in cow-hidin' of him. Folks don't look like wild creatur's for nothin'.
Is'iah's got fox blood in him, an' p'r'haps 't is his misfortune. His own mother
always favored the looks of an old fox, true 's the world; she was a poor
tool,—a poor tool! I d' know's we ought to blame him same 's we do.

"I 've always been a master proud woman, if I was riz among the pastures," Mrs. Peet added, half to herself. There was no use in saying much to
her; she was conscious of little beside her own thoughts and the smouldering excitement caused by this great crisis in her simple existence. Yet the
atmosphere of her loneliness, uncertainty, and sorrow was so touching that
after scolding again at her nephew's treachery, and finding the tears come
fast to my eyes as she talked, I looked intently out of the car window, and
tried to think what could be done for the poor soul. She was one of the old-
time people, and I hated to have her go away; but even if she could keep
her home she would soon be too feeble to live there alone, and some defi-
nite plan must be made for her comfort. Farms in that neighborhood were
not valuable. Perhaps through the agency of the law and quite in secret,
Isaiah Peet could be forced to give up his unrighteous claim. Perhaps, too,
the Winn girls, who were really no longer young, might have saved some-

thing, and would come home again. But it was easy to make such pictures in one's mind, and I must do what I could through other people, for I was just leaving home for a long time. I wondered sadly about Mrs. Peet's future, and the ambitious Isabella, and the favorite Sister Winn's daughters, to whom, with all their kindliness of heart, the care of so old and perhaps so dependent an aunt might seem impossible. The truth about life in Shrewsbury would soon be known; more than half the short journey was already past.

To my great pleasure, my fellow-traveler now began to forget her own troubles in looking about her. She was an alert, quickly interested old soul, and this was a bit of neutral ground between the farm and Shrewsbury, where she was unattached and irresponsible. She had lived through the last tragic moments of her old life, and felt a certain relief, and Shrewsbury might be as far away as the other side of the Rocky Mountains for all the consciousness she had of its real existence. She was simply a traveler for the time being, and began to comment, with delicious phrases and shrewd understanding of human nature, on two or three persons near us who attracted her attention.

"Where do you s'pose they be all goin'?" she asked contemptuously. "There ain't none on 'em but what looks kind o' respectable. I 'll warrant they 've left work to home they 'd ought to be doin'. I knowed, if ever I stopped to think, that cars was hived full o' folks, an' wa'n't run to an' fro for nothin'; but these can't be quite up to the average, be they? Some on 'em 's real thrif'less? guess they 've be'n shoved out o' the last place, an' goin' to try the next one,—*like me,* I suppose you'll want to say! Jest see that flauntin' old creatur' that looks like a stopped clock. There! everybody can't be o' one goodness, even preachers."

I was glad to have Mrs. Peet amused, and we were as cheerful as we could be for a few minutes. She said earnestly that she hoped to be forgiven for such talk, but there were some kinds of folks in the cars that she never had seen before. But when the conductor came to take her ticket she relapsed into her first state of mind, and was at a loss.

"You'll have to look after me, dear, when we get to Shrewsbury," she said, after we had spent some distracted moments in hunting for the ticket, and the cat had almost escaped from the basket, and the bundle-handkerchief had become untied and all its miscellaneous contents scattered about our laps and the floor. It was a touching collection of the last odds and ends of Mrs. Peet's housekeeping: some battered books, and singed holders for flatirons, and the faded little shoulder shawl that I had seen her wear many a day about her bent shoulders. There were her old tin match-box spilling all its matches, and a goose-wing for brushing up ashes, and her much-thumbed Leavitt's Almanac. It was most pathetic to see these poor trifles out of their places. At last the ticket was found in her left-hand woolen glove, where her stiff, work-worn hand had grown used to the feeling of it.

"I should n't wonder, now, if I come to like living over to Shrewsbury first-rate," she insisted, turning to me with a hopeful, eager look to see if I differed. "You see 't won't be so tough for me as if I had n't always felt it lurking within me to go off some day or 'nother an' see how other folks did things. I do' know but what the Winn gals have laid up somethin' sufficient for us to take a house, with the little mite I've got by me. I might keep house for us all, 'stead o' boardin' round in other folks' houses. That I ain't never been demeaned to, but I dare say I should find it pleasant in some ways. Town folks has got the upper hand o' country folks, but with all their work an' pride they can't make a dandelion. I do' know the times when I 've set out to wash Monday mornin's, an' tied out the line betwixt the old pucker-pear tree and the corner o' the barn, an' thought, 'Here I be with the same kind o' week's work right over again.' I'd wonder kind o' f'erce if I could n't git out of it noways; an' now here I be out of it, and an uprooteder creatur' never stood on the airth. Just as I got to feel I had somethin' ahead come that spool-factory business. There! you know he never was a fore-handed man; his health was slim, and he got discouraged pretty nigh before ever he begun. I hope he don't know I 'm turned out o' the old place. 'Is'iah's well off; he'll do the right thing by ye,' says he. But my! I turned hot all over when I found out what I'd put my name to,—me that had always be'n counted a smart woman! I did undertake to read it over, but I could n't sense it. I 've told all the folks so when they laid it off on to me some; but hand-writin' is awful tedious readin' and my head felt that day as if the works was gone."

"I ain't goin' to sag on to nobody," she assured me eagerly, as the train rushed along. "I 've got more work in me now than folks expects at my age. I may be consid'able use to Isabella. She's got a family, an' I 'll take right holt in the kitchen or with the little gals. She had four on 'em, last I heared. Isabella was never one that liked housework. Little gals! I do' know now but what they must be about grown, time doos slip away so. I expect I shall look outlandish to 'em. But there! everybody knows me to home, an' nobody knows me to Shrewsbury; 't won't make a mite o' difference, if I take holt willin'.' "

I hoped, as I looked at Mrs. Peet, that she would never be persuaded to cast off the gathered brown silk bonnet and the plain shawl that she had worn so many years; but Isabella might think it best to insist upon more modern fashions. Mrs. Peet suggested, as if it were a matter of little consequence, that she had kept it in mind to buy some mourning; but there were other things to be thought of first, and so she had let it go until winter, any way, or until she should be fairly settled in Shrewsbury.

"Are your nieces expecting you by this train?" I was moved to ask, though with all the good soul's ready talk and appealing manner I could hardly believe that she was going to Shrewsbury for more than a visit; it seemed as if she must return to the worn old farmhouse over by the sheep-lands. She answered that one of the Barnes boys had written a letter for her the day before, and there was evidently little uneasiness about her first reception.

We drew near the junction where I must leave her within a mile of the town. The cat was clawing indignantly at the basket, and her mistress grew as impatient of the car. She began to look very old and pale, my poor fellow-traveler, and said that she felt dizzy, going so fast. Presently the friendly red cheeked young brakeman came along, bringing the carpet-bag and other possessions, and insisted upon taking the alarmed cat beside, in spite of an aggressive paw that had worked its way through the wicker prison. Mrs. Peet watched her goods disappear with suspicious eyes, and clutched her bundle-handkerchief as if it might be all that she could save. Then she anxiously got to her feet, much too soon, and when I said good-by to her at the car door she was ready to cry. I pointed to the car which she was to take next on the branch line of railway, and I assured her that it was only a few minutes' ride to Shrewsbury, and that I felt certain she would find somebody waiting. The sight of that worn, thin figure adventuring alone across the platform gave my heart a sharp pang as the train carried me away.

Some of the passengers who sat near asked me about my old friend with great sympathy, after she had gone. There was a look of tragedy about her, and indeed it had been impossible not to get a good deal of her history, as she talked straight on in the same tone, when we stopped at a station, as if

56

the train were going at full speed, and some of her remarks caused pity and amusements by turns. At the last minute she said, with deep self-reproach, "Why, I have n't asked a word about your folks; but you 'd ought to excuse such an old stray hen as I be."

In the spring I was driving by on what the old people of my native town call the sheep-lands road, and the sight of Mrs. Peet's former home brought our former journey freshly to my mind. I had last heard from her just after she got to Shrewsbury, when she had sent me a message.

"Have you ever heard how she got on?" I eagerly asked my companion.

"Didn't I tell you that I met her in Shrewsbury High Street one day?" I was answered. "She seemed perfectly delighted with everything. Her nieces have laid up a good bit of money, and are soon to leave the mill, and most thankful to have old Mrs. Peet with them. Somebody told me that they wished to buy the farm here, and come back to live, but she wouldn't hear of it, and thought they would miss too many privileges. She has been going to concerts and lectures this winter, and insists that Isaiah did her a good turn."

We both laughed. My own heart was filled with joy, for the uncertain, lonely face of this homeless old woman had often haunted me. The rain-blackened little house did certainly look dreary, and a whole lifetime of patient toil had left few traces. The pucker-pear tree was in full bloom, however, and gave a welcome gayety to the deserted door-yard.

A little way beyond we met Isaiah Peet, the prosperous money-lender, who had cheated the old woman of her own. I fancied that he looked somewhat ashamed, as he recognized us. To my surprise, he stopped his horse in most social fashion.

"Old Aunt Peet's passed away," he informed me briskly. "She had a shock, and went right off sudden yisterday forenoon. I'm about now tendin' to the funeral 'rangements. She 's be'n extry smart, they say, all winter,— out to meetin' last Sabbath; never enjoyed herself so complete as she has this past month. She 'd be'n a very hard-workin' woman. Her folks was glad to have her there, and give her every attention. The place here never was good for nothin'. The old gen'leman,—uncle, you know,—he wore hisself out tryin' to make a livin' off from it."

There was an ostentatious sympathy and half-suppressed excitement from bad news which were quite lost upon us, and we did not linger to hear

John F. Kensett, *Shrewsbury River*

much more. It seemed to me as if I had known Mrs. Peet better than any one else had known her. I had counted upon seeing her again, and hearing her own account of Shrewsbury life, its pleasures and its limitations. I wondered what had become of the cat and contents of the faded bundle-handkerchief.

Nature Calling

NEWTON TOLMAN

Some of our ornithological neighbors are so expert they can identify thirty-four kinds of warblers, just by hearing various peeps and squeaks coming out of the underbrush. With competition like that around, I'm not likely to get classified as a real bird watcher; actually, I'm more of a word botcher. (We also do some birch warding—preventing campers from cutting rings of birchbark to make souvenirs.)

Something about our place high up on this mountain attracts just about every kind of native bird, except whippoorwills, who apparently get vertigo or shortness of breath or something at this altitude. They've been up here only a couple of times in ten years, and their singing sounded sort of quavery, and they didn't stay long.

All the migratory birds that spend summer vacations between here and the North Pole use our mountain as a beacon. Carrier pigeons land on the lawn to rest, their little messages strapped to their ankles. Woodcock actually drop down inside the bird dogs' pens at night to look for angleworms. This infuriates the dogs next morning when they scent the "splash" the birds have left.

Spring and fall, our outside light stays on all night. An occasional early-morning visitor thinks we've forgotten it, but the fact is we leave it lighted on purpose. It gives migrating birds a convenient check point after dark and aids their navigation.

In July, our twelve-year-old nephew, Jim, came to spend a week with us. My wife insisted I teach him something every day from my vast knowledge of birds, animals, reptiles, the woods, and nature generally. But for some reason he seemed quite skeptical about many of the things I told him.

Maybe he was put off the first night when the mosquitoes woke him up. Getting him back to sleep, I told him how a modern version of an old yarn had happened to us recently when we were camping down on Spoonwood Pond. To get away from mosquitoes, we crawled under our aluminum canoe, packing leaves around the edge to keep them out.

60

This worked all right, but soon the canoe started vibrating so loudly we still couldn't sleep. When I turned on my flashlight, there were hundreds of mosquito stingers coming right through the thin, soft metal. I picked up a stone and clinched them all, so they couldn't be withdrawn. I had some notion this might discourage the rest of them. But all of a sudden the canoe rose up and sailed off down the pond. It took us half the next day to find it and paddle it back.

On Jim's first morning, we were eating breakfast out on the porch. Our porch is one of those big, old-fashioned wooden ones, covered by an extension of the main roof but not screened in—fifteen by fifty, with some stone steps at one end, under which live about a hundred garter snakes. I wouldn't trade it for all the modern flagstone terraces and glass-paneled breezeways in the country. Frank Lloyd Wright, Gropius, and Company never in their whole careers invented anything so useful and suitable for this climate, especially for bird watching.

Jim was surprised when a pair of tame barn swallows swooped inside the porch, perched on an aerial wire between the ceiling joists, and made a great racket chirping at each other. They were discussing a nest they were building almost directly above where we were eating.

I explained to Jim how this had happened. For several mornings, we had found a heap of mud and straw on the floor. The birds were trying to build on the wire, but it would sway and down would come the whole works. I told Janet I would just as soon have them out in the garage or some place farther from my morning cup of coffee, and I hung newspapers over the wire.

Next morning they were trying to build on the newspapers, with no better luck. Janet then ordered me to "fix it for them." So I got a cedar shingle, drilled a hole in the butt so it wouldn't split, and made a shelf of it with an eight-penny nail hammered into the bottom of a joist. (I started to do this near the side of the porch, but the female kept flying over and pointing with her beak at a spot in the center, so I moved over. Evidently, she wanted it where the cat couldn't climb up near it.) It would have held up an eagle, and before I had got down from the stepladder, the swallows were on the shingle, laying out new foundations.

The second day Jim was here, he was surprised to see that the walls of the nest—hardly begun the day before—were now just about complete. He couldn't figure out how the birds had built so fast. "They didn't," I told him. "Not by themselves. They hired another pair of swallows to work for them.

61

Gave them ten bumblebees and a couple of June bugs for an eight-hour day."

Jim took this with a grain of salt, as usual. But later on—we were timing their flights and found it took them four minutes per trip from the nearest brook to bring back a snootful of mud and straw—the two of them happened to arrive together. And no sooner had they departed, when in came a third one (to my utter surprise), which also dumped some mud on the nest. After that, Jim became more cautious about doubting my veracity.

Jim also did a good deal of snake watching while he was here. Janet has an old pet garter snake, named Hildegarde, who raises a prodigious brood every summer under the porch. One day, Jim caught Hildegarde and stretched her out on the porch table and measured her with my steel tape. Our reptile book revealed that twenty-four inches was the normal length for this kind of snake, but "in rare instances individuals may reach thirty-six inches." Jim was delighted that Hildegarde measured a full thirty-three.

I explained to Jim why we hadn't been bothered with any bugs in our vegetable garden for years. After sunrise, all the snakes slide down across the lawn and start hunting in the garden. Meanwhile, our army of toads, which has been on duty all night, retires back into the dark, cool dirt under the lilac bush.

I also told Jim about the big milk snake that used to suck one of the cows dry, now and then, when I was a kid down on the farm. And about the hoop snakes that travel downhill by taking their tails in their mouths and rolling along like a hoop. These are very rare in our region, because the ground is so rough and wooded. Hoop snakes often get going too fast on our steep slopes and run into a tree or a rock, breaking their necks.

Altogether, it was really Nature Week around here during Jim's visit. We found a new patch of large purple-fringed orchids, inspected beds of "big-leaved" orchids (the frosted-silver effect on the undersides of the leaves is caused by a thin film of pure mercury the plant miraculously extracts from the soil) and a few others.

Had a dinner of beefsteak mushrooms and chanterelles. Caught a baby snowshoe rabbit about the size of a tennis ball (his mother had been slain by a pair of redtail hawks) and christened him "Everett the leveret." Found three broods of young partridge. Jim learned where to look for dragon lizards and snapping turtles, and I told him about the time I sat down on a four-foot-wide rock one foggy day while trout fishing along the lake-shore. I was starting to get my line out when the rock began to move into deep water, dumping me off. It turned out I was sitting on a big snapper.

Jim is only one of a pretty constant parade of pilgrims who find their way up here, every summer, to sit on our porch and watch the birds and look at the view. And they are all more than welcome. But there is one woman—well, never mind. The next time she comes, I'll just shove a chair directly under that swallow's nest and say, "Sit right here."

Telling the Bees

JOHN GREENLEAF WHITTIER

A remarkable custom, brought from the Old Country, formerly prevailed in the rural districts of New England. On the death of a member of the family, the bees were at once informed of the event, and their hives dressed in mourning. This ceremonial was supposed to be necessary to prevent the swarms from leaving their hives and seeking a new home. [The scene is minutely that of the Whittier homestead.]

Here is the place; right over the hill
    Runs the path I took;
You can see the gap in the old wall still,
    And the stepping-stones in the shallow brook.

There is the house, with the gate red-barred,
    And the poplars tall;
And the barn's brown length, and the cattle-yard,
    And the white horns tossing above the wall.

There are the beehives ranged in the sun;
    And down by the brink
Of the brook are her poor flowers, weed-o'errun,
    Pansy and daffodil, rose and pink.

A year has gone, as the tortoise goes,
    Heavy and slow;
And the same rose blows, and the same sun glows,
    And the same brook sings of a year ago.

There's the same sweet clover-smell in the breeze;
    And the June sun warm
Tangles his wings of fire in the trees,
    Setting, as then, over Fernside farm.

I mind me how with a lover's care
    From my Sunday coat
I brushed off the burrs, and smoothed my hair,
    And cooled at the brookside my brow and throat.

Since we parted, a month had passed,—
    To love, a year;
Down through the beeches I looked at last
    On the little red gate and the well-sweep near.

I can see it all now,—the slantwise rain
    Of light through the leaves,
The sundown's blaze on her window-pane,
    The bloom of her roses under the eaves.

Just the same as a month before,—
    The house and the trees,
The barn's brown gable, the vine by the door,—
    Nothing changed but the hives of bees.

Before them, under the garden wall,
    Forward and back,
Went drearily singing the chore-girl small,
    Draping each hive with a shred of black.

Trembling, I listened: the summer sun
    Had the chill of snow;
For I knew she was telling the bees of one
    Gone on the journey we all must go!

Root Images

Then I said to myself, "My Mary weeps
    For the dead to-day:
Haply her blind old grandsire sleeps
    The fret and the pain of his age away."

But her dog whined low; on the doorway sill,
    With his cane to his chin,
The old man sat; and the chore-girl still
    Sung to the bees stealing out and in.

And the song she was singing ever since
    In my ear sounds on:—
"Stay at home, pretty bees, fly not hence!
    Mistress Mary is dead and gone!"

Willowware Cup

JAMES MERRILL

Mass hysteria, wave after breaking wave
Blueblooded Cantonese upon these shores

Left the gene pool Lux-opaque and smoking
With dimestore mutants. One turned up today.

Plum in bloom, pagoda, blue birds, plume of willow—
Almost the replica of a prewar pattern—

The same boat bearing the gnat-sized lovers away,
The old bridge now bent double where her father signals

Feebly, as from flypaper, minding less and less.
Two smaller retainers with lanterns light him home.

Is that a scroll he carries? He must by now be immensely
Wise, and have given up earthly attachments, and all that.

Soon, of these May mornings, rising in mist, he will ask
Only to blend—like ink in flesh, blue anchor

Needled upon drunkenness while its destroyer
Full steam departs, the stigma throbbing, intricate—

Only to blend into a crazing texture.
You are far away. The leaves tell what they tell.

Root Images

But this lone, chipped vessel, if it fills,
Fills for you with something warm and clear.

Around its inner horizon the old odd designs
Crowd as before, and seem to concentrate on you.

They represent, I fancy, a version of heaven
In its day more trouble to mend than to replace:

Steep roofs aslant, minutely tiled;
Tilted honeycombs, thunderhead blue.

Clipper Ship *Dreadnought*

The Lightning-Rod Man

HERMAN MELVILLE

What grand irregular thunder, thought I, standing on my hearth-stone among the Acroceraunian hills, as the scattered bolts boomed overhead, and crashed down among the valleys, every bolt followed by zigzag irradiations, and swift slants of sharp rain, which audibly rang, like a charge of spear-points, on my low shingled roof. I suppose, though, that the mountains hereabouts break and churn up the thunder, so that it is far more glorious here than on the plain. Hark!—some one at the door. Who is this that chooses a time of thunder for making calls? And why don't he, man-fashion, use the knocker, instead of making that doleful undertaker's clatter with his fist against the hollow panel? But let him in. Ah, here he comes. "Good day, sir:" an entire stranger. "Pray be seated." What is that strange-looking walking-stick he carries: "A fine thunder-storm, sir."

"Fine?—Awful!"

"You are wet. Stand here on the hearth before the fire."

"Not for worlds!"

The stranger still stood in the exact middle of the cottage, where he had first planted himself. His singularity impelled a closer scutiny. A lean, gloomy figure. Hair dark and lank, mattedly streaked over his brow. His sunken pitfalls of eyes were ringed by indigo halos, and played with an innocuous sort of lightning: the gleam without the bolt. The whole man was dripping. He stood in a puddle on the bare oak floor: his strange walking-stick vertically resting at his side.

It was a polished copper rod, four feet long, lengthwise attached to a neat wooden staff, by insertion into two balls of greenish glass, ringed with copper bands. The metal rod terminated at the top tripodwise, in three keen tines, brightly gilt. He held the thing by the wooden part alone.

"Sir," said I, bowing politely, "have I the honor of a visit from that illustrious god, Jupiter Tonans? So stood he in the Greek statue of old, grasping the lightning-bolt. If you be he, or his viceroy, I have to thank you for this noble storm you have brewed among our mountains. Listen: that was a glorious peal. Ah, to a lover of the majestic, it is a good thing to have the Thunderer himself in one's cottage. The thunder grows finer for that. But pray be seated. This old rush-bottomed arm-chair, I grant, is a poor substitute for your evergreen throne on Olympus; but, condescend to be seated."

While I thus pleasantly spoke, the stranger eyed me, half in wonder, and half in a strange sort of horror; but did not move a foot.

"Do, sir, be seated; you need to be dried ere going forth again."

I planted the chair invitingly on the broad hearth, where a little fire had been kindled that afternoon to dissipate the dampness, not the cold; for it was early in the month of September.

But without heeding my solicitation, and still standing in the middle of the floor, the stranger gazed at me portentously and spoke.

"Sir," said he, "excuse me; but instead of my accepting your invitation to be seated on the hearth there, I solemnly warn *you*, that you had best accept *mine*, and stand with me in the middle of the room. Good Heavens!" he cried, starting—"there is another of those awful crashes. I warn you, sir, quit the hearth."

"Mr. Jupiter Tonans," said I, quietly rolling my body on the stone, "I stand very well here."

"Are you so horridly ignorant, then," he cried, "as not to know, that by far the most dangerous part of a house, during such a terrific tempest as this, is the fire-place?"

"Nay, I did not know that," involuntarily stepping upon the first board next to the stone.

The stranger now assumed such an unpleasant air of successful admonition that—quite involuntarily again—I stepped back upon the hearth, and threw myself into the erectest, proudest posture I could command. But I said nothing.

"For Heaven's sake," he cried, with a strange mixture of alarm and intimidation—"for Heaven's sake, get off the hearth! Know you not, that the heated air and soot are conductors;—to say nothing of those immense iron fire-dogs? Quit the spot—I conjure—I command you."

"Mr. Jupiter Tonans, I am not accustomed to be commanded in my own house."

"Call me not by that pagan name. You are profane in this time of terror."

"Sir, will you be so good as to tell me your business? If you seek shelter from the storm, you are welcome, so long as you be civil; but if you come on business, open it forthwith. Who are you?"

"I am a dealer in lightning-rods," said the stranger, softening his tone; "my special business is—— Merciful Heaven! what a crash!—Have you ever been struck—your premises, I mean? No? It's best to be provided,"—significantly rattling his metallic staff on the floor,—"by nature, there are no castles in thunder-storms: yet, say but the word, and of this cottage I can make a Gibraltar by a few waves of this wand. Hark, what Himalayas of concussions!"

"You interrupted yourself; your special business you were about to speak of."

"My special business is to travel the country for orders for lightning-rods. This is my specimen rod;" tapping his staff; "I have the best of references"—fumbling in his pockets. "In Criggan last month, I put up three-and-twenty rods on only five buildings."

"Let me see. Was it not at Criggan last week, about midnight on Saturday, that the steeple, the big elm, and the assembly-room cupola were struck? Any of your rods there?"

"Not on the tree and cupola, but the steeple."

"Of what use is your rod, then?"

"Of life-and-death use. But my workman was heedless. In fitting the rod at top to the steeple, he allowed a part of the metal to graze the tin sheeting. Hence the accident. Not my fault, but his. Hark!"

"Never mind. That clap burst quite loud enough to be heard without finger-pointing. Did you hear of the event at Montreal last year? A servant girl struck at her bed-side with a rosary in her hand; the beads being metal. Does your beat extend into the Canadas?"

"No. And I hear that there, iron rods only are in use. They should have *mine*, which are copper. Iron is easily fused. Then they draw out the rod so slender, that it has not body enough to conduct the full electric current. The metal melts; the building is destroyed. My copper rods never act so. Those Canadians are fools. Some of them knob the rod at the top, which risks a deadly explosion, instead of imperceptibly carrying down the current into the earth, as this sort of rod does. *Mine* is the only true rod. Look at it. Only one dollar a foot."

"This abuse of your own calling in another might make one distrustful with respect to yourself."

"Hark! The thunder becomes less muttering. It is nearing us, and nearing the earth, too. Hark! One crammed crash! All the vibrations made one by nearness. Another flash. Hold."

"What do you?" I said, seeing how now instantaneously relinquishing his staff, lean intently forward towards the window, with his right fore and middle fingers on his left wrist.

But ere the words had well escaped me, another exclamation escaped him.

"Crash! only three pulses—less than a third of a mile off—yonder, somewhere in that wood. I passed three stricken oaks there, ripped out new and glittering. The oak draws lightning more than other timber, having iron in solution in its sap. Your floor here seems oak."

"Heart-of-oak. From the peculiar time of your call upon me, I suppose you purposely select stormy weather for your journeys. When the thunder is roaring, you deem it an hour peculiarly favorable for producing impressions favorable to your trade."

"Hark!—Awful!"

"For one who would arm others with fearlessness, you seem unbeseemingly timorous yourself. Common men choose fair weather for their travels: you choose thunderstorms; and yet————"

"That I travel in thunder-storms, I grant; but not without particular precautions, such as only a lightning-rod man may know. Hark! Quick—look at my specimen rod. Only one dollar a foot."

"A very fine rod, I dare say. But what are these particular precautions of yours? Yet first let me close yonder shutters; the slanting rain is beating through the sash. I will bar up."

"Are you mad? Know you not that yon iron bar is a swift conductor? Desist."

"I will simply close the shutters, then, and call my boy to bring me a wooden bar. Pray, touch the bell-pull there."

"Are you frantic? That bell-wire might blast you. Never touch bell-wire in a thunder-storm, nor ring a bell of any sort."

"Nor those in belfries? Pray, will you tell me where and how one may be safe in a time like this? Is there any part of my house I may touch with hopes of my life?"

"There is; but not where you now stand. Come away from the wall. The current will sometimes run down a wall, and—a man being a better conductor than a wall—it would leave the wall and run into him. Swoop!

That must have fallen very nigh. That must have been globular lightning."

"Very probably. Tell me at once, which is, in your opinion, the safest part of this house?"

"This room, and this one spot in it where I stand. Come hither."

"The reasons first."

"Hark!—after the flash the gust—the sashes shiver—the house, the house!—Come hither to me!"

"The reasons, if you please."

"Come hither to me!"

"Thank you again, I think I will try my old stand—the hearth. And now, Mr. Lightning-rod-man, in the pauses of the thunder, be so good as to tell me your reasons for esteeming this one room of the house the safest, and your own one stand-point there the safest spot in it."

There was now a little cessation of the storm for a while. The Lightning-rod man seemed relieved, and replied:—

"Your house is a one-storied house, with an attic and a cellar; this room is between. Hence its comparative safety. Because lightning sometimes passes from the clouds to the earth, and sometimes from the earth to the clouds. Do you comprehend?—and I choose the middle of the room, because, if the lightning should strike the house at all, it would come down the chimney or walls; so, obviously, the further you are from them, the better. Come hither to me, now."

"Presently. Something you just said, instead of alarming me, has strangely inspired confidence."

"What have I said?"

"You said that sometimes lightning flashes from the earth to the clouds."

"Aye, the returning-stroke, as it is called; when the earth, being over-charged with the fluid, flashes its surplus upward."

"The returning-stroke; that is, from earth to sky. Better and better. But come here on the hearth and dry yourself."

"I am better here, and better wet."

"How?"

"It is the safest thing you can do—Hark, again!—to get yourself thoroughly drenched in a thunder-storm. Wet clothes are better conductors than the body; and so, if the lightning strike, it might pass down the wet clothes without touching the body. The storm deepens again. Have you a rug in the house? Rugs are non-conductors. Get one, that I may stand on it here, and you, too. The skies blacken—it is dusk at noon. Hark!—the rug, the rug!"

I gave him one; while the hooded mountains seemed closing and tumbling into the cottage.

"And now, since our being dumb will not help us," said I, resuming my place, "let me hear your precautions in traveling during thunder-storms."

"Wait till this one is passed."

"Nay, proceed with the precautions. You stand in the safest possible place according to your own account. Go on."

"Briefly, then. I avoid pine-trees, high houses, lonely barns, upland pastures, running water, flocks of cattle and sheep, a crowd of men. If I travel on foot—as to-day—I do not walk fast; if in my buggy, I touch not its back or sides; if on horseback, I dismount and lead the horse. But of all things, I avoid tall men."

"Do I dream? Man avoid man? and in danger-time, too."

"Tall men in a thunder-storm I avoid. Are you so grossly ignorant as not to know, that the height of a six-footer is sufficient to discharge an electric cloud upon him? Are not lonely Kentuckians, ploughing, smit in the unfinished furrow? Nay, if the six-footer stand by running water, the cloud will sometimes *select* him as its conductor to that running water. Hark! Sure, yon black pinnacle is split. Yes, a man is a good conductor. The lightning goes through and through a man, but only peels a tree. But sir, you have kept me so long answering your questions, that I have not yet come to business. Will you order one of my rods? Look at this specimen one? See: it is of the best of copper. Copper's the best conductor. Your house is low; but being upon the mountains, that lowness does not one whit depress it. You mountaineers are most exposed. In mountainous countries the lightning-rod man should have most business. Look at the specimen, sir. One rod will answer for a house so small as this. Look over these recommendations. Only one rod, sir; cost, only twenty dollars. Hark! There go all the granite Taconics and Hoosics dashed together like pebbles. By the sound, that must have struck something. An elevation of five feet above the house, will protect twenty feet radius all about the rod. Only twenty dollars, sir—a dollar a foot. Hark!—Dreadful!—Will you order? Will you buy? Shall I put down your name? Think of being a heap of charred offal, like a haltered horse burnt in his stall; and all in one flash!"

"You pretended envoy extraordinary and minister plenipotentiary to and from Jupiter Tonans," laughed I; "you mere man who come here to put you and your pipestem between clay and sky, do you think that because you can strike a bit of green light from the Leyden jar, that you can thoroughly avert the supernal bolt? Your rod rusts, or breaks, and where are you? Who has empowered you, you Tetzel, to peddle round your indulgences from divine ordinations? The hairs of our heads are numbered, and the days of our lives. In thunder as in sunshine, I stand at ease in the hands of my God. False negotiator, away! See, the scroll of the storm is rolled back; the house is unharmed; and in the blue heavens I read in the rainbow, that the Deity will not, of purpose, make war on man's earth."

"Impious wretch!"foamed the stranger, blackening in the face as the rainbow beamed, "I will publish your infidel notions."

"Begone! move quickly! if quickly you can, you that shine forth into sight in moist times like the worm."

The scowl grew blacker on his face; the indigo-circles enlarged round his eyes as the storm-rings round the midnight moon. He sprang upon me, his tri-forked thing at my heart.

I seized it; I snapped it; I dashed it; I trod it; and dragging the dark lightning-king out of my door, flung his elbowed, copper sceptre after him.

But spite of my treatment, and spite of my dissuasive talk of him to my neighbors, the Lightning-rod man still dwells in the land; still travels in storm-time, and drives a brave trade with the fears of man.

A Route of Evanescence

EMILY DICKINSON

A Route of Evanescence
With a revolving Wheel—
A Resonance of Emerald—
A Rush of Cochineal—
And every Blossom on the Bush
Adjusts its tumbled Head—
The mail from Tunis, probably,
An easy Morning's Ride—

Civilization Versus Wilderness

Throughout the ages people have been confronted with the questions, "What kind of place do I want to live in? What qualities must a place have to make it pleasing to me?" Answers to these very basic questions will vary with the individual. Some will hate city life; some will shun the suburbs; others will choose the countryside. Relatively few will choose the isolated life of the wilderness. Yet many people have been attracted to the wilderness for a time.

The wilderness seems to have held the promise of a place for a new start, for untrammeled communication with nature, for unconditional struggle with the forces of nature, for a chance to be isolated, for a source of seemingly unrestricted abundance, for a chance to live life freely.

The wilderness, regardless of one's reason for being there, will always be modified by the presence of a human being. The Puritans wanted to start anew "in wilde America" where they could live their lives freely. They found forests and plains almost untouched by the Indians. Since God had led them here, they felt that God had given them the land in custody to be *improved* until the time it was to be returned to Him. Since that time, people have conceived of the wilderness as a place to be "improved."

In the first half of the seventeenth century, people began talking of a "civilized wilderness," of "smiling lawns" and "tasteful cottages." Many farmers, ignoring the knowledge of conservation that then existed, exploited their reasonably productive soil and virgin forests to the point that when land to the west became available, they were happy to abandon their then "barren" land in New England. Thus land once more became wilderness which is now attracting people again.

Civilization Versus Wilderness

We see, then, where the tensions arise in this never ending contest. People need the wilderness and people need civilization. The problem is how to modify as much of the wilderness as is needed without destroying that important segment required for a balance in nature.

The writers appearing in this section respond to varying views. Some consider what nature means to them; others are sensitive to the conflict; others recognize the destructiveness of the excesses of civilization; at least one is aware of the age-old cycle of life and the resulting modifications.

What does the reader learn from these points of view? What balance in the contest can he find possible?

Night Watch
in the City of Boston

ARCHIBALD MacLEISH

Old colleague,
Puritan New England's famous scholar
half intoxicated with those heady draughts of God,
come walk these cobble-stones John Cotton trod,

and you, our Yankee Admiral of the Ocean Sea,
come too, come walk with me.
You know, none better, how the Bay wind blows
fierce in the soul as in the streets its ocean snows.

Lead me between you in the night, old friends,
one living and one dead, and where the journey ends
show me the city built as on a hill
John Winthrop saw long since and you see still.

I almost saw it once, a law school boy
born west beyond the Lakes in Illinois.
Walking down Milk Street in a summer dawn,
the sidewalks empty and the truckers gone,

I thought the asphalt turned to country lane
and climbed toward something, glimpsed and lost again—
some distance not of measure but of mind,
of meaning, Oh, of man, I could not find.

*

What city is it where the heart comes home?

*

Statue of John Adams, Boston

City of God they called it on the hills of Rome
when empire changed to church and kings were crowned
to rule in God's name all the world around.

City of God!
 Was this the city, then, of man?—
this new found city where the hope began
that Eve who spins and Adam's son who delves
might make their peace with God and rule themselves?—

this shanty city on a granite shore,
the woods behind it and the sea before,
where human hope first challenged Heaven's will
and piled a blazing beacon on a little hill?—

city where man, poor naked actor on his narrow stage,
confronted in the wilderness the God of Ages?

 *

Lead me between you to that holy ground
where man and God contended and the hope was found.

Moses upon the Sinai in the cloud
faced God for forty days and nights and bowed;
received the Law, obedient and mute;
brought back to Israel the Decalogue of Duty.

Not so New England's prophets. When their arguments were
 done
they answered thundering skies with their own thunder:
"We have the Lord," wrote Hooker with his wild goose quill,
"We have the Lord in bonds for the fulfilling."

 *

Civilization Versus Wilderness

City of Man! Before the elms came down
no village in America, no prairie town,
but planted avenues of elms against the sky
to praise, to keep the promise, to remember by—

remember that small city of great men
where man himself had walked the earth again:
Warren at Bunker Hill who stood and died
not for a flag—there was none—but for human pride;

Emerson who prayed and quit the church,
choosing not Heaven's answer but the human search;
Thoreau who followed footprints in the snow
to find his own—the human journey he had still to go;

Holmes dissenting in a sordid age,
the Court against him and the rich man's rage—
Holmes who taught the herd how human liberty is won:
by man alone, minority of one.

City of Man, Oh, city of the famous dead
where Otis spoke and Adams' heart was bred:
Mother of the great Republic—mother town
before the elm trees sickened and came down . . .

*

The darkness deepens. Shrieking voices cry
below these fantasies of glass that crowd our sky
and hatred like a whirling paper in a street
tears at itself where shame and hatred meet.

*

Show me, old friends, where in the darkness still
stands the great Republic on its hill!

Walden

E. B. WHITE

Miss Nims, take a letter to Henry David Thoreau. Dear Henry: I thought of you the other afternoon as I was approaching Concord doing fifty on Rote 62. That is a high speed at which to hold a philosopher in one's mind, but in this century we are a nimble bunch.

On one of the lawns in the outskirts of the village a woman was cutting the grass with a motorized lawn mower. What made me think of you was that the machine had rather got away from her, although she was game enough, and in the brief glimpse I had of the scene it appeared to me that the lawn was mowing the lady. She kept a tight grip on the handles, which throbbed violently with every explosion of the one-cylinder motor, and as she sheered around bushes and lurched along at a reluctant trot behind her impetuous servant, she looked like a puppy who had grabbed something that was too much for him. Concord hasn't changed much, Henry; the farm implements and the animals still have the upper hand.

I may as well admit that I was journeying to Concord with the deliberate intention of visiting your woods; for although I have never knelt at the grave of a philosopher nor placed wreaths on moldy poets, and have often gone a mile out of my way to avoid some place of historical interest, I have always wanted to see Walden Pond. The account which you left of your sojourn there is, you will be amused to learn, a document of increasing pertinence; each year it seems to gain a little headway, as the world loses ground. We may all be trascendental yet, whether we like it or not. As our common complexities increase, any tale of individual simplicity (and yours is the best written and the cockiest) acquires a new fascination; as our goods accumulate, but not our well-being, your report of an existence without material adornment takes on a certain awkward credibility.

My purpose in going to Walden Pond, like yours, was not to live cheaply or to live dearly there, but to transact some private business with the fewest obstacles. Approaching Concord, doing forty, doing forty-five, doing fifty, the steering wheel held snug in my palms, the highway held grimly in my vision, the crown of the road now serving me (on the right-hand curves), now defeating me (on the lefthand curves), I began to rouse myself from the stupefaction which a day's motor journey induces. It was a delicious evening, Henry, when the whole body is one sense, and imbibes delight through every pore, if I may coin a phrase. Fields were richly brown where the harrow, drawn by the stripped Ford, had lately sunk its teeth; pastures were green; and overhead the sky had that same everlasting great look which you will find on Page 144 of the Oxford pocket edition. I could feel the road entering me, through tire, wheel, spring, and cushion; shall I not have intelligence with earth too? Am I not partly leaves and vegetable mold myself?—a man of infinite horsepower, yet partly leaves.

Stay with me on 62 and it will take you into Concord. As I say, it was a delicious evening. The snake had come forth to die in a bloody S on the highway, the wheel upon its head, its bowels flat now and exposed. The turtle had come up too to cross the road and die in the attempt, its hard shell smashed under the rubber blow, its intestinal yearning (for the other side of the road) forever squashed. There was a sign by the wayside which announced that the road had a "cotton surface." You wouldn't know what that is, but neither, for that matter, did I. There is a cryptic ingredient in many of our modern improvements—we are awed and pleased without knowing quite what we are enjoying. It is something to be traveling on a road with a cotton surface.

The civilization round Concord to-day is an odd distillation of city, village, farm, and manor. The houses, yards, fields look not quite suburban, not quite rural. Under the bronze beech and the blue spruce of the departed baron grazes the milch goat of the heirs. Under the porte-cochère stands the reconditioned station wagon; under the grape arbor sit the puppies for sale. (But why do men degenerate ever? What makes families run out?)

It was June and everywhere June was publishing her immemorial stanza; in the lilacs, in the syringa, in the freshly edged paths and the sweetness of moist beloved gardens, and the little wire wickets that preserve the tulips' front. Farmers were already moving the fruits of their toil into their yards, arranging the rhubarb, the asparagus, the strictly fresh eggs on the painted stands under the little shed roofs with the patent shingles. And though it was almost a hundred years since you had taken your ax and started cutting out your home on Walden Pond, I was interested to observe that the philosophical spirit was still alive in Massachusetts: in the center of a vacant lot some boys were assembling the framework of a rude shelter, their whole mind and skill concentrated in the rather inauspicious helter-skeleton of studs and rafters. They too were escaping from town, to live naturally, in a rich blend of savagery and philosophy.

That evening, after supper at the inn, I strolled out into the twilight to dream my shapeless transcendental dreams and see that the car was locked up for the night (first open the right front door, then reach over, straining, and pull up the handles of the left rear and the left front till you hear the click, then the handle of the right rear, then shut the right front but open it again, remembering that the key is still in the ignition switch, remove the key, shut the right front again with a bang, push the tiny keyhole cover to one side, insert key, turn, and withdraw). It is what we all do, Henry. It is called locking the car. It is said to confuse thieves and keep them from making off with the laprobe. Four doors to lock behind one robe. The driver himself never uses a laprobe, the free movement of his legs being vital to the operation of the vehicle; so that when he locks the car it is a pure and unselfish act. I have in my life gained very little essential heat from laprobes, yet I have ever been at pains to lock them up.

The evening was full of sounds, some of which would have stirred your memory. The robins still love the elms of New England villages at sundown. There is enough of the thrush in them to make song inevitable at the end of day, and enough of the tramp to make them hang round the dwellings of men. A robin, like many another American, dearly loves a white house with green blinds. Concord is still full of them.

Your fellow-townsmen were stirring abroad—not many afoot, most of them in their cars; and the sound which they made in Concord at evening was a rustling and a whispering. The sound lacks steadfastness and is wholly unlike that of a train. A train, as you know who lived so near the Fitchburg line, whistles once or twice sadly and is gone, trailing a memory in smoke, soothing to ear and mind. Automobiles, skirting a village green, are like flies that have gained the inner ear—they buzz, cease, pause, start, shift, stop, halt, brake, and the whole effect is a nervous polytone curiously disturbing.

As I wandered along, the toc toc of ping pong balls drifted from an attic window. In front of the Reuben Brown house a Buick was drawn up. At the wheel, motionless, his hat upon his head, a man sat, listening to Amos and Andy on the radio (it is a drama of many scenes and without an end). The deep voice of Andrew Brown, emerging from the car, although it originated more than two hundred miles away, was unstrained by distance. When you used to sit on the shore of your pond on Sunday morning, listening to the church bells of Acton and Concord, you were aware of the excellent filter of the intervening atmosphere. Science has attended to that, and sound now maintains its intensity without regard for distance. Properly sponsored, it goes on forever.

A fire engine, out for a trial spin, roared past Emerson's house, hot with readiness for public duty. Over the barn roofs the martins dipped and chittered. A swarthy daughter of an asparagus grower, in culottes, shirt, and bandanna, pedalled past on her bicycle. It was indeed a delicious evening, and I returned to the inn (I believe it was your house once) to rock with the old ladies on the concrete veranda.

Next morning early I started afoot for Walden, out Main Street and down Thoreau, past the depot and the Minuteman Chevrolet Company. The morning was fresh, and in a bean field along the way I flushed an agriculturalist, quietly studying his beans. Thoreau Street soon joined Number 126, an artery of the State. We number our highways nowadays, our speed being so great we can remember little of their quality or character and are lucky to remember their number. (Men have an indistinct notion that if they keep up this activity long enough all will at length ride somewhere, in next to no time.) Your pond is on 126.

I knew I must be nearing your woodland retreat when the Golden Pheasant lunchroom came into view—Sealtest ice cream, toasted sandwiches, hot frankfurters, waffles, tonics, and lunches. Were I the proprietor, I should add rice, Indian meal, and molasses—just for old time's sake. The Pheasant, incidentally, is for sale: a chance for some nature lover who wishes to set himself up beside a pond in the Concord atmosphere and live deliberately, fronting only the essential facts of life on Number 126. Beyond the Pheasant was a place called Walden Breezes, an oasis whose porch pillars were made of old green shutters sawed into lengths. On the porch was a distorting mirror, to give the traveler a comical image of himself, who had miraculously learned to gaze in an ordinary glass without smiling. Behind the Breezes, in a sun-parched clearing, dwelt your philosophical descendants in their trailers, each trailer the size of your hut, but all grouped together for the sake of congeniality. Trailer people leave the city, as you did, to discover solitude and in any weather, at any hour of the day or night, to improve the nick of time; but they soon collect in villages and get bogged deeper in the mud than ever. The camp behind Walden Breezes was just rousing itself to the morning. The ground was packed hard under the heel, and the sun came through the clearing to bake the soil and enlarge the wry smell of cramped housekeeping. Cushman's bakery truck had stopped to deliver an early basket of rolls. A camp dog, seeing me in the road, barked petulantly. A man emerged from one of the trailers and set forth with a bucket to draw water from some forest tap.

Leaving the highway I turned off into the woods toward the pond, which was apparent through the foliage. The floor of the forest was strewn with dried old oak leaves and *Transcripts*. From beneath the flattened pop-corn wrapper (*granum explosum*) peeped the frail violet. I followed a footpath and descended to the water's edge. The pond lay clear and blue in the morning light, as you have seen it so many times. In the shallows a man's waterlogged shirt undulated gently. A few flies came out to greet me and convoy me to your cove, past the No Bathing signs on which the fellows and the girls had scrawled their names. I felt strangely excited suddenly to be snooping around your premises, tiptoeing along watchfully, as though not to tread by mistake upon the intervening century. Before I got to the cove I heard something which seemed to me quite wonderful: I heard your frog, a full, clear *troonk*, guiding me, still hoarse and solemn, bridging the years as the robins had bridged them in the sweetness of the village evening. But he soon quit, and I came on a couple of young boys throwing stones at him.

Your front yard is marked by a bronze tablet set in a stone. Four small granite posts, a few feet away, show where the house was. On top of the tablet was a pair of faded blue bathing trunks with a white stripe. Back of it is a pile of stones, a sort of cairn, left by your visitors as a tribute I suppose. It is a rather ugly little heap of stones, Henry. In fact the hillside itself seems faded, browbeaten; a few tall skinny pines, bare of lower limbs, a smattering of young maples in suitable green, some birches and oaks, and a number of trees felled by the last big wind. It was from the bole of one of these fallen pines, torn up by the roots, that I extracted the stone which I added to the cairn—a sentimental act in which I was interrupted by a small terrier from a nearby picnic group, who confronted me and wanted to know about the stone.

I sat down for a while on one of the posts of your house to listen to the bluebottles and the dragonflies. The invaded glade sprawled shabby and mean at my feet, but the flies were tuned to the old vibration. There were the remains of a fire in your ruins, but I doubt that it was yours; also two beer bottles trodden into the soil and become part of earth. A young oak had taken root in your house, and two or three ferns, unrolling like the ticklers at a banquet. The only other furnishings were a DuBarry pattern sheet, a page torn from a picture magazine, and some crusts in wax paper.

Before I quit I walked clear round the pond and found the place where you used to sit on the northeast side to get the sun in the fall, and the beach where you got sand for scrubbing your floor. On the eastern side of the pond, where the highway borders it, the State has built dressing rooms for swimmers, a float with diving towers, drinking fountains of porcelain, and rowboats for hire. The pond is in fact a State Preserve, and carries a twenty-dollar fine for picking wild flowers, a decree signed in all solemnity by your fellow-citizens Walter C. Wardwell, Erson B. Barlow, and Nathaniel I. Bowditch. There was a smell of creosote where they had been building a wide wooden stairway to the road and the parking area. Swimmers and boaters were arriving; bodies plunged vigorously into the water and emerged wet and beautiful in the bright air. As I left, a boatload of town boys were splashing about in mid-pond, kidding and fooling, the young fellows singing at the tops of their lungs in a wild chorus:

Amer-ica, Amer-i-ca, God shed his grace on thee,
And crown thy good with brotherhood
From sea to shi-ning sea!

I walked back to town along the railroad, following your custom. The rails were expanding noisily in the hot sun, and on the slope of the roadbed the wild grape and the backberry sent up their creepers to the track.

The expense of my brief sojourn in Concord was:

Canvas shoes	. . . .	$1.95
Baseball bat	. . . .	.25 ⎱ gifts to take back
Left-handed fielder's glove	. . . .	1.25 ⎰ to a boy
Hotel and meals	. . . .	4.25
In all	. . . .	$7.70

As you see, this amount was almost what you spent for food for eight months. I cannot defend the shoes or the expenditure for shelter and food: they reveal a meanness and grossness in my nature which you would find contemptible. The baseball equipment, however, is the kind of impediment with which you were never on even terms. You must remember that the house where you practiced the sort of economy which I respect was haunted only by mice and squirrels. You never had to cope with a shortstop.

All Day I Was with Trees

MAY SARTON

Across wild country on solitary roads
Within a fugue of parting, I was consoled
By birches' sovereign whiteness in sad woods,
Dark glow of pines, a single elm's distinction—
I was consoled by trees.

In February we see the structure change—
Or the light change, and so the way we see it.
Tensile and delicate, the trees stand now
Against the early skies, the frail fresh blue,
In an attentive stillness.

Naked, the trees are singularly present,
Although their secret force is still locked in.
Who could believe that the new sap is rising
And soon we shall draw up amazing sweetness
From stark maples?

All day I was with trees, a fugue of parting,
All day I lived in long cycles, not brief hours.
A tenderness of light before new falls of snow
Lay on the barren landscape like a promise.
Love nourished every vein.

Stones

MAXINE KUMIN

The moving of stones, that sly jockeying thrust
takes place at night underground, shoulders first.

They bud in their bunkers like hydras. They puff
up head after head and allow them to drop off

on their own making quahogs, cow flops, eggs and knee
caps. In this way one stone can infuse a colony.

Eyeless and unsurprised they behave
in the manner of stones: swallow turnips, heave graves

rise up openmouthed into walls and from time
to time imitate oysters or mushrooms.

The doors of my house are held open by stones
and to see the tame herd of them hump their backbones

as cumbrous as bears across the pasture in
an allday rain is to believe for an afternoon

of objects that waver and blur
in some dark obedient order.

Nature

RALPH WALDO EMERSON

The rounded world is fair to see,
Nine times folded in mystery:
Though baffled seers cannot impart
The secret of its laboring heart,
Throb thine with Nature's throbbing breast,
And all is clear from east to west.
Spirit that lurks each form within
Beckons to spirit of its kin;
Self-kindled every atom glows,
And hints the future which it owes.

There are days which occur in this climate, at almost any season of the year, wherein the world reaches its perfection; when the air, the heavenly bodies and the earth, make a harmony, as if nature would indulge her offspring; when, in these bleak upper sides of the planet, nothing is to desire that we have heard of the happiest latitudes, and we bask in the shining hours of Florida and Cuba; when everything that has life gives sign of satisfaction, and the cattle that lie on the ground seem to have great and tranquil thoughts. These halcyons may be looked for with a little more assurance in that pure October weather which we distinguish by the name of the Indian summer. The day, immeasurably long, sleeps over the broad hills and warm wide fields. To have lived through all its sunny hours, seems longevity enough. The solitary places do not seem quite lonely. At the gates of the forest, the surprised man of the world is forced to leave his city estimates of great and small, wise and foolish. The knapsack of custom falls off his back with the first step he takes into these precincts. Here is sanctity which shames our religions, and reality which discredits our heroes. Here we find Nature to be the circumstance which dwarfs every other circumstance, and judges like a god all men that come to her. We have crept out of our close and crowded houses into the night and morning, and we see what majestic beauties daily wrap us in their bosom. How willingly we would es-

93

cape the barriers which render them comparatively impotent, escape the sophistication and second thought, and suffer nature to intrance us. The tempered light of the woods is like a perpetual morning, and is stimulating and heroic. The anciently-reported spells of these places creep on us. The stems of pines, hemlocks and oaks almost gleam like iron on the excited eye. The incommunicable trees begin to persuade us to live with them, and quit our life of solemn trifles. Here no history, or church, or state, is interpolated on the divine sky and the immortal year. How easily we might walk onward into the opening landscape, absorbed by new pictures and by thoughts fast succeeding each other, until by degrees the recollection of home was crowded out of the mind, all memory obliterated by the tyranny of the present, and we were led in triumph by nature.

These enchantments are medicinal, they sober and heal us. These are plain pleasures, kindly and native to us. We come to our own, and make friends with matter, which the ambitious chatter of the schools would persuade us to despise. We never can part with it; the mind loves its old home: as water to our thirst, so is the rock, the ground, to our eyes and hands and feet. It is firm water; it is cold flame; what health, what affinity! Ever an old friend, ever like a dear friend and brother when we chat affectedly with strangers, comes in this honest face, and takes a grave liberty with us, and shames us out of our nonsense. Cities give not the human senses room enough. We go out daily and nightly to feed the eyes on the horizon, and require so much scope, just as we need water for our bath. There are all degrees of natural influence, from these quarantine powers of nature, up to her dearest and gravest ministrations to the imagination and the soul. There is the bucket of cold water from the spring, the wood-fire to which the chilled traveller rushes for safety,—and there is the sublime moral of autumn and of noon. We nestle in nature, and draw our living as parasites from her roots and grains, and we receive glances from the heavenly bodies, which call us to solitude and foretell the remotest future. The blue zenith is the point in which romance and reality meet. I think if we should be rapt away into all that and dream of heaven, and should converse with Gabriel and Uriel, the upper sky would be all that would remain of our furniture.

It seems as if the day was not wholly profane in which we have given heed to some natural object. The fall of snowflakes in a still air, preserving to each crystal its perfect form; the blowing of sleet over a wide sheet of water, and over plains; the waving rye-field; the mimic waving of acres of houstonia, whose innumerable florets whiten and ripple before the eye; the reflections of trees and flowers in glassy lakes; the musical, steaming, odorous south wind, which converts all trees to wind-harps; the crackling and spurting of hemlock in the flames, or of pine logs, which yield glory to the walls and faces in the sitting-room,—these are the music and pictures of the most ancient religion. My house stands in low land, with limited out-look, and on the skirt of the village. But I go with my friend to the shore of our little river, and with one stroke of the paddle I leave the village politics and personalities, yes, and the world of villages and personalities, behind, and pass into a delicate realm of sunset and moonlight, too bright almost for spotted man to enter without novitiate and probation. We penetrate bodily this incredible beauty; we dip our hands in this painted element; our eyes are bathed in these lights and forms. A holiday, a *villeggiatura*, a royal revel, the proudest, most heart-rejoicing festival that valor and beauty, power and taste, ever decked and enjoyed, establishes itself on the instant. These sunset clouds, these delicately emerging stars, with their private and ineffable glances, signify it and proffer it. I am taught the poorness of our in-vention, the ugliness of towns and palaces. Art and luxury have early learned that they must work as enhancement and sequel to this original beauty. I am over-instructed for my return. Henceforth I shall be hard to please. I cannot go back to toys. I am grown expensive and sophisticated. I can no longer live without elegance, but a countryman shall be my master of revels. He who knows the most; he who knows what sweets and virtues are in the ground, the waters, the plants, the heavens, and how to come at these enchantments,—is the rich and royal man. Only as far as the masters of the world have called in nature to their aid, can they reach the height of magnificence. This is the meaning of their hanging-gardens, villas, garden-houses, islands, parks and preserves, to back their faulty personality with these strong accessories. I do not wonder that the landed interest should be invincible in the State with these dangerous auxiliaries. These bribe and in-vite; not kings, not palaces, not men, not women, but these tender and po-etic stars, eloquent of secret promises. We heard what the rich man said, we knew of his villa, his grove, his wine and his company, but the provoca-tion and point of the invitation came out of these beguiling stars. In their soft glances I see what men strove to realize in some Versailles, or Paphos, or Ctesiphon. Indeed, it is the magical lights of the horizon and the blue sky for the background which save all our works of art, which were otherwise bawbles. When the rich tax the poor with servility and obsequiousness, they should consider the effect of men reputed to be the possessors of nature, on imaginative minds. Ah! if the rich were rich as the poor fancy riches! A boy hears a military band play on the field at night, and he has kings and queens and famous chivalry palpably before him. He hears the echoes of a horn in a hill country, in the Notch Mountains, for example, which converts the mountains into an Æolian harp,—and this supernatural *tiralira* restores to him the Dorian mythology, Apollo, Diana, and all divine hunters and huntresses. Can a musical note be so lofty, so haughtily beautiful! To the poor young poet, thus fabulous is his picture of society; he is loyal; he respects the rich; they are rich for the sake of his imagination; how poor his fancy would be, if they were not rich! That they have some high-fenced grove which they call a park; that they live in larger and better-garnished saloons than he has visited, and go in coaches, keeping only the society of the elegant, to watering-places and to distant cities,—these make the groundwork from which he has delineated estates of romance, compared with which their actual possessions are shanties and paddocks. The muse herself betrays her son, and enhances the gifts of wealth and well-born beauty by a radiation out of the air, and clouds, and forests that skirt the road,—a certain haughty favor, as if from patrician genii to patricians, a kind of aristocracy in nature, a prince of the power of the air.

The moral sensibility which makes Edens and Tempes so easily, may not be always found, but the material landscape is never far off. We can find these enchantments without visiting the Como Lake, or the Madeira Islands. We exaggerate the praises of local scenery. In every landscape the point of astonishment is the meeting of the sky and the earth, and that is seen from the first hillock as well as from the top of the Alleghanies. The stars at night stoop down over the brownest, homeliest common with all the spiritual magnificence which they shed on the Campagna, or on the marble deserts of Egypt. The uprolled clouds and the colors of morning and evening will transfigure maples and alders. The difference between landscape and landscape is small, but there is great difference in the beholders. There is nothing so wonderful in any particular landscape as the necessity of being beautiful under which every landscape lies. Nature cannot be surprised in undress. Beauty breaks in everywhere.

But it is very easy to outrun the sympathy of readers on this topic, which schoolmen called *natura naturata*, or nature passive. One can hardly speak directly of it without excess. It is as easy to broach in mixed companies what is called "the subject of religion." A susceptible person does not like to indulge his tastes in this kind without the apology of some trivial necessity: he goes to see a wood-lot, or to look at the crops, or to fetch a plant or a mineral from a remote locality, or he carries a fowling-piece or a fishing-rod. I suppose this shame must have a good reason. A dilettanteism in nature is barren and unworthy. The fop of fields is no better than his brother of Broadway. Men are naturally hunters and inquisitive of wood-craft, and I suppose that such a gazetteer as wood-cutters and Indians should furnish facts for, would take place in the most sumptuous drawing-rooms of all the "Wreaths" and "Flora's chaplets" of the bookshops; yet ordinarily, whether we are too clumsy for so subtle a topic, or from whatever cause, as soon as men begin to write on nature, they fall into euphuism. Frivolity is a most unfit tribute to Pan, who ought to be represented in the mythology as the most continent of gods. I would not be frivolous before the admirable reserve and prudence of time, yet I cannot renounce the right of returning often to this old topic. The multitude of false churches accredits the true religion. Literature, poetry, science are the homage of man to this unfathomed secret, concerning which no sane man can affect an indifference or incuriosity. Nature is loved by what is best in us. It is loved as the city of God, although, or rather because there is no citizen. The sunset is unlike anything that is underneath it: it wants men. And the beauty of nature must always seem unreal and mocking, until the landscape has human figures that are as good as itself. If there were good men, there would never be this rapture in nature. If the king is in the palace, nobody looks at the walls. It is when he is gone, and the house is filled with grooms and gazers, that we turn from the people to find relief in the majestic men that are suggested by the pictures and the architecture. The critics who complain of the sickly separation of the beauty of nature from the thing to be done, must consider that our hunting of the picturesque is inseparable from our protest against false society. Man is fallen; nature is erect, and serves as a differential thermometer, detecting the presence or absence of the divine sentiment in man. By fault of our dulness and selfishness we are looking up to nature, but when we are convalescent, nature will look up to us. We see the foaming brook with compunction: if our own life flowed with the right energy, we should shame the brook. The stream of zeal sparkles with real fire, and not with reflex rays of sun and moon. Nature may be as selfishly studied as trade. Astronomy to the selfish becomes astrology; psychology, mesmerism (with intent to show where our spoons are gone); and anatomy and physiology become phrenology and palmistry.

But taking timely warning, and leaving many things unsaid on this topic, let us not longer omit our homage to the Efficient Nature, *natura naturans,* the quick cause before which all forms flee as the driven snows; itself secret, its works driven before it in flocks and multitudes, (as the ancients represented nature by Proteus, a shepherd,) and in undescribable variety. It publishes itself in creatures, reaching from particles and spiculæ through transformation on transformation to the highest symmetries, arriving at consummate results without a shock or a leap. A little heat, that is a little motion, is all that differences the bald, dazzling white and deadly cold poles of the earth from the prolific tropical climates. All changes pass without violence, by reason of the two cardinal conditions of boundless space and boundless time. Geology has initiated us into the secularity of nature, and taught us to disuse our dame-school measures, and exchange our Mosaic and Ptolemaic schemes for her large style. We knew nothing rightly, for want of perspective. Now we learn what patient periods must round themselves before the rock is formed; then before the rock is broken, and the first lichen race has disintegrated the thinnest external plate into soil, and opened the door for the remote Flora, Fauna, Ceres, and Pomona to come in. How far off yet is the trilobite! how far the quadruped! how inconceivably remote is man! All duly arrive, and then race after race of men. It is a long way from granite to the oyster; farther yet to Plato and the preaching of the immortality of the soul. Yet all must come, as surely as the first atom has two sides.

The Summer Farmer

JOHN CHEEVER

The Nor'easter is a train the railroad christened at a moment when its directors were imbued with the mystery of travel. Memory is often more appealing than fact, and a passenger who had long ridden the train might overlook its noise and dirt each time he entered the Grand Central Station and saw there the name of a northerly three-day rain. This, at least, was the case with Paul Hollis, who rode the Nor'easter on nearly every Thursday or Friday night of his summer. He was a bulky man, who suffered in all Pullmans, but in none so much as he did on this ride. As a rule, he stayed in the club car until ten, drinking Scotch. The whiskey ordinarily kept him asleep until they reached the tumultuous delays of Springfield, past midnight. North of Springfield, the train fell into the balky and malingering stride of an old local, and Paul lay in his berth between wakefulness and sleep, like a partially anesthetized patient. The ordeal ended when, after breakfast, he left the Nor'easter, in Meridian Junction, and was met by his gentle wife. There was this to be said about the journey: It made one fully conscious of the terrestrial distance that separated the hot city from the leafy and ingenuous streets of the junction village.

The conversation between Paul and Virginia Hollis during the drive from the Junction to their farm, north of Hiems, was confined to the modest properties and affections they shared; more than this, it seemed to aim at a deliberate inconsequence, as if to mention the checking balance or the wars might ruin the spell of a mild morning and an open car. The drain in the downstairs shower was leaking, Virginia told Paul one morning in July, his sister Ellen was drinking too much, the Marstons had been over for lunch, and the time had come for the children to have a pet. This was a subject to which she had obviously given some thought. No country dog would last in a New York apartment when they returned in the fall, she said, cats were a nuisance, and she had concluded that rabbits were the best they could do. There was a house on the road with a rabbit cage on its lawn, and they could stop there that morning and buy a pair. They would be a present from

Village of Burke Hollow, Vermont

Paul to the children, and so much the better for that. The purchase would make that weekend the weekend when they had bought the rabbits, and distinguish it from the weekend when they had transplanted the Christmas fern or the weekend when they had removed the dead juniper. They could put the rabbits into the old duckhouse, Virginia said, and when they went back to the city in the fall, Kasiak could eat them. Kasiak was the hired man.

They were driving upland. From the Junction north, one never quite lost the sense of a gradual climb. Hills blocked off the delicate, the vitiated New Hampshire landscape, with its omnipresence of ruin, but every few miles a tributary of the Merrimack opened a broad valley, with elms, farms, and stone fences. "It's along here," Virginia said. Paul didn't know what she meant until she reminded him of the rabbits. "If you'll slow down here . . . Here, Paul, *here*." He bumped the car over the shoulder of the road and stopped. On the lawn of a white, neat house, darkened by rock maples, there was a rabbit cage. "Hello," Paul shouted, "hello," and a man in overalls came out of a side door, chewing on something, as if he'd been interrupted at a meal. White rabbits were two dollars, he said. Browns and grays were a dollar and a half. He swallowed, and wiped his mouth with his fist. He spoke uneasily, as if he had wanted to keep the simple transaction from someone, and after Paul had picked a brown and a gray, he ran to the barn for a box. As Paul turned the car back onto the road, they heard behind them a heartbroken shout. A boy ran from the house to the rabbit cage, and they saw the source of the farmer's uneasiness.

The cash market and the antique store, the Civil War cannon and the post office of Hiems fell behind them, and Paul accelerated the car happily when they escaped from the narrow streets of the village and drove into the fresh lake winds. The road brought them, first, along the unfashionable, or gregarious, end of the lake; then the houses thinned and gave way to pine groves and empty fields as they drove north. The sense of home-coming—of returning to a place where he had summered all his life—became for Paul so violent that the difference between the pace of his imagination and the speed of the car annoyed him until they turned off the road onto grass ruts and saw, literally at the road's end, their farm.

The gentle shadow of a cloud was passing the face of the Hollis house. At the edge of the lawn, there was an upside-down piece of porch furniture that had been abandoned in a thundershower and that seemed to have been drying there since Paul's youth. The light and heat increased and the shade deepened as the moving shadow of the cloud darkened the barn and the clothesyard and vanished into the woods. "Hello, Brother." It was Paul's sister Ellen calling to him from one of the open windows. His business suit bound at the shoulders when he left the car, as if he had taken on height, for the place told him that he was ten years younger; the maples, the house, the simple mountains all told him this. His two small children stormed around the edge of the barn and collided against his legs. Taller, browner, healthier, more handsome, more intelligent—they seemed to him to be all these things each weekend when he was reunited with them. A sere branch on a maple caught his eye. That would have to be cut. He stooped down to pick up his little boy and girl in a scalding rush of love, for which he was unarmed and, it seemed, unprepared.

The duckhouse, where they put the rabbits that morning, had been empty for years, but there was a cage and a shelter, and it would do. "Now, these are your pets, these are your rabbits," Paul told the children. His sternness transfixed them, and the little boy began to suck his thumb. "These are your responsibility, and if you take good care of them, perhaps you can have a dog when we get back to New York. You'll have to feed them and clean their house." His love for the children and his desire to draw for them, even faintly, the mysterious shapes of responsibility reduced him to a fatuity that he was conscious of himself. "I don't want you to expect someone else to help you," he said. "You'll have to give them water twice a day. They're supposed to like lettuce and carrots. Now you can put them in the house yourself. Daddy has to get to work."

Paul Hollis was a summer farmer. He mowed, cultivated, and waxed angry about the price of scratch feed, and at that instant when the plangent winds of Labor Day began to sound he hung up his blunted scythe to rust in the back hall, where the kerosene was kept, and happily shifted his interest to the warm apartments of New York. On that day—the day when he bought the rabbits—he went to his bedroom after he had lectured the children, and changed into a pair of coveralls that were still dimly stencilled with his name, rank, and serial number. Virginia sat on the edge of the bed while he dressed, and talked about his sister Ellen, who was spending a month with them. Ellen needed the rest; Ellen drank too much. But there was no suggestion of correction or change in what Virginia said about Ellen, and when Paul glanced at his wife, he thought how forgiving and comely she was. The room was old and pleasant—it had been his parents' room— and what light reached it reached it through the leaves. They lingered there talking about Ellen, the children, tasting the astringency of their content-ment and their worthiness, but not so long as to seem idle. Paul was going to help Kasiak scythe the highest field, and Virginia wanted to pick some flowers.

The Hollis property was high, and it was Paul's long-dead father who had called the highest pasture Elysian, because of its unearthly stillness. This pasture was mowed on alternate years to keep the scrub from taking hold. When Paul reached it that morning, Kasiak was there, and Paul judged that he had been working for about three hours; Kasiak was paid by the hour. The two men spoke briefly—the hired man and the vacationist—and picked up the tacit bond of people who happen to be working together. Paul mowed below and a little to Kasiak's right. He used a scythe well, but there was no confusing, even at a distance, Kasiak's diligent figure with Paul's.

Kasiak was Russian-born. This and everything else Paul knew about him he had been told while they worked. Kasiak had landed in Boston, worked in a shoe factory, studied English at night, rented, and eventually bought, the farm below the Hollis place. They had been neighbors for twenty years. He was doing the Hollises' work that year for the first time. Up until then, he had been merely a persevering and colorful figure on their landscape. He dressed his deaf wife in salt bags and potato sacks. He was miserly. He was bitter. Even on that summer morning, he cut a figure of chagrin and discontent. He kept his woods clear and stored his hay at precisely the right moment, and his fields, his gardens, his compost heap, and the sour smell of milk in his immaculate kitchen conveyed the sense of security that lies in the power of intelligent husbandry. He mowed, he walked, like a prisoner in a prison yard. From the time he went to the barn, an hour before dawn, until his day ended, there was no hesitation in his thought or in his step, and this flawless link of chores was part of a larger chain of responsibilities and aspirations that had begun with his youth in Russia and that would end, he believed, with the birth of a just and peaceable world, delivered in bloodshed and arson.

Virginia had been amused when Paul told her that Kasiak was a Com-munist. Kasiak had told Paul himself. Two weeks after he had begun to work for them, he had taken to cutting editorials from a Communist news-paper and handing them to Paul or slipping them under the kitchen door. Reasonableness was Paul's watchword with Kasiak, he liked to think. Twice, in the feed store, when Kasiak's politics had been under discussion, Paul had defended Kasiak's right to draw his own conclusions about the future, and in their conversations he always asked Kasiak lightly when he was going to have his revolution.

That day fell at the end of the haying weather. As it got late in the morning, they could hear dull blasts of thunder. A wind rose in the neighborhood, but there was none to speak of in the field. Kasiak trailed after him a rich blend of citronella and vinegar, and both men were plagued with flies. They did not let the chance of a storm change the pace of their scything. It was as if there were some significance, hidden, surely, to them, in completing the field. Then the wet wind climbed the hill behind them, and Paul, taking one hand off the snath, straightened his back. While they had been working, clouds had blackened the sky from the horizon to above his head, so he was given the illusion of a country divided evenly between the lights of catastrophe and repose. The shade of the storm was travelling as rapidly up the field as a man walks, but the hay it had not touched was yellow, and there was no portent of the storm in the delicate sky ahead of him or in the clouds there or in anything he could see except the green wood, whose color the storm had begun to deepen. Then he felt against his skin a coldness that belonged to no part of the day, and heard at his back the rain begin to drop through the trees.

Paul ran for the woods. Kasiak followed slowly, with the storm at his heels. They sat beside each other on stones in the shelter of the dense foliage, watching the moving curtain of rain. Kasiak took off his hat—for the first time that summer to Paul's knowledge. His hair and forehead were gray. Ruddiness began on his high cheekbones and shaded down to a dark brown that spread from his jaw to his neck.

"How much will you charge me for using your horse to cultivate the garden?" Paul asked.

"Four dollars." Kasiak didn't raise his voice, and Paul couldn't hear him above the noise the rain made crashing into the field.

"How much?"

"Four dollars."

"Let's try it tomorrow morning if it's clear. Shall we?"

"You'll have to do it early. It's too hot for her in the afternoon."

"Six o'clock."

"You want to get up that early?" Kasiak smiled at his gibe at the Hollis family and their disorderly habits. Lightning tipped the woods, so close to them that they could smell the galvanic discharge, and a second later there was an explosion of thunder that sounded as if it had destroyed the county. The front of the storm passed then, the wind died down, and the shower fell around them with the dogged gloom of an autumn rain.

"Have you heard from your family recently, Kasiak?" Paul asked.

"For two years—not for two years."

"Would you like to go back?"

"Yes, yes." There was an intent light in his face. "On my father's farm, there are some big fields. My brothers are still there. I would like to go there in an airplane. I would land the airplane in these big fields, and they would all come running to see who it was and they would see it was me."

"You don't like it here, do you?"

"It's a capitalist country."

"Why did you come, then?"

"I don't know. I think over there they made me work too hard. Over there, we cut the rye at night, when there is some moisture in the air. They put me to work in the fields when I was twelve years old. We get up at three in the morning to cut the rye. My hands are all bleeding, and swollen so I can't sleep. My father beat me like a convict. In Russia, they used to beat convicts. He beat me with a whip for horses until my back was bleeding." Kasiak felt his back, as if the welts still bled. "After that, I decided to go away. I waited six years. That's why I came, I guess—they set me to work in the fields too soon."

"When are you going to have your revolution, Kasiak?"

"When the capitalists make another war."

"What's going to happen to me, Kasiak? What's going to happen to people like me?"

"It depends. If you work on a farm or in a factory, I guess it will be all right. They'll only get rid of useless people."

"All right, Kasiak," Paul said heartily, "I'll work for you," and he slapped the farmer on the back. He frowned at the rain. "I guess I'll go down and get some lunch," he said. "We won't be able to scythe any more today, will we?" He ran down the wet field to the barn. Kasiak followed him a few minutes later, but he did not run. He entered the barn and began to repair a cold frame, as if the thunderstorm fitted precisely into his scheme of things.

Before dinner that night, Paul's sister Ellen drank too much. She was late coming to the table, and when Paul went into the pantry for a spoon, he found her there, drinking out of the silver cocktail shaker. Seated at the table, high in her firmament of gin, she looked critically at her brother and his wife, remembering some real or imagined injustice of her youth, for with any proximity the constellations of some families generate among themselves an asperity that nothing can sweeten. Ellen was a heavy-featured woman who held her strong blue eyes at a squint. She had had her second divorce that spring. She had wrapped a bright scarf around her head for dinner that night and put on an old dress she had found in one of the attic trunks, and, reminded by her faded clothes of a simpler time of life, she talked uninterruptedly about the past and, particularly, about Father—Father this and Father that. The shabby dress and her reminiscent mood made Paul impatient, and it seemed to him that a vast crack had appeared magically in Ellen's heart the night Father died.

A northwest wind had driven the thunderstorm out of the county and left in the air a poignant chill, and when they went out on the piazza after dinner to watch the sun go down, there were a hundred clouds in the west—clouds of gold, clouds of silver, clouds like bone and tinder and filth under the bed. "It's so *good* for me to be up here," Ellen said. "It does so much for me." She sat on the rail against the light, and Paul couldn't see her face. "I can't find Father's binoculars," she went on, "and his golf clubs have disappeared." From the open window of the children's room, Paul heard his daughter singing, "How many miles is it to Babylon? Three score miles and ten. Can we get there by candlelight? . . ." Immense tenderness and contentment fell to him with her voice from the open window.

It was so good for them all, as Ellen said; it did so much for them. It was a phrase Paul had heard spoken on that piazza since his memory had become retentive. Ellen was the mote on that perfect evening. There was something wrong, some half-known evil in her worship of the bucolic scene—some measure of her inadequacy and, he supposed, of his.

"Let's have a brandy," Ellen said. They went into the house to drink. In the living room, there was a lot of talk about what they would have—brandy, mint, Cointreau, Scotch. Paul went into the kitchen and put glasses and bottles on a tray. The screen door was shaken by something—the wind, he guessed, until the thumping was repeated and he saw Kasiak standing in the dark. He would offer him a drink. He would settle him in the wing chair and play out that charade of equality between vacationist and hired man that is one of the principal illusions of the leafy months. "Here's something you ought to read," Kasiak said, before Paul could speak, and he passed him a newspaper clipping. Paul recognized the type face of the Communist paper that was mailed to Kasiak from Indiana. LUXURY LIVING WEAKENS U.S. was the headline, and the story described with traitorous joy the hardy and purposeful soldiers of Russia. Paul's face got warm in anger at Kasiak and at the uprush of chauvinism he felt. "Is that all you want?" His voice broke dryly. Kasiak nodded. "I'll see you tomorrow morning at six," Paul said, master to hired man, and he hooked the screen door and turned his back.

Paul liked to think that his patience with the man was inexhaustible—for, after all, Kasiak not only believed in Bakunin, he believed that stones grow and that thunder curdles milk. In his dealings with Kasiak, he had unconsciously sacrificed some independence, and in order to get to the garden at six the next morning, he got up at five. He made himself some breakfast, and at half past five he heard the rattle of a cart on the road. The puerile race of virtue and industry had begun. Paul was in the garden when Kasiak brought the cart into view. Kasiak was disappointed.

Paul had seen the mare only in pasture, and, aside from the fact that she was costing him four dollars, he was curious about the animal, for, along with a cow and a wife, she made up Kasiak's family. Her coat was dusty, he saw; her belly was swollen; her hoofs were unshod and uncut and had shredded like paper. "What's her name?" he asked, but Kasiak didn't answer. He hitched the mare to the cultivator, and she sighed and labored up the hill. Paul led the mare by the bridle, and Kasiak held down the cultivator.

Halfway along the first row in the garden, a stone stopped them, and when it had been dislodged and rolled away, Kasiak called "Gee-up" to the mare. She didn't move. "Gee-up," he shouted. His voice was harsh, but there was some tenderness hidden in it. "Gee-up, gee-up, gee-up." He slapped her sides lightly with the reins. He looked anxiously at Paul, as if he were ashamed that Paul should notice the mare's extreme decrepitude and reach a mistaken judgment on an animal he loved. When Paul suggested that he might use a whip, Kasiak said no. "Gee-up, gee-up, gee-up," he shouted again, and when she still failed to respond, he struck her rump with the reins. Paul pulled at her bit. They stood for ten minutes in the middle of the row pulling and shouting, and it seemed that the life had gone out of the mare. Then, when they were hoarse and discouraged, she began to stir

107

and gather wind in her lungs. Her carcass worked like a bellows and the wind whistled in her nostrils, and, like the bag Aeolus gave to Ulysses, she seemed to fill with tempests. She shook the flies off her head and pulled the cultivator a few feet forward.

This made for slow work, and by the time they finished, the sun was hot. Paul heard voices from his house as he and Kasiak led the infirm mare back to the cart, and he saw his children, still in their night clothes, feeding their rabbits in the lettuce patch. When Kasiak harnessed the mare to the cart, Paul again asked him her name.

"She has no name," Kasiak said.

"I've never heard of a farm horse without a name."

"To name animals is bourgeois sentimentality," Kasiak said, and he started to drive away.

Paul laughed.

"You never come back!" Kasiak called over his shoulder. It was the only meanness at hand; he knew how deeply Paul loved the hill. His face was dark. "You never come back next year. You wait and see."

There is a moment early on Sunday when the tide of the summer day turns inexorably toward the evening train. You can swim, play tennis, or take a nap or a walk, but it doesn't make much difference. Immediately after lunch, Paul was faced with his unwillingness to leave. This became so strong that he was reminded of the intensity and the apprehensiveness he had felt on furloughs. At six, he put on his tight business suit and had a drink with Virginia in the kitchen. She asked him to buy nail scissors and candy in New York. While they were there, he heard that noise that he lived in dread of above all others—his innocent and gentle children screaming in pain.

He ran out, letting the screen door slam in Virginia's face. Then he turned back and held the door open for her, and she came out and ran up the hill at his side. The children were coming down the road, under the big trees. Lost in their crystalline grief, blinded with tears, they stumbled and ran toward their mother and searched in her dark skirts for a shape to press their heads against. They were howling. But it was nothing serious, after all. Their rabbits were dead.

"There, there, there, there . . ." Virginia drew the children down toward the house. Paul went on up the road and found the limp rabbits in the hutch. He carried them to the edge of the garden and dug a hole. Kasiak

108

came by, carrying water for the chickens, and when he had sized up the situation, he spoke mournfully. "Why you dig a grave?" he asked. "The skunks will dig them up tonight. Throw them in Cavis's pasture. They'll dig them up again. . . ." He went on toward the chicken house. Paul stamped down the grave. Dirt got into his low shoes. He went back to the rabbit house to see if he could find any trace of what had killed them, and in the feeding trough, below some wilted vegetables that the children had uprooted, he saw the crystals of a mortal poison that they used to kill rats in the winter.

Paul made a serious effort to remember whether he could have left the poison there himself. The stifling heat in the hutch raised and sent the sweat rolling down his face. Could Kasiak have done it? Could Kasiak have been so mean, so perverse? Could he, through believing that on some fall evening fires on the mountain would signal the diligent and the reliable to seize power from the hands of those who drank Martinis, have become shrewd enough to put his finger on the only interest in the future Paul had?

Kasiak was in the chicken house. Shadow had begun to cover the ground, and some of the happy and stupid fowl were roosting. "Did you poison the rabbits, Kasiak?" Paul called. "Did you? Did you?" His loud voice maddened the fowl. They spread their heavy wings and cawed. "Did you, Kasiak?" Kasiak didn't speak. Paul put his hands on the man's shoulders and shook him. "Don't you know how strong that poison is? Don't you know that the children might have got into it? Don't you know that it might have killed them?" The fowl involved themselves in the fracas. Signals went from the house to the yard; they pushed one another off the congested gangway and thumped their wings. As if the life in Kasiak hid slyly from violence behind cartilage and bone, there was no apparent resistance in him, and Paul shook him until he creaked. "Did you, Kasiak?" Paul shouted. "Did you? Oh, Kasiak, if you touch my children, if you harm them in any way—in any way—I'll cut your head open." He pushed the man away from him and he sprawled in the dirt.

When Paul got back to the kitchen, there was no one there, and he drank two glasses of water. From the living room he could hear his mourning children, and his sister Ellen, who had no children of her own, struggling awkwardly to distract them with a story about a cat she had once owned. Virginia came into the kitchen and closed the door after her. She asked if the rabbits had been poisoned, and he said yes. She sat in a chair by the kitchen table. "I put it there," she said. "I put it there last fall. I never thought we'd use that house again, and I wanted to keep the rats out of it. I forgot. I never thought we'd use that house again. I completely forgot."

It is true of even the best of us that if an observer can catch us boarding a train at a way station; if he will mark our faces, stripped by anxiety of their self-possession; if he will appraise our luggage, our clothing, and look out of the window to see who has driven us to the station; if he will listen to the harsh or tender things we say if we are with our families, or notice the way we put our suitcase onto the rack, check the position of our wallet, our key ring, and wipe the sweat off the back of our necks; if he can judge sensibly the self-importance, diffidence, or sadness with which we settle ourselves, he will be given a broader view of our lives than most of us would intend.

Paul barely made the train that Sunday night. When he pulled himself up the high steps of the coach, he was short-winded. There was still some straw on his shoes from the violence in the chicken house. The drive had not completely cooled his temper, and his face was red. No harm had been done, he thought. "No harm," he said under his breath as he swung his suitcase onto the rack—a man of forty with signs of mortality in a tremor of his right hand, signs of obsoleteness in his confused frown, a summer farmer with blistered hands, a sunburn, and lame shoulders, so visibly shaken by some recent loss of principle that it would have been noticed by a stranger across the aisle.

Private Transaction

WILLIAM MUNDELL

When Truman sold his farm to younger folks
he sought to make the deed out by himself,
he didn't hold to trite legal descriptions.
"It took me fifty years," he said, "to learn
what I had bought because it wa'n't on paper."
A certain piece of land, described To Wit:
—he smiled to think how much the law left out.
It mentioned nowhere that his hillside rose
highest above the valley for its view,
or that one half his field stood up on edge,
pinned to the mountain's steepness, so it seemed,
by two outcropping points of rusty ledge.
It never mentioned that the morning sun
most often chose to climb his pasture's line,
or that the moon, friendly and dallying,
at times played hide and seek among his pine.
He wanted to write in what he was selling:
those gnarled and twisted beech along the ridge
that never would be lumber worth the cutting.
Yet by their steadfast leaning to the weather,
for him, they held a worth beyond the telling;
that knoll of brush he had been quick to call
a waste, that ripened to wild blueberries in fall.
He'd name the alder swamp, lush and wild growing:
it took him years to learn that he had bought
a wealth in mountain springs, pure and full flowing.

Civilization Versus Wilderness

Nowhere was it mentioned, when he bought
the land, of rights of animals to passage,
food and shelter; or that one rocky mound
long had been claimed by foxes as a den;
or that a falling acorn might belong
to him whose ears first heard it hit the ground.
Somewhere he'd write in the observation
that trees didn't care who they were growing for,
they'd go on meeting season after season.
He'd add one final sentence and admit
really the land could not be owned, by reason
that one life is too short quite to possess it.

FROM *The Journals of Francis Parkman*

Aug. 2nd, Captain Brag[g]'s Settlement [Errol, N. H.]. We left Colebrook and civilization this morning, and now a new epoch of this interesting history commences. Our journey lieth not, henceforward, through pleasant villages and cultivated fields, but through the wild forest and among lakes and streams which have borne no bark but the canoe of the Indian or the hunter. This is probably the last night for some time which we shall spend under a roof. Our road ran eastward towards Maine. A few farm houses were at first scattered along its side, but they became more and more distant as we went on, and at last the way was flanked by a forest so thickset and tangled that we could scarcely see two rods in any direction, excepting before and behind. We were traveling what was called a road, but the term was grievously misapplied. By dint of great exertion, a strong waggon might possibly be forced over the stones and stumps and roots and through the overhanging boughs which formed a complete arch overhead, but the attempt would be destruction to a carriage or chaise. Ruts on each side showed that it was occasionally travelled, but that this was very seldom was evident from the grass which almost covered it. As we were sitting on a log to rest, we heard a clatter of hoofs, and in a moment a man, mounted and bearing a gun, appeared through the trees, advancing toward us. He was from Brag's settlement, thirteen miles further on, and going to Colebrook for employment. The pass, he told us, was but a few miles before us, and accordingly, through an opening in the trees, we saw the mountains extended before us like a green wall and apparently blocking our passage. A little further, and we emerged upon a plain almost free of wood; and now a gap in the range appeared, with bare and pointed rocks starting upward from the forests that covered the mountains and looking down upon us as we entered the passage. These rocks were many hundred feet high and the pass between extremely narrow. Looking upward on either side, the mountains were almost perpendicular. Fire had stripped them of their verdure and left them covered with blackened trunks and rocks rolled from the

113

Winslow Homer, *The North Woods*

sharp peaks above. In picturesque effect the scene was superior to the Notch of the White Mountains, but in grandeur it fell far below it. Instead of the vast rounded summits of the Notch, these mountains were surmounted by peaks and needles of rock, which from below looked like ruined towers standing out in relief against the sky.

We were in want of a dinner, and so, catching some trout and shooting some pigeons, we cooked them after a style wholly original, and stayed for a time the inroads of appetite. While Dan sat still to digest his dinner, I ascended one of the mountains and had a fine view of the pass and the neighboring country. We proceeded, passed some few houses, mostly log cabins, and reached at sunset the settlement of Capt. Brag on the Amorescoggin [Androscoggin]. Here we got tolerable accommodation, and slept to the roar of the rapids of the river which ran close to the house.

The Captain slew a bear day before yesterday, and his fresh skin was nailed on the barn to dry. I write this on the morning of the 4th—having got somewhat behind-hand—by the blaze of our campfire in the forest.

And now, the life I have led for the past week having prevented my recording my experiences from day to day, I take this first opportunity for making up for former neglect. Beginning where I left off:

Tuesday, Aug. 3rd. Brag's settlement is on the Amariscoggin River, not far from Lake Umbagog and a few miles west of the mouth of the Margalloway. The Amariscoggin at this place is a succession of rapids extending more than a mile. On the Margalloway, too, some miles above its junction with the Ameriscoggin, are rapids of two miles in length and passable only by means of a rugged and difficult portage. Our intention was to take a boat and a guide at Brag's, ascend the Margalloway as far as the rapids, have the boat drawn round them and launched above, and then keep on up the river, which is navigable for thirty miles above without serious obstruction. But we found it impossible to procure here a good guide and boat, though both, they told us, were to be had at settlements on the Margalloway. Could they convey us to these settlements? Brag had but few men with him and these occupied in necessary work; moreover, there was a path through the forest several miles less than the passage by water, and by this we might reach the settlements in half a day. We determined on this route, and Brag accompanied us a mile or two on our way to point out its difficulties and to prevent our plunging into quagmires or mistaking a rabbit track or a cattle path for the road.

"The first house," said he, "is five or six miles further on. When you get about a mile, you will have to cross a brook. On the other side there are logging paths and one thing another branching out like, right and left. All you have got to do is to pick out the one that you see has been most travelled by the cattle, because all the others run a little ways and then come to nothing. Then go on a little further and you will come to a guzzle that they say is pretty bad this season, though I ha'nt seen it myself. However it a'nt more than two rods wide, so I guess you can get across. Just keep, all along, where the cattle have been most, and you can't miss the way."

With these direction we set out. The path was about four inches wide, through the dense forest, choked up with undergrowth, and obstructed by logs that had fallen across it. As may well be imagined, five miles by such a road were equivalent to twenty by any other. We crossed the brook, and following the cow-tracks, fortunately took the right turning and found to our infinite satisfaction that the path became a little more distinct and passable than before. Passing over a swampy tract, we saw deer and bear tracks in abundance. Two miles further (which two miles it took us as many hours to accomplish) and we had our first view of the Margalloway—a broad, still river whose sloping banks are, and for centuries will be, clothed with deep forests. We had forgotten the threatened "guzzle," and our very ideas of its nature were somewhat vague and mystified, though the Captain had been at great pains to explain it. But now we came upon it and our doubts were set at rest. A kind of muddy creek, very deep and dirty, extended from the river directly across the path. It was, as the Captain said, about two rods wide, with muddy and slippery banks and no earthly means of crossing but two slender poles, laid one from each bank and resting on a floating log in the middle. On the opposite bank, however, lay a heap of logs with their ends in the water, and bearing to the careless eye an appearance of tolerable solidity. With a commendable spirit of prudence, I induced Dan to make the first attempt. He cut him a long pole to steady himself, and, adding two or three additional supports to the frail bridge, essayed to cross. He planted his pole firmly in the mud and leaned hard against it, but he was not a foot from shore before the bridge began to sink, inch by inch. Daniel's ponderous frame was too much for it and, wherever he stepped, down sunk logs, poles, and branches, and resting place for his foot he had none. Dan got flurried. He splashed here and there, lost his balance, gave a leap in desperation at the treacherous pier of logs on the other side, they tilted up, and in plunged Dan, floundering among the fragments of the demolished bridge and sputtering the dirty water from his mouth. He gained the bank and shook himself like a dog. "Ha! Ha! Ha!" laughed I from one side. "Haw! Haw! Haw!" responded he from the other. "Now let's see you cross," said Dan. I accordingly rearranged the bridge with his assistance and succeeded in getting over, though wet to the knees.

We at length came to a log house with a small clearing about it, where dwell a famous hunter in those parts, one Mr. Bennet[t]; a man strong and hardy and handsome, moreover, though I never saw an Indian darker than exposure had made his features. He should like nothing better than to go, he said, but he was in the midst of his haying and could not think of leaving home. "I know who will go with you, though. There's Joshua Lumber [Lombard]—he's got a boat and a team of oxen to drag it round the falls." "Where does Joshua Lumber live?" "Just at the foot of the falls, about five miles from here." Bennet's son paddled us over the river, for the path to Lumber's was on the other side; and passing a log cabin or two, we arrived in due time at that sturdy farmer's abode. His house was the last but one on the river, Captain Wilson holding a "clearing" a mile further up—all above as far as the Canada settlements is one vast forest varied, as yet, with not the slightest trace of man's hand, unless it be the remains of the hunter's encampment. Lumber's habitation, like all in these parts, was of logs. He was blessed with a wife and a number of stout boys to whose charge he confided the farm during his absence. His place is situated just within the borders of Maine. A high and picturesque mountain rises on the west, with summits some rounded, some steep and broken. The river flows at its base through fertile plains which Lumber's industry has cleared of timber and covered with a growth of grain and grass. Asesquoss [Aziscoos] is the name of the mountain.

As an initiation into the mode of life which we were about to enter upon, we determined to spend the night in the forest. Accordingly we repaired thither, built a fire, and arranged our camp. Soon we received a visit from Lumber and his sons, and with them came another man whom by his speech I discovered to be an Indian, for our fire cast but a dubious light on the assembly. This Indian [Jerome], who was a nephew of Anantz and an excellent hunter, said that he was going on a hunting expedition up the river in the course of a few days. Thinking that his services might be useful,

I appointed a place thirty miles up the river where he should meet us, and where we might engage him to guide us through the forest to Canada, in case we should prefer that course to returning the way we had come.

Aug. 4th, Wednesday.   Early in the morning, a light skiff, built after the fashion of a birch canoe and weighing scarce more, was placed on a sledge and drawn up the portage by a team of oxen. The length of the portage was three miles and so encumbered was it with logs and fallen trees that the axe had to be employed more than once to open a way. "Considerable of an enterprise, sir," said the farmer when his oxen at length stood panting on the bank of the river above the rapids. Here lay the canoe of Jerome, the Indian, ready for his hunting expedition.

Our boat needed some repairs after its rough passage, but in the course of half an hour we were embarked and on our way up the river. Our stock of provisions was exceedingly limited. Six pounds of bread, some salt, and some butter were all we had; but there was a certainty of procuring fish and a chance of meeting larger game. The Indian, moreover, had a large stock of dried moose-meat concealed near the place where we were to meet him. After half an hour's paddling, we reached the mouth of a cold stream which entered the river; and here we got a dinner of trout, the chief drawback to the pleasure of fishing being that the flies bit infinitely more than the fish. After a paddle of an hour or two more, we stopped; and cutting down wood, built a fire and made a tolerable dinner of our fish. Then resuming our course, we kept on until dark, when we stopped, hauled the boat on shore, cleared a space of a few yards in the forest, built a roaring fire, got ready a scanty supper, and prepared to spend the night as comfortably as circumstances would allow. Our bed was a heap of spruce boughs and our fire warmed the cold night air. Several trees were cut down to maintain the blaze and our camp being of [on] a bank elevated far above the river, there was little apprehension from the cold. Soon the moon came up and glistened on the still river and half lighted the black forest. An owl, disturbed by the glare of our fire, sent forth a long wild cry from the depths of the woods and was answered by the shrill bark of some other habitant of the forest. Thus far, the river bank has been clothed with huge trees and the summits of considerable mountains appeared on the right and left; but tomorrow we pass "the meadows," a flat and marshy tract of ground covered with low bushes through which the stream runs in a winding course for many miles. We have paddled today eighteen miles. Along the banks, moose and bear tracks have appeared in abundance—not so, unfortunately, the animals themselves.

Thursday, Aug. 5th.   We resumed our journey but our rate of proceeding was slow, for, by reason of the bends of the river, five miles by water were equivalent to one in a direct line. The stream began to grow shallow, too, and the current swift—so much so that the united force of paddles and poles was barely sufficient, in some places, to propel the boat. We often ran aground on shallows or among rocks, and were obliged to get out into the water to lighten our bark. Once we were stopped by a huge barricade of timber, over which we lifted the boat by main force. The bites of the flies were intolerable, so we made a fire of rotten wood in our frying pan, and, placing it in the bow of the boat, its smoke prevented any further annoyance from that source. We could get no trout today and were obliged to rest content with a dinner of chubs, of which we took some very fine ones. We passed the meadows at length, and again our way was through the forest, and a most wild and beautiful appearance did the river shores present. From the high banks huge old pines stooped forward over the water, the moss hanging from their aged branches, and behind rose a wall of foliage, green and thick, with no space or opening which the eye could penetrate. The river was not here, as some miles below, an expanse of still deep water, but came down over a rocky and gravelly bed in a swift current and some times broke in cascades—a change which, how much soever it might improve the effect of the scene, was of no advantage to the navigation. However, we reached our destination at last. This was the fork of the river, where, branching to the right and left, it preserves on the one side its original title and, on the other, takes that of the "Little Margalloway." This was the place we had appointed to meet the Indian and where he was to appear at sunrise the next day. We made our camp—this time with a little more care, for Lumber erected a shed of boughs as a protection against the dews. We procured a mess of most magnificent trout, none of them being less than a foot in length, though this is an unfavorable season for them; supped, and went to sleep. Our camp was on the tongue of land between the two streams, and the tumbling of the water was no ways unfavorable to repose. As usual, our chief annoyance was from flies and mosquitoes, of which the latter swarmed in numbers unprecedented, but their attacks were as nothing in comparison with that of clouds of black flies—animals not much larger than the head of a pin, but inflicting a wound twice as large as themselves and assaulting with such eagerness that nothing but being in the midst of a thick smoke will keep them off. They seemed to take a special liking to me, and I was bitten to such a degree that I am now—nearly four days after—covered with their wounds as if I had the small-pox. There is another cursed race, yet smaller, denominated from their microscopic dimensions "no-see-ems." Their bite is like the prick of a needle, but not half so endurable, and they insinuate themselves through pantaloons, stockings, and everything else.

We slept in spite of them. Morning was on the point of breaking when a shout sounded from the river, Jerome's canoe touched the shore, and in a moment he was amongst us. He had seen a moose, he said, as he came up, had fired at and, he believed, wounded her, and he would go down in the morning to see if he could find her. He wrapped him[self] in his blanket, head and all, and in two minutes was fast asleep. Well he might be, for he had been paddling since nine o'clock of the morning before.

Friday, Aug. 6th. Our bread had almost failed and, still worse, we were unprovided with blankets; we therefore abandoned our half-formed intention of going on to Canada, and determined to return by the way we had come. My chief object in coming so far was merely to have a taste of the half-savage kind of life necessary to be led, and to see the wilderness where it was as yet uninvaded by the hand of man. I had had some hope of shooting a moose; but that hope seemed doomed to be disappointed, although, had we kept on, there was a very considerable chance of finding them. Slade, however, became utterly discouraged and refused to proceed; and this alone would have prevented me, even if there had been no other obstacles. We breakfasted, cleared out the boat, and began our return voyage, the Indian having set out before us, whirling down the swift current like a bubble in his bark canoe. Our descent was nothing compared to our ascent. The mist was rising from the river, and the scenes we had passed the day before with toil and difficulty bore an appearance twice as inviting, now that we were borne by them with no effort.

The canoe was quickly out of sight. We had gone about five miles when a sudden splash into the water arrested our attention, and we saw a young moose, far in front, leap from the bank and wade the river. He ascended the opposite shore, shook the water from his flanks, and disappeared in the woods. I dropped my paddle, cocked my gun, and stood in the prow of the boat. We bore down swiftly and silently to the spot where he had disappeared, but there was no trace of him but the broad tracks which marked the place where he had left the water. A bend in the river prevented our seeing farther on. An instant after we heard another plunge. The snap of a gun missing fire followed, and, sweeping round the bend, we saw a large moose on the point of climbing the bank, while Jerome stood on the opposite shore hastily and eagerly picking the lock of his gun. The bank was steep, and the moose stood half way up, nearly hidden in the bushes. I took a quick aim at the back, fired, and the moose tumbled into the river with her spine severed by my bullet. Jerome had fired at her the night before and wounded her in the lower part of the belly. He had just tracked her by means of his dog; she had leaped into the river and he had aimed at her as she was wading across; but, his gun missing fire, she had gained the shore and was attempting to ascend the bank when we approached. The poor beast lay an instant in the water and then, with a convulsive effort, staggered to her feet and stood in the river where it was about a foot deep. Jerome aimed at her head, fired, and missed altogether. I reloaded and, aiming at the eye, struck the head just below the root of the ear. Still the moose stood motionless. Jerome took a long aim and fired again. He hit her fair and full between the eyes. For an instant she did not move; then her body declined slowly to one side and she fell, gave a short plunge, and lay dead on the bottom. Being a female, she had no horns, but her body was larger than a horse's. Each siezed a leg and she was drawn to shore. Jerome shouldered the huge dead trunk of a tree, brought it from the forest, chopped it up, and kindled a fire to keep off the flies. He and Lumber then flayed and cut her up—a process which occupied an hour or more; and then we got under way again, taking with us as much of the meat as we had occasion for. Jerome stayed behind to load his canoe with the rest.

We stopped at our camp of the first night, and, finding our fire still smouldering, we rekindled it and cooked a dinner of moose meat. Getting again under way, we reached our starting place at the head of the rapids half an hour before sunset, having paddled almost unceasingly since early morning and travelled, by the river, a distance of more than thirty miles. We walked to Lumber's and, though he offered beds, preferred the fresh hay of his barn to the chance of what we might encounter in the shape of log-cabin sheets.

Covered Bridge, Bath, New Hampshire

Meeting-House Hill

AMY LOWELL

I must be mad, or very tired,
When the curve of a blue bay beyond a railroad track
Is shrill and sweet to me like the sudden springing of a tune,
And the sight of a white church above thin trees in a city
    square
Amazes my eyes as though it were the Parthenon.
Clear, reticent, superbly final,
With the pillars of its portico refined to a cautious elegance,
It dominates the weak trees,
And the shot of its spire
Is cool, and candid,
Rising into an unresisting sky.
Strange meeting-house
Pausing a moment upon a squalid hill-top.
I watch the spire sweeping the sky,
I am dizzy with the movement of the sky,
I might be watching a mast
With its royals set full
Straining before a two-reef breeze.
I might be sighting a tea-clipper,
Tacking into the blue bay,
Just back from Canton
With her hold full of green and blue porcelain,
And a Chinese coolie leaning over the rail
Gazing at the white spire
With dull, sea-spent eyes.

FROM *Night on the Great Beach*

HENRY BESTON

Our fantastic civilization has fallen out of touch with many aspects of nature, and with none more completely than with night. Primitive folk, gathered at a cave mouth round a fire, do not fear night; they fear, rather, the energies and creatures to whom night gives power; we of the age of the machines, having delivered ourselves of nocturnal enemies, now have a dislike of night itself. With lights and ever more lights, we drive the holiness and beauty of night back to the forests and the sea; the little villages, the crossroads even, will have none of it. Are modern folk, perhaps, afraid of night? Do they fear that vast serenity, the mystery of infinite space, the austerity of stars? Having made themselves at home in a civilization obsessed with power, which explains its whole world in terms of energy, do they fear at night for their dull acquiescence and the pattern of their beliefs? Be the answer what it will, to-day's civilization is full of people who have not the slightest notion of the character or the poetry of night, who have never even seen night. Yet to live thus, to know only artificial night, is as absurd and evil as to know only artificial day.

Night is very beautiful on this great beach. It is the true other half of the day's tremendous wheel; no lights without meaning stab or trouble it; it is beauty, it is fulfilment, it is rest. Thin clouds float in these heavens, islands of obscurity in a splendour of space and stars: the Milky Way bridges earth and ocean; the beach resolves itself into a unity of form, its summer lagoons, its slopes and uplands merging; against the western sky and the falling bow of sun rise the silent and superb undulations of the dunes.

My nights are at their darkest when a dense fog streams in from the sea under a black, unbroken floor of cloud. Such nights are rare, but are most to be expected when fog gathers off the coast in early summer; this last Wednesday night was the darkest I have known. Between ten o'clock and two in the morning three vessels stranded on the outer beach—a fisherman, a four-masted schooner, and a beam trawler. The fisherman and the schooner have been towed off, but the trawler, they say, is still ashore.

124

I went down to the beach that night just after ten o'clock. So utterly black, pitch dark it was, and so thick with moisture and trailing showers, that there was no sign whatever of the beam of Nauset; the sea was only a sound, and when I reached the edge of the surf the dunes themselves had disappeared behind. I stood as isolate in that immensity of rain and night as I might have stood in interplanetary space. The sea was troubled and noisy, and when I opened the darkness with an outlined cone of light from my electric torch I saw that the waves were washing up green coils of sea grass, all coldly wet and bright in the motionless and unnatural radiance. Far off a single ship was groaning its way along the shoals. The fog was compact of the finest moisture; passing by, it spun itself into my lens of light like a kind of strange, aerial, and liquid silk. Effin Chalke, the new coast guard, passed me going north, and told me that he had news at the halfway house of the schooner at Cahoon's.

It was dark, pitch dark to my eye, yet complete darkness, I imagine, is exceedingly rare, perhaps unknown in outer nature. The nearest natural approximation to it is probably the gloom of forest country buried in night and cloud. Dark as the night was here, there was still light on the surface of the planet. Standing on the shelving beach, with the surf breaking at my feet, I could see the endless wild uprush, slide, and withdrawal of the sea's white rim of foam. The men at Nauset tell me that on such nights they follow along this vague crawl of whiteness, trusting to habit and a sixth sense to warn them of their approach to the halfway house.

Animals descend by starlight to the beach. North, beyond the dunes, muskrats forsake the cliff and nose about in the driftwood and weed, leaving intricate trails and figure eights to be obliterated by the day; the lesser folk—the mice, the occasional small sand-coloured toads, the burrowing moles—keep to the upper beach and leave their tiny footprints under the overhanging wall. In autumn skunks, beset by a shrinking larder, go beach combing early in the night. The animal is by preference a clean feeder and turns up his nose at rankness. I almost stepped on a big fellow one night as I was walking north to meet the first man south from Nauset. There was a scamper, and the creature ran up the beach from under my feet; alarmed he certainly was, yet was he contained and continent. Deer are frequently seen, especially north of the light. I find their tracks upon the summer dunes.

Years ago, while camping on this beach north of Nauset, I went for a stroll along the top of the cliff at break of dawn. Though the path followed close enough along the edge, the beach below was often hidden, and I looked directly from the height to the flush of sunrise at sea. Presently the path, turning, approached the brink of the earth precipice, and on the beach below, in the cool, wet rosiness of dawn, I saw three deer playing. They frolicked, rose on their hind legs, scampered off, and returned again, and were merry. Just before sunrise they trotted off north together down the beach toward a hollow in the cliff and the path that climbs it.

Occasionally a sea creature visits the shore at night. Lone coast guardsmen, trudging the sand at some deserted hour, have been startled by seals. One man fell flat on a creature's back, and it drew away from under him, flippering toward the sea, with a sound "halfway between a squeal and a bark." I myself once had rather a start. It was long after sundown, the light dying and uncertain, and I was walking home on the top level of the beach and close along the slope descending to the ebbing tide. A little more than halfway to the Fo'castle a huge unexpected something suddenly writhed horribly in the darkness under my bare foot. I had stepped on a skate left stranded by some recent crest of surf, and my weight had momentarily annoyed it back to life.

Facing north, the beam of Nauset becomes part of the dune night. As I walk toward it, I see the lantern, now as a star of light which waxes and wanes three mathematic times, now as a lovely pale flare of light behind the rounded summits of the dunes. The changes in the atmosphere change the colour of the beam; it is now whitish, now flame golden, now golden red; it changes its form as well, from a star to a blare of light, from a blare of light to a cone of radiance sweeping a circumference of fog. To the west of Nauset I often see the apocalyptic flash of the great light at the Highland reflected on the clouds or even on the moisture in the starlit air, and, seeing it, I often think of the pleasant hours I have spent there when George and Mary Smith were at the light and I had the good fortune to visit as their guest. Instead of going to sleep in the room under the eaves, I would lie awake, looking out of a window to the great spokes of light revolving as solemnly as a part of the universe.

All night long the lights of coastwise vessels pass at sea, green lights going south, red lights moving north. Fishing schooners and flounder draggers anchor two or three miles out, and keep a bright riding light burning on the mast. I see them come to anchor at sundown, but I rarely see them go, for they are off at dawn. When busy at night, these fishermen illumine their decks with a scatter of oil flares. From shore, the ships might be

John F. Kensett, *Beacon Rock, Newport Harbor*

thought afire. I have watched the scene through a night glass. I could see no smoke, only the waving flares, the reddish radiance on sail and rigging, an edge of reflection overside, and the enormous night and sea beyond.

One July night, as I returned at three o'clock from an expedition north, the whole night, in one strange, burning instant, turned into a phantom day. I stopped and, questioning, stared about. An enormous meteor, the largest I have ever seen, was consuming itself in an effulgence of light west of the zenith. Beach and dune and ocean appeared out of nothing, shadowless and motionless, a landscape whose every tremor and vibration were stilled, a landscape in a dream.

The beach at night has a voice all its own, a sound in fullest harmony with its spirit and mood—with its little, dry noise of sand forever moving, with its solemn, overspilling, rhythmic seas, with its eternity of stars that sometimes seem to hang down like lamps from the high heavens—and that sound the piping of a bird. As I walk the beach in early summer my solitary coming disturbs it on its nest, and it flies away, troubled, invisible, piping its sweet, plaintive cry. The bird I write of is the piping plover, *Charadrius melodus,* sometimes called the beach plover or the mourning bird. Its note is a whistled syllable, the loveliest musical note, I think, sounded by any North Atlantic bird.

Now that summer is here I often cook myself a camp supper on the beach. Beyond the crackling, salt-yellow driftwood flame, over the pyramid of barrel staves, broken boards, and old sticks all atwist with climbing fire, the unseen ocean thunders and booms, the breaker sounding hollow as it falls. The wall of the sand cliff behind, with its rim of grass and withering roots, its sandy crumblings and erosions, stands gilded with flame; wind cries over it; a covey of sandpipers pass between the ocean and the fire. There are stars, and to the south Scorpio hangs curving down the sky with ringed Saturn shining in his claw.

Learn to reverence night and to put away the vulgar fear of it, for, with the banishment of night from the experience of man, there vanishes as well a religious emotion, a poetic mood, which gives depth to the adventure of humanity. By day, space is one with the earth and with man—it is his sun that is shining, his clouds that are floating past; at night, space is his no more. When the great earth, abandoning day, rolls up the deeps of the heavens and the universe, a new door opens for the human spirit, and there are few so clownish that some awareness of the mystery of being does not touch them as they gaze. For a moment of night we have a glimpse of ourselves and of our world islanded in its stream of stars—pilgrims of mortality, voyaging between horizons across eternal seas of space and time. Fugitive though the instant be, the spirit of man is, during it, ennobled by a genuine moment of emotional dignity, and poetry makes its own both the human spirit and experience.

At the Natural History Museum

WILLIAM MEREDITH

Past a swim-by of deep-sea fish,
cold rockets in a tank of air, tamed
by their right names and their Latin underneath,
he walks toward the cafeteria. It grows dark.
October clouds shadow the frosted-glass roof,
the dinosaurs appear, mahogany bones.
The family died out.

On the far wall, a fierce one rears erect,
his shoulders thrown back like a man's
when he is loved or seeks high office.
His jaws are strong pliers. Dawn men watch in awe
from the bushes this blood cousin
in a world of crusty things.

But the family dies out before his eyes,
grass-eaters first, then taloned meat-eaters.
Some of the bones have been fleshed out with plaster
but Hazard and the guard are the oldest living things
here. Even the author of the comic verse
about extinction, copied at the monster's feet,
has gone his bony way.

We descend by chosen cells that are not lost,
though they wander off in streams and rivulets.
Not everyone has issue in this creation.
Cousins-german are everywhere in the shale
and marshes under this dry house. In slime, in sperm,
our living cousins flow.

And grazers or killers, each time we must stoop low
and enter by some thigh-lintel, gentle as rills.
Who consents to his own return, Nietzsche says,
participates in the divinity of the world.
Perhaps I have already eddied on, out of this backwater,
man, on my way to the cafeteria, Hazard thinks.
Perhaps nothing dies but husks.

The Mud Turtle

HOWARD NEMEROV

Out of the earth beneath the water,
Dragging over the stubble field
Up to the hilltop in the sun
On his way from water to water,
He rests an hour in the garden,
His alien presence observed by all:
His lordly darkness decked in filth
Bearded with weed like a lady's favor,
He is a black planet, another world
Never till now appearing, even now
Not quite believably old and big,
Set in the summer morning's midst
A gloomy gemstone to the sun opposed.
Our measures of him do not matter,
He would be huge at any size;
And neither does the number of his years,
The time he comes from doesn't count.

When the boys tease him with sticks
He breaks the sticks, striking with
As great a suddenness as speed;
Fingers and toes would snap as soon,
Says one of us, and the others shudder.
Then when they turn him on his back
To see the belly heroically yellow,
He throws himself fiercely to his feet,
Brings down the whole weight of his shell,
Spreads out his claws and digs himself in

Immovably, invulnerably,
But for the front foot on the left,
Red-budded, with the toes torn off.
So over he goes again, and shows
Us where a swollen leech is fastened.
Softly between plastron and shell.
Nobody wants to go close enough
To burn it loose; he can't be helped
Either, there is no help for him
As he makes it to his feet again
And drags away to the meadow's edge.
We see the tall grass open and wave
Around him, it closes, he is gone
Over the hill toward another water,
Bearing his hard and chambered hurt
Down, down, down, beneath the water,
Beneath the earth beneath. He takes
A secret wound out of the world.

Appearance Versus Reality

What is real? Is what you see, taste, hear, feel, or touch real? Or is reality something behind appearances? Can you trust what you are told, or do you have to search beyond the words? Throughout the ages, people have experienced grave uncertainty about what they can believe. The Elizabethans, Shakespeare especially, pondered the question of the difference between what *seems* and what actually *is*. Hamlet's tragedy, you may remember, began with his uncertainty whether to interpret his father's ghost as a revelation of his unnatural murder, or as some foul delusion prompted by the devil. The early Puritans questioned whether their delight in the beauties of this physical world was sensual or a reaction to God's glory. What first seems obvious can suddenly take on an entirely different meaning from the one originally perceived. Appearances, people have found, can be misleading.

That the evidence of the five senses can turn out to be quite opposite to what is actually the truth is a fact frequently used by playwrights to create ironic situations. Eugene O'Neill's "The Rope" illustrates such use of irony. Language, too, often shifts in meaning, depending on the circumstances. Figurative language, particularly metaphor, does not actually mean what it literally says. By using metaphor the writer tries to picture one thing so that the reader will recognize in it a certain relationship with something else and thus understand the second more clearly. Edward Taylor, Emily Dickinson, Robert Frost, Anne Bradstreet, Wallace Stevens, and Anne Sexton, in their poems, reveal a constant questioning of the realities hidden by the appearances of things. In "Bewitched" Edith Wharton deals with the delusions that can generate appearances far from realities.

Appearance Versus Reality

When readers become involved with the selections in this section, they will find a number of approaches to this most fascinating of problems.

A Visitor in Marl–

EMILY DICKINSON

A Visitor in Marl—
Who influences Flowers—
Till they are orderly as Busts—
And Elegant—as Glass—

Who visits in the Night—
And just before the Sun—
Concludes his glistening interview—
Caresses—and is gone—

But whom his fingers touched—
And where his feet have run—
And whatsoever Mouth he kissed—
Is as it had not been—

For Once, Then, Something

ROBERT FROST

Others taunt me with having knelt at well-curbs
Always wrong to the light, so never seeing
Deeper down in the well than where the water
Gives me back in a shining surface picture
Me myself in the summer heaven godlike
Looking out of a wreath of fern and cloud puffs.
Once, when trying with chin against a well-curb,
I discerned, as I thought, beyond the picture,
Through the picture, a something white, uncertain,
Something more of the depths—and then I lost it.
Water came to rebuke the too clear water.
One drop fell from a fern, and lo, a ripple
Shook whatever it was lay there at bottom,
Blurred it, blotted it out. What was that whiteness?
Truth? A pebble of quartz? For once, then, something.

Huswifery

EDWARD TAYLOR

Make me, O Lord, thy Spining Wheele compleate.
    Thy Holy Worde my Distaff make for mee.
Make mine Affections thy Swift Flyers neate
    And make my Soule thy holy Spoole to bee.
    My Conversation make to be thy Reele
    And reele the yarn thereon spun of thy Wheele.

Make me thy Loome then, knit therein this Twine:
    And make thy Holy Spirit, Lord, winde quills:
Then weave the Web thyselfe. The yarn is fine.
    Thine Ordinances make my Fulling Mills.
    Then dy the same in Heavenly Colours Choice,
    All pinkt with Varnisht Flowers of Paradise.

Then cloath therewith mine Understanding, Will,
    Affections, Judgment, Conscience, Memory
My Words, and Actions, that their shine may fill
    My wayes with glory and thee glorify.
    Then mine apparell shall display before yee
    That I am Cloathd in Holy robes for glory.

The Rope

EUGENE O'NEILL

CHARACTERS

ABRAHAM BENTLEY

ANNIE, *his daughter*

PAT SWEENEY, *her husband*

MARY, *their child*

LUKE BENTLEY, *Abe's son by a second marriage*

SCENE. *The interior of an old barn situated on top of a high headland of the seacoast. In the rear, to the left, a stall in which lumber is stacked up. To the right of it, an open double doorway looking out over the ocean. Outside the doorway, the faint trace of what was once a road leading to the barn. Beyond the road, the edge of a cliff which rises sheer from the sea below. On the right of the doorway, three stalls with mangers and hay-ricks. The first of these is used as a woodbin and is half full of piled-up cordwood. Near this bin, a chopping-block with an ax driven into the top of it.*

The left section of the barn contains the hayloft, which extends at a height of about twelve feet from the floor as far to the right as the middle of the doorway. The loft is bare except for a few scattered mounds of dank-looking hay. From the edge of the loft, half-way from the door, a rope about five feet long with an open running noose at the end, is hanging. A rusty plow and various other farming implements, all giving evidence of long disuse, are lying on the floor near the left wall. Farther forward an old cane-bottomed chair is set back against the wall.

In front of the stalls on the right stands a long, roughly constructed carpenter's table, evidently home-made. Saws, a lathe, a hammer, chisel, a keg

141

*containing nails and other tools of the carpentry trade are on the table.
Two benches are placed, one in front, one to the left of it.*

The right side of the barn is a bare wall.

*It is between six and half-past in the evening of a day in early spring. At the
rising of the curtain some trailing clouds near the horizon, seen through
the open doorway, are faintly tinged with gold by the first glow of the
sunset. As the action progresses this reflected light gradually becomes
brighter, and then slowly fades into a smoky crimson. The sea is a dark
slate color. From the rocks below the headland sounds the muffled
monotone of breaking waves.*

As the curtain rises MARY *is discovered squatting cross-legged on the floor,
her back propped against the right side of the doorway, her face in
profile. She is a skinny, overgrown girl of ten, with thin, carroty hair
worn in a pigtail. She wears a shabby gingham dress. Her face is stupidly expressionless. Her hands flutter about aimlessly in relaxed, flabby
gestures.*

*She is staring fixedly at a rag doll which she has propped up against the
doorway opposite her. She hums shrilly to herself.*

*At a sudden noise from outside she jumps to her feet, peeks out, and quickly
snatches up the doll, which she hugs fiercely to her breast. Then, after a
second's fearful hesitation, she runs to the carpenter's table and crawls
under it.*

As she does so ABRAHAM BENTLEY *appears in the doorway and stands,
blinking into the shadowy barn. He is a tall, lean, stoop-shouldered old
man of sixty-five. His thin legs, twisted by rheumatism, totter feebly
under him as he shuffles slowly along by the aid of a thick cane. His face
is gaunt, chalky-white, furrowed with wrinkles, surmounted by a shiny
bald scalp fringed with scanty wisps of white hair. His eyes peer weakly
from beneath bushy, black brows. His mouth is a sunken line drawn in
under his large, beak-like nose. A two weeks' growth of stubby patches
of beard covers his jaws and chin. He has on a threadbare brown over-
coat but wears no hat.*

BENTLEY [*comes slowly into the barn, peering around him suspiciously. As
he reaches the table and leans one hand on it for support,* MARY *darts
from underneath and dashes out through the doorway.* BENTLEY *is
startled; then shakes his cane after her*]: Out o' my sight, you Papist

brat! Spawn o' Satan! Spyin' on me! They set her to it. Spyin' to watch me! [*He limps to the door and looks out cautiously. Satisfied, he turns back into the barn*] Spyin' to see—what they'll never know. [*He stands staring up at the rope and taps it testingly several times with his stick, talking to himself as he does so*] It's tied strong—strong as death— [*He cackles with satisfaction*] They'll see, then! They'll see! [*He laboriously creeps over to the bench and sits down wearily. He looks toward the sea and his voice quavers in a doleful chant*] "Woe unto us! for the day goeth away, for the shadows of the evening are stretched out." [*He mumbles to himself for a moment—then speaks clearly*] Spyin' on me! Spawn o' the Pit! [*He renews his chant*] "They hunt our steps that we cannot go in our streets: our end is near, our days are fulfilled; for our end is come."

[*As he finishes* ANNIE *enters. She is a thin, slovenly, worn-out-looking woman of about forty with a drawn, pasty face. Her habitual expression is one of a dulled irritation. She talks in a high-pitched, sing-song whine. She wears a faded gingham dress and a torn sunbonnet.*]

ANNIE [*comes over to her father but warily keeps out of range of his stick*]: Paw! [*He doesn't answer or appear to see her*] Paw! You ain't fergittin' what the doctor told you when he was here last, be you? He said you was to keep still and not go a-walkin' round. Come on back to the house, Paw. It's gittin' near supper-time and you got to take your medicine b'fore it, like he says.

BENTLEY [*his eyes fixed in front of him*]: "The punishment of thine iniquity is accomplished, O daughter of Zion: he will visit thine iniquity, O daughter of Edom; he will discover thy sins."

ANNIE [*waiting resignedly until he has finished—wearily*]: You better take watch on your health, Paw, and not be sneakin' up to this barn no more. Lord sakes, soon 's my back is turned you goes sneakin' off agen. It's enough to drive a body outa their right mind.

BENTLEY: "Behold, every one that useth proverbs shall use this proverb against thee, saying, As is the mother, so is her daughter!" [*He cackles to himself*] So is her daughter!

ANNIE [*her face flushing with anger*]: And if I am, I'm glad I take after her and not you, y' old wizard! [*Scornfully*] A fine one you be to be shoutin' Scripture in a body's ears all the live-long day—you that druv Maw to her death with your naggin', and pinchin', and miser stinginess. If

143

you've a mind to pray, it's down in the medder you ought to go, and kneel down by her grave, and ask God to forgive you for the meanness you done to her all her life.

BENTLEY [*mumbling*]: "As is the mother, so is her daughter."

ANNIE [*enraged by the repetition of this quotation*]: *You* quotin' Scripture! Why, Maw wasn't cold in the earth b'fore you was down in the port courtin' agen—courtin' that harlot that was the talk o' the whole town! And then you disgraces yourself and me by marryin' her—*her*—and bringin' her back home with you; and me still goin' every day to put flowers on Maw's grave that you'd fergotten. [*She glares at him vindictively, pausing for breath*] And between you you'd have druv me into the grave like you done Maw if I hadn't married Pat Sweeney so's I could git away and live in peace. Then you took on so high and mighty 'cause he was a Cath'lic—*you* gittin' religion all of a moment just for spite on me 'cause I'd left—and b'cause she egged you on against me; *you* sayin' it was a sin to marry a Papist, after not bein' at Sunday meetin' yourself for more'n twenty years!

BENTLEY [*loudly*]: "He will visit thine iniquity—"

ANNIE [*interrupting*]: And the carryin's-on you had the six years at home after I'd left you—the shame of the whole county! Your wife, indeed, with a child she *claimed* was your'n, and her goin' with this farmer and that, and even men off the ships in the port, and you blind to it! And then when she got sick of you and ran away—only to meet her end at the hands of God a year after—she leaves you alone with that—*your* son, Luke, *she* called him—and him only five years old!

BENTLEY [*babbling*]: Luke? Luke?

ANNIE [*tauntingly*]: Yes, Luke! "As is the mother, so is her son"—that's what you ought to preach 'stead of puttin' curses on me. You was glad enough to git me back home agen, and Pat with me, to tend the place, and help bring up that brat of hers. [*Jealously*] You was fond enough of him all them years—and how did he pay you back? Stole your money and ran off and left you just when he was sixteen and old enough to help. Told you to your face he'd stolen and was leavin'. He only laughed when you was took crazy and cursed him; and he only laughed harder when you hung up that silly rope there [*she points*] and told him to hang himself on it when he ever came home agen.

BENTLEY [*mumbling*]: You'll see, then. You'll see!

ANNIE [*wearily—her face becoming dull and emotionless again*]: I s'pose I'm

144

a bigger fool than you be to argy with a half-witted body. But I tell you agen that Luke of yours ain't comin' back; and if he does he ain't the kind to hang himself, more's the pity. He's like her. He'd hang *you* more likely if he s'pected you had any money. So you might 's well take down that ugly rope you've had tied there since he run off. He's probably dead anyway by this.

BENTLEY [*frightened*]: No! No!

ANNIE: Them as bad as him comes to a sudden end. [*Irritably*] Land sakes, Paw, here I am argyin' with your lunatic notions and the supper not ready. Come on and git your medicine. You can see no one ain't touched your old rope. Come on! You can sit 'n' read your Bible. [*He makes no movement. She comes closer to him and peers into his face— uncertainly*] Don't you hear me? I do hope you ain't off in one of your fits when you don't know nobody. D'you know who's talkin'? This is Annie—your Annie, Paw.

BENTLEY [*bursting into senile rage*]: None o'mine! Spawn o' the Pit! [*With a quick movement he hits her viciously over the arm with his stick. She gives a cry of pain and backs away from him, holding her arm.*]

ANNIE [*weeping angrily*]: That's what I git for tryin' to be kind to you, you ugly old devil! [*The sound of a man's footsteps is heard from outside, and* SWEENEY *enters. He is a stocky, muscular, sandy-haired Irishman dressed in patched corduroy trousers shoved down into high laced boots, and a blue flannel shirt. The bony face of his bullet head has a pressed-in appearance except for his heavy jaw, which sticks out pugnaciously. There is an expression of mean cunning and cupidity about his mouth and his small, round, blue eyes. He has evidently been drinking and his face is flushed and set in an angry scowl.*]

SWEENEY: Have ye no supper at all made, ye lazy slut? [*Seeing that she has been crying*] What're you blubberin' about?

ANNIE: It's all his fault. I was tryin' to git him home but he's that set I couldn't budge him; and he hit me on the arm with his cane when I went near him.

SWEENEY: He did, did he? I'll soon learn him better. [*He advances toward* BENTLEY *threateningly.*]

ANNIE [*grasping his arm*]: Don't touch him, Pat. He's in one of his fits and you might kill him.

SWEENEY: An' good riddance!

BENTLEY [*hissing*]: Papist! [*Chants*] "Pour out thy fury upon the heathen

145

that know thee not, and upon the families that call not on thy name: for they have eaten up Jacob, and devoured him, and consumed him, and made his habitation desolate."

SWEENEY [*instinctively crosses himself—then scornfully*]: Spit curses on me till ye choke. It's not likely the Lord God'll be listenin' to a wicked auld sinner the like of you. [*To* ANNIE] What's got into him to be roamin' up here? When I left for the town he looked too weak to lift a foot.

ANNIE: Oh, it's the same crazy notion he's had ever since Luke left. He wanted to make sure the rope was still here.

BENTLEY [*pointing to the rope with his stick*]: He-he! Luke'll come back. Then you'll see. You'll see!

SWEENEY [*nervously*]: Stop that mad cacklin', for the love of heaven! [*With a forced laugh*] It's great laughter I should be havin' at you, mad as you are, for thinkin' that thief of a son of yours would come back to hang himself on account of your curses. It's five years he's been gone, and not a sight of him; an' you cursin' an callin' down the wrath o' God on him by day an' by night. That shows you what God thinks of your curses— an' Him deaf to you!

ANNIE: It's no use talkin' to him, Pat.

SWEENEY: I've small doubt but that Luke is hung long since—by the police. He's come to no good end, that lad. [*His eyes on the rope*] I'll be pullin' that thing down, so I will; an' the auld loon'll stay in the house, where he belongs, then, maybe. [*He reaches up for the rope as if to try and yank it down.* BENTLEY *waves his stick frantically in the air, and groans with rage.*]

ANNIE [*frightened*]: Leave it alone, Pat. Look at him. He's liable to hurt himself. Leave his rope be. It don't do no harm.

SWEENEY [*reluctantly moves away*]: It looks ugly hangin' there open like a mouth. [*The old man sinks back into a relieved immobility.* SWEENEY *speaks to his wife in a low tone*] Where's the child? Get her to take him out o' this. I want a word with you he'll not be hearin'. [*She goes to the door and calls out*] Ma-ry! Ma-ry! [*A faint, answering cry is heard and a moment later* MARY *rushes breathlessly into the barn.* SWEENEY *grabs her roughly by the arm. She shrinks away, looking at him with terrified eyes*] You're to take your grandfather back to the house—an' see to it he stays there.

ANNIE: And give him his medicine.

SWEENEY [*as the child continues to stare at him silently with eyes stupid*

146

from fear, he shakes her impatiently]: D'you hear me, now? [*To his wife*] It's soft-minded she is, like I've always told you, an' stupid; and you're not too firm in the head yourself at times, God help you! An' look at him! It's the curse is in the wits of your family, not mine.

ANNIE: You've been drinkin' in town or you wouldn't talk that way.

MARY [*whining*]: Maw! I'm skeered!

SWEENEY [*lets go of her arm and approaches* BENTLEY]: Get up out o' this, ye auld loon, an' go with Mary. She'll take you to the house. [BENTLEY *tries to hit him with the cane*] Oho, ye would, would ye? [*He wrests the cane from the old man's hands*] Bad cess to ye, you're the treach'rous one! Get up, now! [*He jerks the old man to his feet*] Here, Mary, take his hand. Quick now! [*She does so tremblingly*] Lead him to the house.

ANNIE: Go on, Paw! I'll come and git your supper in a minute.

BENTLEY [*stands stubbornly and begins to intone*]: "O Lord, thou hast seen my wrong; judge thou my cause. Thou hast seen all their vengeance and all their imaginations against me—"

SWEENEY [*pushing him toward the door.* BENTLEY *tries to resist.* MARY *pulls at his hand in a sudden fit of impish glee, and laughs shrilly*]: Get on now an' stop your cursin'.

BENTLEY: "Render unto them a recompense, O Lord, according to the work of their hands."

SWEENEY: Shut your loud quackin! Here's your cane. [*He gives it to the old man as they come to the doorway and quickly steps back out of reach*] An' mind you don't touch the child with it or I'll beat you to a jelly, old as ye are.

BENTLEY [*resisting* MARY'S *efforts to pull him out, stands shaking his stick at* SWEENEY *and his wife*]: "Give them sorrow of heart, thy curse unto them. Persecute and destroy them in anger from under the heavens of the Lord."

MARY [*tugging at his hand and bursting again into shrill laughter*]: Come on, Gran'paw. [*He allows himself to be led off, right.*]

SWEENEY [*making the sign of the cross furtively—with a sigh of relief*]: He's gone, thank God! What a snake's tongue he has in him! [*He sits down on the bench to the left of table*] Come here, Annie, till I speak to you. [*She sits down on the bench in front of table.* SWEENEY *winks mysteriously*] Well, I saw him, sure enough.

ANNIE [*stupidly*]: Who?

147

SWEENEY [*sharply*]: Who? Who but Dick Waller, the lawyer, that I went to see. [*Lowering his voice*] An' I've found out what we was wishin' to know. [*With a laugh*] Ye said I'd been drinkin'—which was true; but 'twas all in the plan I'd made. I've a head for strong drink, as ye know, but he hasn't. [*He winks cunningly*] An' the whiskey loosened his tongue till he'd told all he knew.

ANNIE: He told you—about Paw's will?

SWEENEY: He did. [*Disappointedly*] But for all the good it does us we might as well be no wiser than we was before. [*He broods for a moment in silence—then hits the table furiously with his fist*] God's curse on the auld miser!

ANNIE: What did he tell you?

SWEENEY: Not much at the first. He's a cute one, an' he'd be askin' a fee to tell you your own name, if he could get it. His practice is all dribbled away from him lately on account of the drink. So I let on I was only payin' a friendly call, havin' known him for years. Then I asked him out to have a drop o' drink, knowin' his weakness; an' we had rashers of them, an' I payin' for it. Then I come out with it straight and asked him about the will—because the auld man was crazy an' on his last legs, I told him, an' he was the lawyer made out the will when Luke was gone. So he winked at me an' grinned—he was drunk by this—an' said: "It's no use, Pat. He left the farm to the boy." "To hell with the farm," I spoke back. "It's mortgaged to the teeth; but how about the money?" "The money?" an' he looks at me in surprise, "What money?" "The cash he has," I says. "You're crazy," he says. "There wasn't any cash—only the farm." "D'you mean to say he made no mention of money in his will?" I asked. You could have knocked me down with a feather. "He did not—on my oath," he says. [SWEENEY *leans over to his wife—indignantly*] Now what d'you make o' that? The auld divil!

ANNIE: Maybe Waller was lyin'.

SWEENEY: He was not. I could tell by his face. He was surprised to hear me talkin' of money.

ANNIE: But the thousand dollars Paw got for the mortgage just before that woman ran away—

SWEENEY: An' that I've been slavin' me hands off to pay the int'rist on!

ANNIE: What could he have done with that? He ain't spent it. It was in twenty-dollar gold pieces he got it, I remember Mr. Kellar of the bank tellin' me once.

SWEENEY: Divil a penny he's spent. Ye know as well as I do if it wasn't for my hammerin', an' sawin', an' nailin', he'd be in the poorhouse this minute—or the madhouse, more likely.

ANNIE: D'you suppose that harlot ran off with it?

SWEENEY: I do not; I know better—an' so do you. D'you not remember the letter she wrote tellin' him he could support Luke on the money he'd got on the mortgage she'd signed with him; for he'd made the farm over to her when he married her. An' where d'you suppose Luke got the hundred dollars he stole? The auld loon must have had cash with him then, an' it's only five years back.

ANNIE: He's got it hid some place in the house most likely.

SWEENEY: Maybe you're right. I'll dig in the cellar this night when he's sleepin'. He used to be down there a lot recitin' Scripture in his fits.

ANNIE: What else did Waller say?

SWEENEY: Nothin' much; except that we should put notices in the papers for Luke, an' if he didn't come back by sivin years from when he'd left— two years from now, that'd be—the courts would say he was dead an' give us the farm. Divil a lot of use it is to us now with no money to fix it up; an' himself ruinin' it years ago by sellin' everythin' to buy that slut new clothes.

ANNIE: Don't folks break wills like his'n in the courts?

SWEENEY: Waller said 'twas no use. The auld divil was plain in his full senses when he made it; an' the courts cost money.

ANNIE [*resignedly*]: There ain't nothin' we can do then.

SWEENEY: No—except wait an' pray that young thief is dead an' won't come back; an' try an' find where it is the auld man has the gold hid, if he has it yet. I'd take him by the neck an' choke him till he told it, if he wasn't your father. [*He takes a full quart flask of whiskey from the pocket of his coat and has a big drink*] Aahh! If we'd on'y the thousand we'd stock the farm good an' I'd give up this dog's game [*He indicates the carpentry outfit scornfully*] an' we'd both work hard with a man or two to help, an' in a few years we'd be rich; for 'twas always a payin' place in the auld days.

ANNIE: Yes, yes, it was always a good farm then.

SWEENEY: He'll not last long in his senses, the doctor told me. His next attack will be very soon an' after it he'll be a real lunatic with no legal claims to anythin'. If we on'y had the money— 'Twould be the divil an' all if the auld fool should forget where he put it, an' him takin' leave of his senses altogether. [*He takes another nip at the bottle and puts it back in his pocket—with a sigh*] Ah, well, I'll save what I can an' at the end of two years, with good luck in the trade, maybe we'll have enough. [*They are both startled by the heavy footsteps of someone approaching outside. A shrill burst of* MARY'S *laughter can be heard and the deep voice of a man talking to her.*]

SWEENEY [*uneasily*]: It's Mary; but who could that be with her? It's not himself. [*As he finishes speaking* LUKE *appears in the doorway, holding the dancing* MARY *by the hand. He is a tall, strapping young fellow about twenty-five with a coarse-featured, rather handsome face bronzed by the sun. What his face lacks in intelligence is partly forgiven for his good-natured, half-foolish grin, his hearty laugh, his curly dark hair, a certain devil-may-care recklessness and irresponsible youth in voice and gesture. But his mouth is weak and characterless; his brown eyes are large but shifty and acquisitive. He wears a dark blue jersey, patched blue pants, rough sailor shoes, and a gray cap. He advances into the stable with a mocking smile on his lips until he stands directly under the rope. The man and woman stare at him in petrified amazement.*]

ANNIE: Luke!

SWEENEY [*crossing himself*]: Glory be to God—it's him!

MARY [*hopping up and down wildly*]: It's Uncle Luke, Uncle Luke, Uncle Luke! [*She runs to her mother, who pushes her away angrily.*]

LUKE [*regarding them both with an amused grin*]: Sure, it's Luke—back after five years of bummin' round the rotten old earth in ships and things. Paid off a week ago—had a bust-up—and then took a notion to come out here—bummed my way—and here I am. And you're both of you tickled to death to see me, ain't yuh?—like hell! [*He laughs and walks over to* ANNIE] Don't yuh even want to shake flippers with your dear, long-lost brother, Annie? I remember you and me used to git on so fine together—like hell!

ANNIE [*giving him a venomous look of hatred*]: Keep your hands to yourself.

LUKE [*grinning*]: You ain't changed, that's sure—on'y yuh're homelier'n ever. [*He turns to the scowling* SWEENEY] How about you, brother Pat?

SWEENEY: I'd not lower myself to take the hand of a—

LUKE [*with a threat in his voice*]: Easy goes with that talk! I'm not so soft to lick as I was when I was a kid; and don't forget it.

150

ANNIE [*to* MARY, *who is playing catch with a silver dollar which she has had clutched in her hand—sharply*]: Mary! What have you got there? Where did you get it? Bring it here to me this minute! [MARY *presses the dollar to her breast and remains standing by the doorway in stubborn silence.*]

LUKE: Aw, let her alone! What's bitin' yuh? That's on'y a silver dollar I give her when I met her front of the house. She told me you was up here; and I give her that as a present to buy candy with. I got it in Frisco— cart-wheels, they call 'em. There ain't none of them in these parts I ever seen, so I brung it along on the voyage.

ANNIE [*angrily*]: I don't know or care where you got it—but I know you ain't come by it honest. Mary! Give that back to him this instant! [*As the child hesitates, she stamps her foot furiously*] D'you hear me? [MARY *starts to cry softly, but comes to* LUKE *and hands him the dollar.*]

LUKE [*taking it—with a look of disgust at his half-sister*]: I was right when I said you ain't changed, Annie. You're as stinkin' mean as ever. [*To* MARY, *consolingly*] Quit bawlin', kid. You 'n' me'll go out on the edge of the cliff here and chuck some stones in the ocean same's we useter, remember? [MARY'S *tears immediately cease. She looks up at him with shining eyes, and claps her hands.*]

MARY [*pointing to the dollar he has in his hand*]: Throw that! It's flat 'n' it'll skip.

LUKE [*with a grin*]: That's the talk, kid. That's all it's good for—to throw away; not buryin' it like your miser folks'd tell you. Here! You take it and chuck it away. It's your'n. [*He gives her the dollar and she hops to the doorway. He turns to* PAT *with a grin*] I'm learnin' your kid to be a sport, Tight-Wad. I hope you ain't got no objections.

MARY [*impatiently*]: Come on, Uncle Luke. Watch me throw it.

LUKE: Aw right. [*To* PAT] I'll step outside a second and give you two a chanct to git all the dirty things yuh're thinkin' about me off your chest. [*Threateningly*] And then I'm gointer come and talk turkey to you, see? I didn't come back here for fun, and the sooner you gets that in your beans, the better.

MARY: Come on and watch me!

LUKE: Aw right, I'm comin'. [*He walks out and stands, leaning his back against the doorway, left.* MARY *is about six feet beyond him on the other side of the road. She is leaning down, peering over the edge of the cliff and laughing excitedly.*]

MARY: Can I throw it now? Can I?

LUKE: Don't git too near the edge, kid. The water's deep down there, and you'd be a drowned rat if you slipped. [*She shrinks back a step*] You chuck it when I say three. Ready, now! [*She draws back her arm*] One! Two! Three! [*She throws the dollar away and bends down to see it hit the water.*]

MARY [*clapping her hands and laughing*]: I seen it! I seen it splash! It's deep down now, ain't it?

LUKE: Yuh betcher it is! Now watch how far I kin chuck rocks. [*He picks up a couple and goes to where she is standing. During the following conversation between* SWEENEY *and his wife he continues to play this way with* MARY. *Their voices can be heard but the words are indistinguishable.*]

SWEENEY [*glancing apprehensively toward the door—with a great sigh*]: Speak of the divil an' here he is! [*Furiously*] Flingin' away dollars, the dirty thief, an' us without—

ANNIE [*interrupting him*]: Did you hear what he said? A thief like him ain't come back for no good. [*Lowering her voice*] D'you s'pose he knows about the farm bein' left to him?

SWEENEY [*uneasily*]: How could he? An' yet—I dunno—[*With sudden decision*] You'd best lave him to me to watch out for. It's small sense you have to hide your hate from him. You're as loony as the rist of your breed. An' he needs to be blarneyed round to fool him an' find out what he's wantin'. I'll pritind to make friends with him, God roast his soul! An' do you run to the house an' break the news to the auld man; for if he seen him suddin it's likely the little wits he has left would leave him; an' the thief could take the farm from us tomorrow if himself turned a lunatic.

ANNIE [*getting up*]: I'll tell him a little at a time till he knows.

SWEENEY: Be careful, now, or we'll lose the farm this night. [*She starts towards the doorway.* SWEENEY *speaks suddenly in a strange, awed voice*] Did you see Luke when he first came in to us? He stood there with the noose of the rope almost touchin' his head. I was almost wishin'—[*He hesitates.*]

ANNIE [*viciously*]: I was wishin' it was round his neck chokin' him, that's what I was—hangin' him just as Paw says.

SWEENEY: Ssshh! He might hear ye. Go along, now. He's comin' back.

MARY [*pulling at* LUKE's *arm as he comes back to the doorway*]: Lemme throw 'nother! Lemme throw 'nother!

152

LUKE [*enters just as* ANNIE *is going out and stops her*]: Goin' to the house? Do we get any supper? I'm hungry.

ANNIE [*glaring at him but restraining her rage*]: Yes.

LUKE [*jovially*]: Good work! And tell the old man I'm here and I'll see him in a while. He'll be glad to see me, too—like hell! [*He comes forward.* ANNIE *goes off, right.*]

MARY [*in an angry whine, tugging at his hand*]: Lemme throw 'nother. Lemme—

LUKE [*shaking her away*]: There's lots of rocks, kid. Throw them. Dollars ain't so plentiful.

MARY [*screaming*]: No! No! I don' wanter throw rocks. Lemme throw 'nother o' them.

SWEENEY [*severely.*]: Let your uncle in peace, ye brat! [*She commences to cry*] Run help your mother now or I'll give ye a good hidin'. [MARY *runs out of the door, whimpering.* PAT *turns to* LUKE *and holds out his hand.*]

LUKE [*looking at it in amazement*]: Ahoy, there! What's this?

SWEENEY [*with an ingratiating smile*]: Let's let bygones be bygones. I'm harborin' no grudge agen you these past years. Ye was only a lad when ye ran away an' not to be blamed for it. I'd have taken your hand a while back, an' glad to, but for her bein' with us. She has the divil's own tongue, as ye know, an' she can't forget the rowin' you an' her used to be havin'.

LUKE [*still looking at* SWEENEY's *hand*]. So that's how the wind blows! [*With a grin*] Well, I'll take a chanct. [*They shake hands and sit down by the table,* SWEENEY *on the front bench and* LUKE *on the left one.*]

SWEENEY [*pulls the bottle from his coat pocket—with a wink*]: Will ye have a taste? It's real stuff.

LUKE: Yuh betcher I will! [*He takes a big gulp and hands the bottle back.*]

SWEENEY [*after taking a drink himself, puts bottle on table*]: I wasn't wishin' herself to see it or I'd have asked ye sooner. [*There is a pause, during which each measures the other with his eyes.*]

LUKE: Say, how's the old man now?

SWEENEY [*cautiously*]: Oh, the same as ivir—older an' uglier, maybe.

LUKE: I thought he might be in the bug-house by this time.

SWEENEY [*hastily*]: Indeed not; he's foxy to pritind he's loony, but he's his wits with him all the time.

153

LUKE [*insinuatingly*]: Is he as stingy with his coin as he used to be?

SWEENEY: If he owned the ocean he wouldn't give a fish a drink; but I doubt if he's any money left at all. Your mother got rid of it all I'm thinkin'. [LUKE *smiles a superior, knowing smile*] He has on'y the farm, an' that mortgaged. I've been payin' the int'rist an' supportin' himself an' his doctor bills by the carpentryin' these five years past.

LUKE [*with a grin*]: Huh! Yuh're slow. Yuh oughter get wise to yourself.

SWEENEY [*inquisitively*]: What d'ye mean by that?

LUKE [*aggravatingly*]: Aw, nothin'. [*He turns around and his eyes fix themselves on the rope*] What the hell—[*He is suddenly convulsed with laughter and slaps his thigh*] Haha! If that don't beat the Dutch! The old nut!

SWEENEY: What?

LUKE: That rope. Say, has he had that hangin' there ever since I skipped?

SWEENEY [*smiling*]: Sure; an' he thinks you'll be comin' home to hang yourself.

LUKE: Hahaha! Not this chicken! And you say he ain't crazy! Gee, that's too good to keep. I got to have a drink on that. [SWEENEY *pushes the bottle toward him. He raises it toward the rope*] Here's how, old chum! [*He drinks.* SWEENEY *does likewise*] Say, I'd almost forgotten about that. Remember how hot he was that day when he hung that rope up and cussed me for pinchin' the hundred? He was standin' there shakin' his stick at me, and I was laughin' 'cause he looked so funny with the spit dribblin' outa his mouth like he was a mad dog. And when I turned round and beat it he shouted after me: "Remember, when you come home again there's a rope waitin' for yuh to hang yourself on, yuh bastard!" [*He spits contemptuously*] What a swell chanct. [*His manner changes and he frowns*] The old slave-driver! That's a hell of a fine old man for a guy to have!

SWEENEY [*pushing the bottle toward him*]: Take a sup an' forgit it. 'Twas a long time past.

LUKE: But the rope's there yet, ain't it? And he keeps it there. [*He takes a large swallow.* SWEENEY *also drinks*] But I'll git back at him aw right, yuh wait 'n' see. I'll git every cent he's got this time.

SWEENEY [*slyly*]: If he has a cent. I'm not wishful to discourage ye, but— [*He shakes his head doubtfully, at the same time fixing* LUKE *with a keen glance out of the corner of his eye.*]

LUKE [*with a cunning wink*]: Aw, he's got it aw right. You watch me! [*He is *beginning to show the effects of the drink he has had. He pulls out tobacco and a paper and rolls a cigarette and lights it. As he puffs he continues boastfully*] You country jays oughter wake up and see what's goin' on. Look at me. I was green as grass when I left here, but bummin' round the world, and bein' in cities, and meetin' all kinds, and keepin' your two eyes open—that's what'll learn yuh a cute trick or two.

SWEENEY: No doubt but you're right. Us country folks is stupid in most ways. We've no chance to learn the things a travelin' lad like you'd be knowin'.

LUKE [*complacently*]: Well, you watch me and I'll learn yuh. [*He snickers*] So yuh thinks the old man's flat broke, do yuh?

SWEENEY: I do so.

LUKE: Then yuh're simple; that's what—simple! Yuh're lettin' him kid yuh.

SWEENEY: If he has any, it's well hid, I know that. He's a sly old bird.

LUKE: And I'm a slyer bird. D'yuh hear that? I c'n beat his game any time. You watch me! [*He reaches out his hand for the bottle. They both drink again.* SWEENEY *begins to show signs of getting drunk. He hiccoughs every now and then and his voice grows uncertain and husky.*]

SWEENEY: It'd be a crafty one who'd find where he'd hidden it, sure enough.

LUKE: You watch me. I'll find it. I betcher anything yuh like I find it. You watch me! Just wait till he's asleep and I'll show yuh—ternight. [*There is a noise of shuffling footsteps outside and* ANNIE's *whining voice raised in angry protest.*]

SWEENEY: Ssshh! It's himself comin' now. [LUKE *rises to his feet and stands, waiting in a defensive attitude, a surly expression on his face. A moment later* BENTLEY *appears in the doorway, followed by* ANNIE. *He leans against the wall, in an extraordinary state of excitement, shaking all over, gasping for breath, his eyes devouring* LUKE *from head to foot.*]

ANNIE: I couldn't do nothin' with him. When I told him *he'd* come back there was no holdin' him. He was a'most frothin' at the mouth till I let him out. [*Whiningly*] You got to see to him, Pat, if you want any supper. I can't—

SWEENEY: Shut your mouth! We'll look after him.

ANNIE: See that you do. I'm goin' back. [*She goes off, right.* LUKE *and his father stand looking at each other. The surly expression disappears from* LUKE's *face, which gradually expands in a broad grin.*]

LUKE [*jovially*]: Hello, old sport! I s'pose yuh're tickled to pieces to see me—like hell! [*The old man stutters and stammers incoherently as if the very intensity of his desire for speech had paralyzed all power of articulation.* LUKE *turns to* PAT] I see he ain't lost the old stick. Many a crack on the nut I used to get with that.

BENTLEY [*suddenly finding his voice—chants*]: "Bring forth the best robe, and put it on him; and put a ring on his hand, and shoes on his feet: And bring hither the fatted calf, and kill it; and let us eat and be merry: For this my son was dead, and is alive again; he was lost, and is found." [*He ends up with a convulsive sob.*]

LUKE [*disapprovingly*]: Yuh're still spoutin' the rotten old Word o' God same's ever, eh? Say, give us a rest on that stuff, will yuh? Come on and shake hands like a good sport. [*He holds out his hand. The old man totters over to him, stretching out a trembling hand.* LUKE *seizes it and pumps it up and down*] That's the boy!

SWEENEY [*genuinely amazed*]: Look at that, would ye—the two-faced auld liar. [BENTLEY *passes his trembling hand all over* LUKE, *feeling of his arms, his chest, his back. An expression of overwhelming joy suffuses his worn features.*]

LUKE [*grinning at* SWEENEY]: Say, watch this. [*With tolerant good-humor*] On the level I b'lieve the old boy's glad to see me at that. He looks like he was tryin' to grin; and I never seen him grin in my life, I c'n remember. [*As* BENTLEY *attempts to feel of his face*] Hey, cut it out! [*He pushes his hand away, but not roughly*] I'm all here, yuh needn't worry. Yuh needn't be scared I'm a ghost. Come on and sit down before yuh fall down. Yuh ain't got your sea-legs workin' right. [*He guides the old man to the bench at left of table*] Squat here for a spell and git your wind. [BENTLEY *sinks down on the bench.* LUKE *reaches for the bottle*] Have a drink to my makin' port. It'll buck yuh up.

SWEENEY [*alarmed*]: Be careful, Luke. It might likely end him.

LUKE [*holds the bottle up to the old man's mouth, supporting his head with the other hand.* BENTLEY *gulps, the whiskey drips over his chin, and he goes into a fit of convulsive coughing.* LUKE *laughs*]: Hahaha! Went down the wrong way, did it? I'll show yuh the way to do it. [*He drinks*] There yuh are—smooth as silk. [*He hands the bottle to* SWEENEY, *who drinks and puts it back on the table.*]

SWEENEY: He must be glad to see ye or he'd not drink. 'Tis dead against it he's been these five years past. [*Shaking his head*] An' him cursin' you

156

day an' night! I can't put head or tail to it. Look out he ain't meanin' some bad to ye underneath. He's crafty at pretendin'.

LUKE [*as the old man makes signs to him with his hand*]: What's he after now? He's lettin' on he's lost his voice again. What d'yuh want? [BENT-LEY *points with his stick to the rope. His lips move convulsively as he makes a tremendous effort to utter words.*]

BENTLEY [*mumbling incoherently*]: Luke—Luke—rope—Luke—hang.

SWEENEY [*appalled*]: There ye are! What did I tell you? It's to see you hang yourself he's wishin', the auld fiend!

BENTLEY [*nodding*]: Yes—Luke—hang.

LUKE [*taking it as a joke—with a loud guffaw*]: Hahaha! If that don't beat the Dutch! The old nanny-goat! Aw right, old sport. Anything to oblige. Hahaha! [*He takes the chair from left and places it under the rope. The old man watches him with eager eyes and seems to be trying to smile.* LUKE *stands on the chair.*]

SWEENEY: Have a care, now! I'd not be foolin' with it in your place.

LUKE: All out for the big hangin' of Luke Bentley by hisself. [*He puts the noose about his neck with an air of drunken bravado and grins at his father. The latter makes violent motions for him to go on*] Look at him, Pat. By God, he's in a hurry. Hahaha! Well, old sport, here goes nothin'. [*He makes a movement as if he were going to jump and kick the chair from under him.*]

SWEENEY [*half starts to his feet—horrified*]: Luke! Are ye gone mad?

LUKE [*stands staring at his father, who is still making gestures for him to jump. A scowl slowly replaces his good-natured grin*]: D'yuh really mean it—that yuh want to see me hangin' myself? [BENTLEY *nods vigorously in the affirmative.* LUKE *glares at him for a moment in silence*] Well, I'll be damned! [*To* PAT] An' I thought he was only kiddin'. [*He removes the rope gingerly from his neck. The old man stamps his foot and gesticulates wildly, groaning with disappointment.* LUKE *jumps to the floor and looks at his father for a second. Then his face grows white with a vicious fury*] I'll fix your hash, you stinkin' old murderer! [*He grabs the chair by its back and swings it over his head as if he were going to crush* BENTLEY'*s skull with it. The old man cowers on the bench in abject terror.*]

SWEENEY [*jumping to his feet with a cry of alarm*]: Luke! For the love of God! [LUKE *hesitates; then hurls the chair in back of him under the loft,*

157

and stands menacingly in front of his father, his hands on his hips.]

LUKE [*grabbing* BENTLEY'S *shoulder and shaking him—hoarsely*]: Yuh wanted to see me hangin' there in real earnest, didn't yuh? You'd hang me yourself if yuh could, wouldn't yuh? And you my own father! Yuh damned son-of-a-gun! Yuh would, would yuh? I'd smash your brains out for a nickel! [*He shakes the old man more and more furiously.*]

SWEENEY: Luke! Look out! You'll be killin' him next.

LUKE [*giving his father one more shake, which sends him sprawling on the floor*]: Git outa here! Git outa this b'fore I kill yuh dead! [SWEENEY *rushes over and picks the terrified old man up*] Take him outa here, Pat! [*His voice rises to a threatening roar*] Take him outa here or I'll break every bone in his body! [*He raises his clenched fists over his head in a frenzy of rage.*]

SWEENEY: Ssshh! Don't be roarin'! I've got him. [*He steers the whimpering, hysterical* BENTLEY *to the doorway*] Come out o' this, now. Get down to the house! Hurry now! Ye've made enough trouble for one night! [*They disappear off right.* LUKE *flings himself on a bench, breathing heavily. He picks up the bottle and takes a long swallow.* SWEENEY *re-enters from rear. He comes over and sits down in his old place*] Thank God he's off down to the house, scurryin' like a frightened hare as if he'd never a kink in his legs in his life. He was moanin' out loud so you could hear him a long ways. [*With a sigh*] It's a murd'rous auld loon he is, sure enough.

LUKE [*thickly*]: The damned son-of-a-gun!

SWEENEY: I thought you'd be killin' him that time with the chair.

LUKE [*violently*]: Serve him damn right if I done it.

SWEENEY: An' you laughin' at him a moment sooner! I thought 'twas jokin' ye was.

LUKE [*suddenly*]: So I was kiddin'; but I thought he was tryin' to kid me, too. And then I seen by the way he acted he really meant it. [*Banging the table with his fist*] Ain't that a hell of a fine old man for yuh!

SWEENEY: He's a mean auld swine.

LUKE: He meant it aw right, too. Yuh shoulda seen him lookin' at me. [*With sudden lugubriousness*] Ain't he a hell of a nice old man for a guy to have? Ain't he?

SWEENEY [*soothingly*]: Hush! It's all over now. Don't be thinkin' about it.

LUKE [*on the verge of drunken tears*]: How kin I help thinkin'—and him my own father? After me bummin' and starvin' round the rotten earth, and workin' myself to death on ships and things—and when I come home he tries to make me bump off—wants to see me a corpse—my own father, too! Ain't he a hell of an old man to have? The rotten son-of-a-gun!

SWEENEY: It's past an' done. Forgit it. [*He slaps* LUKE *on the shoulder and pushes the bottle toward him*] Let's take a drop more. We'll be goin' to supper soon.

LUKE [*takes a big drink—huskily*]: Thanks. [*He wipes his mouth on his sleeve with a snuffle*] But I'll tell yuh something you can put in your pipe and smoke. It ain't past and done, and it ain't goin' to be! [*More and more aggressively*] And I ain't goin' to fergit it, either! Yuh kin betcher life on that, pal. And *he* ain't goin' to ferget it—not if he lives a million—not by a damned sight! [*With sudden fury*] I'll fix his hash! I'll git even with him, the old skunk! You watch me! And this very night, too!

SWEENEY: How'd you mean?

LUKE: You just watch me, I tell yuh! [*Banging the table*] I said I'd git even and I will git even—this same night, with no long waits, either! [*Frowning*] Say, you don't stand up for him, do yuh?

SWEENEY [*spitting—vehemently*]: That's child's talk. There's not a day passed I've not wished him in his grave.

LUKE [*excitedly*]: Then we'll both git even on him—you 'n' me. We're pals, ain't we?

SWEENEY: Sure.

LUKE: And yuh kin have half what we gits. That's the kinda feller I am! That's fair enough, ain't it?

SWEENEY: Surely.

LUKE: I don't want no truck with this rotten farm. You kin have my share of that. I ain't made to be no damned dirt-puncher—not me! And I ain't goin' to loaf round here more'n I got to, and when I goes this time I ain't never comin' back. Not me! Not to punch dirt and milk cows. You kin have the rotten farm for all of me. What I wants is cash—regular coin yuh kin spend—not dirt. I want to show the gang a real time, and then ship away to sea agen or go bummin' agen. I want coin yuh kin throw away—same's your kid chucked that dollar of mine overboard, remember? A real dollar, too! She's a sport, aw right!

SWEENEY [*anxious to bring him back to the subject*]: But where d'you think to find his money?

LUKE [*confidently*]: Don't yuh fret. I'll show yuh. You watch me! I know his hidin' places. I useter spy on him when I was a kid—Maw used to make me—and I seen him many a time at his sneakin'. [*Indignantly*] He used to hide stuff from the old lady. What d'yuh know about him—the mean skunk.

SWEENEY: That was a long time back. You don't know—

LUKE [*assertively*]: But I do know, see! He's got two places. One was where I swiped the hundred.

SWEENEY: It'll not be there, then.

LUKE: No; but there's the other place; and he never knew I was wise to that. I'd have left him clean on'y I was a kid and scared to pinch more. So you watch me! We'll git even on him, you 'n' me, and go halfs, and yuh kin start the rotten farm goin' agen and I'll beat it where there's some life.

SWEENEY: But if there's no money in that place, what'll you be doin' to find out where it is, then?

LUKE: Then you 'n' me 'ull make him tell!

SWEENEY: Oho, don't think it! 'Tis not him'd be tellin'.

LUKE: Aw, say, you're simple! You watch me! I know a trick or two about makin' people tell what they don't wanter. [*He picks up the chisel from the table*] Yuh see this? Well, if he don't answer up nice and easy we'll show him! [*A ferocious grin settles over his face*] We'll git even on him, you 'n' me—and he'll tell where it's hid. We'll just shove this into the stove till it's red-hot and take off his shoes and socks and warm the bottoms of his feet for him. [*Savagely*] He'll tell then—anything we wants him to tell.

SWEENEY: But Annie?

LUKE: We'll shove a rag in her mouth so's she can't yell. That's easy.

SWEENEY [*his head lolling drunkenly—with a cruel leer*]: 'Twill serve him right to heat up his hoofs for him, the limpin' auld miser!—if ye don't hurt him too much.

LUKE [*with a savage scowl*]: We won't hurt him—more'n enough. [*Suddenly raging*] I'll pay him back aw right! He won't want no more people to hang themselves when I git through with him. I'll fix his hash! [*He sways to his feet, the chisel in his hand*] Come on! Let's git to work. Sooner we starts the sooner we're rich. [SWEENEY *rises. He is steadier on his feet than* LUKE. *At this moment* MARY *appears in the doorway.*]

MARY: Maw says supper's ready. I had mine. [*She comes into the room and jumps up, trying to grab hold of the rope*] Lift me, Uncle Luke. I wanter swing.

160

LUKE [*severely*]: Don't yuh dare touch that rope, d'yuh hear?

MARY [*whining*]: I wanter swing.

LUKE [*with a shiver*]: It's bad, kid. Yuh leave it alone, take it from me.

SWEENEY: She'll get a good whalin' if I catch her jumpin' at it.

LUKE: Come on, pal. T'hell with supper. We got work to do first. [*They go to the doorway.*]

SWEENEY [*turning back to the sulking* MARY]: And you stay here, d'you hear, ye brat, till we call ye—or I'll skin ye alive.

LUKE: And termorrer mornin', kid, I'll give yuh a whole handful of them shiny, bright things yuh chucked in the ocean—and yuh kin be a real sport.

MARY [*eagerly*]: Gimme 'em now! Gimme 'em now, Uncle Luke. [*As he shakes his head—whiningly*] Gimme one! Gimme one!

LUKE: Can't be done, kid. Termorrer. Me 'n' your old man is goin' to git even now—goin' to make him pay for—

SWEENEY [*interrupting—harshly*]: Hist with your noise! D'you think she's no ears? Don't be talkin' so much. Come on, now.

LUKE [*permitting himself to be pulled out the doorway*]: Aw right! I'm with yuh. We'll git even—you 'n' me. The damned son-of-a-gun! [*They lurch off to the right.*]

[MARY *skips to the doorway and peeps after them for a moment. Then she comes back to the center of the floor and looks around her with an air of decision. She sees the chair in under the loft and runs over to it, pulling it back and setting it on its legs directly underneath the noose of the rope. She climbs and stands on the top of the chair and grasps the noose with both her upstretched hands. Then with a shriek of delight she kicks the chair from under her and launches herself for a swing. The rope seems to part where it is fixed to the beam. A dirty gray bag tied to the end of the rope falls to the floor with a muffled, metallic thud.* MARY *sprawls forward on her hands and knees, whimpering. Straggly wisps from the pile of rank hay fall silently to the floor in a mist of dust.* MARY, *discovering she is unhurt, glances quickly around and sees the bag. She pushes herself along the floor and, untying the string at the top, puts in her hand. She gives an exclamation of joy at what she feels and, turning the bag upside down, pours its contents in her lap. Giggling to herself, she gets to her feet and goes to the doorway, where she dumps what she has in her lap in a heap on the floor just inside the barn. They lie there* in a glittering pile, shimmering in the faint sunset glow—fifty twenty-dollar gold pieces. MARY claps her hands and sings to herself: "Skip—skip—skip." Then she quickly picks up four or five and runs out to the edge of the cliff. She throws them one after another into the ocean as fast as she can and bends over to see them hit the water. Against the background of horizon clouds still tinted with blurred crimson she hops up and down in a sort of grotesque dance, clapping her hands and laughing shrilly. After the last one is thrown she rushes back into the barn to get more.]

MARY [picking up a handful—giggling ecstatically]: Skip! Skip! [She turns and runs out to throw them as the curtain falls.]

Go Fly a Saucer

DAVID McCORD

I've seen one flying saucer. Only when
It flew across our sight in 1910
We little thought about the little men.

But let's suppose the little men were there
To cozy such a disc through foreign air:
Connecticut was dark, but didn't scare.

I wonder what they thought of us, and why
They chose the lesser part of Halley's sky,
And went away and let the years go by

Without return? Or did they not get back
To Mars or Venus through the cosmic flak?
At least they vanished, every spaceman Jack.

Now they are with us in the books, in air,
In argument, in hope, in fear, in spare
Reports from men aloft who saw them there.

The day one saucer cracks, the greatest egg
Since dinosaur and dodo shook a leg
Will give new meaning to the prefix *meg*.

Some say the saucers with their little race
Of little men from Littlesphere in space
Have sensed our international disgrace.

Appearance Versus Reality

And when the thing blows over, up, or what,
They'll gladly land and give us all they've got
So Earth shall cease to be a trouble spot.

One fact as old as Chaucer, Saucer Men:
You may be little as a bantam hen,
But Earth has specialized in little men.

A. C. Goodwin, *Mt. Vernon Street, Boston*

Before the Birth of One of Her Children

ANNE BRADSTREET

All things within this fading world hath end,
Adversity doth still our joys attend;
No ties so strong, no friends so dear and sweet,
But with death's parting blow is sure to meet.
The sentence past is most irrevocable,
A common thing, yet oh, inevitable.
How soon, my Dear, death may my steps attend,
How soon't may be thy lot to lose thy friend,
We both are ignorant, yet love bids me
These farewell lines to recommend to thee,
That when that knot's untied that made us one,
I may seem thine, who in effect am none.
And if I see not half my days that's due,
What nature would, God grant to yours and you;
The many faults that well you know I have
Let be interred in my oblivious grave;
If any worth or virtue were in me,
Let that live freshly in thy memory
And when thou feel'st no grief, as I no harms,
Yet love thy dead, who long lay in thine arms.
And when thy loss shall be repaid with gains
Look to my little babes, my dear remains.
And if thou love thyself, or loved'st me,
These O protect from step-dame's injury.
And if chance to thine eyes shall bring this verse,
With some sad sighs honour my absent hearse;
And kiss this paper for thy love's dear sake,
Who with salt tears this last farewell did take.

Bewitched

EDITH WHARTON

The snow was still falling thickly when Orrin Bosworth, who farmed the land south of Lonetop, drove up in his cutter to Saul Rutledge's gate. He was surprised to see two other cutters ahead of him. From them descended two muffled figures. Bosworth, with increasing surprise, recognized Deacon Hibben, from North Ashmore, and Sylvester Brand, the widower, from the old Bearcliff farm on the way to Lonetop.

It was not often that anybody in Hemlock County entered Saul Rutledge's gate; least of all in the dead of winter, and summoned (as Bosworth, at any rate, had been) by Mrs. Rutledge, who passed, even in that unsocial region, for a woman of cold manners and solitary character. The situation was enough to excite the curiosity of a less imaginative man than Orrin Bosworth.

As he drove in between the broken-down white gateposts topped by fluted urns the two men ahead of him were leading their horses to the adjoining shed. Bosworth followed, and hitched his horse to a post. Then the three tossed off the snow from their shoulders, clapped their numb hands together, and greeted each other.

"Hallo, Deacon."

"Well, well, Orrin—" They shook hands.

" 'Day, Bosworth," said Sylvester Brand, with a brief nod. He seldom put any cordiality into his manner, and on this occasion he was still busy about his horse's bridle and blanket.

Orrin Bosworth, the youngest and most communicative of the three, turned back to Deacon Hibben, whose long face, queerly blotched and moldy-looking, with blinking peering eyes, was yet less forbidding than Brand's heavily-hewn countenance.

"Queer, our all meeting here this way. Mrs. Rutledge sent me a message to come," Bosworth volunteered.

The Deacon nodded. "I got a word from her too—Andy Pond come with it yesterday noon. I hope there's no trouble here—"

He glanced through the thickening fall of snow at the desolate front of the Rutledge house, the more melancholy in its present neglected state because, like the gateposts, it kept traces of former elegance. Bosworth had often wondered how such a house had come to be built in that lonely stretch between North Ashmore and Cold Corners. People said there had once been other houses like it, forming a little township called Ashmore, a sort of mountain colony created by the caprice of an Enlish Royalist officer, one Colonel Ashmore, who had been murdered by the Indians, with all his family, long before the Revolution. This tale was confirmed by the fact that the ruined cellars of several smaller houses were still to be discovered under the wild growth of the adjoining slopes, and that the Communion plate of the moribund Episcopal church of Cold Corners was engraved with the name of Colonel Ashmore, who had given it to the church of Ashmore in the year 1723. Of the church itself no traces remained. Doubtless it had been a modest wooden edifice, built on piles, and the conflagration which had burnt the other houses to the ground's edge had reduced it utterly to ashes. The whole place, even in summer, wore a mournful solitary air, and people wondered why Saul Rutledge's father had gone there to settle.

"I never knew a place," Deacon Hibben said, "as seemed as far away from humanity. And yet it ain't so in miles."

"Miles ain't the only distance," Orrin Bosworth answered; and the two men, followed by Sylvester Brand, walked across the drive to the front door. People in Hemlock County did not usually come and go by their front doors, but all three men seemed to feel that, on an ocasion which appeared to be so exceptional, the usual and more familiar approach by the kitchen would not be suitable.

They had judged rightly; the Deacon had hardly lifted the knocker when the door opened and Mrs. Rutledge stood before them.

"Walk right in," she said in her usual dead-level tone; and Bosworth, as he followed the others, thought to himself: "Whatever's happened, she's not going to let it show in her face."

It was doubtful, indeed, if anything unwonted could be made to show in Prudence Rutledge's face, so limited was its scope, so fixed were its features. She was dressed for the occasion in a black calico with white spots, a collar of crochet lace fastened by a gold brooch, and a gray woolen shawl, crossed under her arms and tied at the back. In her small narrow head the only marked prominence was that of the brow projecting roundly over pale spectacled eyes. Her dark hair, parted above this prominence, passed tight

168

Winslow Homer, *A Winter Morning—Shovelling Out*

and flat over the tips of her ears into a small braided coil at the nape; and her contracted head looked still narrower from being perched on a long hollow neck with cord-like throat muscles. Her eyes were of a pale cold gray, her complexion was an even white. Her age might have been anywhere from thirty-five to sixty.

The room into which she led the three men had probably been the dining room of the Ashmore house. It was now used as a front parlor, and a black stove planted on a sheet of zinc stuck out from the delicately fluted panels of an old wooden mantel. A newly-lit fire smoldered reluctantly, and the room was at once close and bitterly cold.

"Andy Pond," Mrs. Rutledge cried out to some one at the back of the house, "Step out and call Mr. Rutledge. You'll likely find him in the woodshed, or round the barn somewheres." She rejoined her visitors. "Please suit yourselves to seats," she said.

The three men, with an increasing air of constraint, took the chairs she pointed out, and Mrs. Rutledge sat stiffly down upon a fourth, behind a rickety beadwork table. She glanced from one to the other of her visitors.

"I presume you folks are wondering what it is I asked you to come here for," she said in her dead-level voice. Orrin Bosworth and Deacon Hibben murmured an assent; Sylvester Brand sat silent, his eyes, under their great thicket of eyebrows, fixed on the huge boot tip swinging before him.

"Well, I allow you didn't expect it was for a party," continued Mrs. Rutledge.

No one ventured to respond to this chill pleasantry, and she continued: "We're in trouble here, and that's the fact. And we need advice—Mr. Rutledge and myself do." She cleared her throat, and added in a lower tone, her pitilessly clear eyes looking straight before her: "There's a spell been cast over Mr. Rutledge."

The Deacon looked up sharply, an incredulous smile pinching his thin lips. "A spell?"

"That's what I said: he's bewitched."

Again the three visitors were silent; then Bosworth, more at ease or less tongue-tied than the others, asked with an attempt at humor: "Do you use the word in the strict Scripture sense, Mrs. Rutledge?"

She glanced at him before replying: "That's how *he* uses it."

The Deacon coughed and cleared his long rattling throat. "Do you care to give us more particulars before your husband joins us?"

Mrs. Rutledge looked down at her clasped hands, as if considering the

170

question. Bosworth noticed that the inner fold of her lids was of the same uniform white as the rest of her skin, so that when she drooped them her rather prominent eyes looked like the sightless orbs of a marble statue. The impression was unpleasing, and he glanced away at the text over the mantelpiece, which read:

The Soul That Sinneth It Shall Die.

"No," she said at length, "I'll wait."

At this moment Sylvester Brand suddenly stood up and pushed back his chair. "I don't know," he said, in his rough bass voice, "as I've got any particular lights on Bible mysteries; and this happens to be the day I was to go down to Starkfield to close a deal with a man."

Mrs. Rutledge lifted one of her long thin hands. Withered and wrinkled by hard work and cold, it was nevertheless of the same leaden white as her face. "You won't be kept long," she said. "Won't you be seated?"

Farmer Brand stood irresolute, his purplish underlip twitching. "The Deacon here—such things is more in his line. . . ."

"I want you should stay," said Mrs. Rutledge quietly; and Brand sat down again.

A silence fell, during which the four persons present seemed all to be listening for the sound of a step; but none was heard, and after a minute or two Mrs. Rutledge began to speak again.

"It's down by that old shack on Lamer's pond; that's where they meet," she said suddenly.

Bosworth, whose eyes were on Sylvester Brand's face, fancied he saw a sort of inner flush darken the farmer's heavy leathern skin. Deacon Hibben learned forward, a glitter of curiosity in his eyes.

"They—*who*, Mrs. Rutledge?"

"My husband, Saul Rutledge . . . and her. . . ."

Sylvester Brand again stirred in his seat. "Who do you mean by *her?*" he asked abruptly, as if roused out of some far-off musing.

Mrs. Rutledge's body did not move; she simply revolved her head on her long neck and looked at him.

"Your daughter, Sylvester Brand."

The man staggered to his feet with an explosion of inarticulate sounds. "My—my daughter? What the hell are you talking about? My daughter? It's a damned lie . . . it's . . . it's. . . ."

"Your daughter *Ora*, Mr. Brand," said Mrs. Rutledge slowly.

171

Bosworth felt an icy chill down his spine. Instinctively he turned his eyes away from Brand, and they rested on the mildewed countenance of Deacon Hibben. Between the blotches it had become as white as Mrs. Rutledge's, and the Deacon's eyes burned in the whiteness like live embers among ashes.

Brand gave a laugh: the rusty creaking laugh of one whose springs of mirth are never moved by gaiety. "My daughter *Ora?*" he repeated.

"Yes."

"My *dead* daughter?"

"That's what he says."

"Your husband?"

"That's what Mr. Rutledge says."

Orrin Bosworth listened with a sense of suffocation; he felt as if he were wrestling with long-armed horrors in a dream. He could no longer resist letting his eyes turn to Sylvester Brand's face. To his surprise it had resumed a natural imperturbable expression. Brand rose to his feet. "Is that all?" he queried contemptuously.

"All? Ain't it enough? How long is it since you folks seen Saul Rutledge, any of you?" Mrs. Rutledge flew out at them.

Bosworth, it appeared, had not seen him for nearly a year; the Deacon had only run across him once, for a minute, at the North Ashmore post office, the previous autumn, and acknowledged that he wasn't looking any too good then. Brand said nothing, but stood irresolute.

"Well, if you wait a minute you'll see with your own eyes; and he'll tell you with his own words. That's what I've got you here for—to see for yourselves what's come over him. Then you'll talk different," she added, twisting her head abruptly toward Sylvester Brand.

The Deacon raised a lean hand of interrogation.

"Does your husband know we've been sent for on this business, Mrs. Rutledge?"

Mrs. Rutledge signed assent.

"It was with his consent, then—?"

She looked coldly at her questioner. "I guess it had to be," she said. Again Bosworth felt the chill down his spine. He tried to dissipate the sensation by speaking with an affectation of energy.

"Can you tell us, Mrs. Rutledge, how this trouble you speak of shows itself . . . what makes you think . . . ?"

She looked at him for a moment; then she leaned forward across the rickety beadwork table. A thin smile of disdain narrowed her colorless lips. "I don't think—I know."

"Well—but how?"

She leaned closer, both elbows on the table, her voice dropping. "I seen 'em."

In the ashen light from the veiling of snow beyond the windows the Deacon's little screwed-up eyes seemed to give out red sparks. "Him and the dead?"

"Him and the dead."

"Saul Rutledge and—and Ora Brand?"

"That's so."

Sylvester Brand's chair fell backward with a crash. He was on his feet again, crimson and cursing. "It's a God-damned fiend-begotten lie. . . ."

"Friend Brand . . . friend Brand . . ." the Deacon protested.

"Here, let me get out of this. I want to see Saul Rutledge himself, and tell him—"

"Well, here he is," said Mrs. Rutledge.

The outer door had opened; they heard the familiar stamping and shaking of a man who rids his garments of their last snowflakes before penetrating to the sacred precincts of the best parlor. Then Saul Rutledge entered.

II

As he came in he faced the light from the north window, and Bosworth's first thought was that he looked like a drowned man fished out from under the ice—"self-drowned," he added. But the snow light plays cruel tricks with a man's color, and even with the shape of his features; it must have been partly that, Bosworth reflected, which transformed Saul Rutledge from the straight muscular fellow he had been a year before into the haggard wretch now before them.

The Deacon sought for a word to ease the horror. "Well, now, Saul—you look's if you'd ought to set right up to the stove. Had a touch of ague, maybe?"

The feeble attempt was unavailing. Rutledge neither moved nor answered. He stood among them silent, incommunicable, like one risen from the dead.

Brand grasped him roughly by the shoulder. "See here, Saul Rutledge, what's this dirty lie your wife tells us you've been putting about?"

Still Rutledge did not move. "It's no lie," he said.

Brand's hand dropped from his shoulder. In spite of the man's rough bullying power he seemed to be undefinably awed by Rutledge's look and tone.

"No lie? You've gone plumb crazy, then, have you?"

Mrs. Rutledge spoke. "My husband's not lying, nor he ain't gone crazy. Don't I tell you I seen 'em?"

Brand laughed again. "Him and the dead?"

"Yes."

"Down by the Lamer pond, you say?"

"Yes."

"And when was that, if I might ask?"

"Day before yesterday."

A silence fell on the strangely assembled group. The Deacon at length broke it to say to Mr. Brand: "Brand, in my opinion we've got to see this thing through."

Brand stood for a moment in speechless contemplation: there was something animal and primitive about him, Bosworth thought, as he hung thus, lowering and dumb, a little foam beading the corners of that heavy purplish underlip. He let himself slowly down into his chair. "I'll see it through."

The two other men and Mrs. Rutledge had remained seated. Saul Rutledge stood before them, like a prisoner at the bar, or rather like a sick man before the physicians who were to heal him. As Bosworth scrutinized that hollow face, so wan under the dark sunburn, so sucked inward and consumed by some hidden fever, there stole over the sound healthy man the thought that perhaps, after all, husband and wife spoke the truth, and that they were all at that moment really standing on the edge of some forbidden mystery. Things that the rational mind would reject without a thought seemed no longer so easy to dispose of as one looked at the actual Saul Rutledge and remembered the man he had been a year before. Yes; as the Deacon said, they would have to see it through. . . .

"Sit down then, Saul; draw up to us, won't you?" the Deacon suggested, trying again for a natural tone.

Mrs. Rutledge pushed a chair forward, and her husband sat down on it. He stretched out his arms and grasped his knees in his brown bony fingers; in that attitude he remained, turning neither his head nor his eyes.

"Well, Saul," the Deacon continued, "your wife says you thought mebbe we could do something to help you through this trouble, whatever it is."

174

Rutledge's gray eyes widened a little. "No; I didn't think that. It was her idea to try what could be done."

"I presume, though, since you've agreed to our coming, that you don't object to our putting a few questions?"

Rutledge was silent for a moment; then he said with a visible effort: "No; I don't object."

"Well—you've heard what your wife says?"

Rutledge made a slight motion of assent.

"And—what have you got to answer? How do you explain. . . ?"

Mrs. Rutledge intervened. "How can he explain? I seen 'em."

There was a silence; then Bosworth, trying to speak in an easy reassuring tone, queried: "That so, Saul?"

"That's so."

Brand lifted up his brooding head. "You mean to say . . . you sit here before us all and say. . . ."

The Deacon's hand again checked him. "Hold on, friend Brand. We're all of us trying for the facts, ain't we?" He turned to Rutledge. "We've heard what Mrs. Rutledge says. What's your answer?"

"I don't know as there's any answer. She found us."

"And you mean to tell me the person with you was . . . was what you took to be . . ." the Deacon's thin voice grew thinner, "Ora Brand?"

Saul Rutledge nodded.

"You knew . . . or thought you knew . . . you were meeting with the dead?"

Rutledge bent his head again. The snow continued to fall in a steady unwavering sheet against the window, and Bosworth felt as if a winding sheet were descending from the sky to envelop them all in a common grave.

"Think what you're saying! It's against our religion! Ora . . . poor child! . . . died over a year ago. I saw you at her funeral, Saul. How can you make such a statement?"

"What else can he do?" thrust in Mrs. Rutledge.

There was another pause. Bosworth's resources had failed him, and Brand once more sat plunged in dark meditation. The Deacon laid his quivering finger tips together, and moistened his lips.

"Was the day before yesterday the first time?" he asked.

The movement of Rutledge's head was negative.

"Not the first? Then when. . . ?"

"Nigh on a year ago, I reckon."

"God! And you mean to tell us that ever since—?"

"Well . . . look at him," said his wife. The three men lowered their eyes.

After a moment Bosworth, trying to collect himself, glanced at the Deacon. "Why not ask Saul to make his own statement, if that's what we're here for?"

"That's so," the Deacon assented. He turned to Rutledge. "Will you try and give us your idea . . . of . . . of how it began?"

There was another silence. Then Rutledge tightened his grasp on his gaunt knees, and still looking straight ahead, with his curiously clear, unseeing gaze: "Well," he said, "I guess it begun away back, afore even I was married to Mrs. Rutledge. . . ." He spoke in a low automatic tone, as if some invisible agent were dictating his words, or even uttering them for him. "You know," he added, "Ora and me was to have been married."

Sylvester Brand lifted his head. "Straighten that statement out first, please," he interjected.

"What I mean is, we kept company. But Ora she was very young. Mr. Brand here he sent her away. She was gone nigh to three years, I guess. When she come back I was married."

"That's right," Brand said, relapsing once more into his sunken attitude.

"And after she came back did you meet her again?" the Deacon continued.

"Alive?" Rutledge questioned.

A perceptible shudder ran through the room.

"Well—of course," said the Deacon nervously.

Rutledge seemed to consider. "Once I did—only once. There was a lot of other people round. At Cold Corners Fair it was."

"Did you talk with her then?"

"Only a minute."

"What did she say?"

His voice dropped. "She said she was sick and knew she was going to die, and when she was dead she'd come back to me."

"And what did you answer?"

"Nothing."

"Did you think anything of it at the time?"

"Well, no. Not till I heard she was dead I didn't. After that I thought of it—and I guess she drew me." He moistened his lips.

"Drew you down to that abandoned house by the pond?"

Rutledge made a faint motion of assent, and the Deacon added: "How did you know it was there she wanted you to come?"

"She . . . just drew me. . . ."

There was a long pause. Bosworth felt, on himself and the other two men, the oppressive weight of the next question to be asked. Mrs. Rutledge opened and closed her narrow lips once or twice, like some beached shell-fish gasping for the tide. Rutledge waited.

"Well, now, Saul, won't you go on with what you was telling us?" the Deacon at length suggested.

"That's all. There's nothing else."

The Deacon lowered his voice. "She just draws you?"

"Yes."

"Often?"

"That's as it happens. . . ."

"But if it's always there she draws you, man, haven't you the strength to keep away from the place?"

For the first time, Rutledge wearily turned his head toward his questioner. A spectral smile narrowed his colorless lips. "Ain't any use. She follers after me. . . ."

There was another silence. What more could they ask, then and there? Mrs. Rutledge's presence checked the next question. The Deacon seemed hopelessly to revolve the matter. At length he spoke in a more authoritative tone. "These are forbidden things. You know that, Saul. Have you tried prayer?"

Rutledge shook his head.

"Will you pray with us now?"

Rutledge cast a glance of freezing indifference on his spiritual adviser. "If you folks want to pray, I'm agreeable," he said. But Mrs. Rutledge intervened.

"Prayer ain't any good. In this kind of thing it ain't no manner of use; you know it ain't. I called you here, Deacon, because you remember the last case in this parish. Thirty years ago it was, I guess; but you remember. Lefferts Nash—did praying help *him*? I was a little girl then, but I used to hear my folks talk of it winter nights. Lefferts Nash and Hannah Cory. They drove a stake through her breast. That's what cured him."

"Oh—" Orrin Bosworth exclaimed.

Sylvester Brand raised his head. "You've speaking of that old story as if this was the same sort of thing?"

"Ain't it? Ain't my husband pining away the same as Lefferts Nash did? The Deacon here knows—"

The Deacon stirred anxiously in his chair. "These are forbidden things," he repeated. "Supposing your husband is quite sincere in thinking himself haunted, as you might say. Well, even then, what proof have we that the . . . the dead woman . . . is the specter of that poor girl?"

"Proof? Don't he say so? Didn't she tell him? Ain't I seen 'em?" Mrs. Rutledge almost screamed.

The three men sat silent, and suddenly the wife burst out: "A stake through the breast! That's the old way; and it's the only way. The Deacon knows it!"

"It's against our religion to disturb the dead."

"Ain't it against your religion to let the living perish as my husband is perishing?" She sprang up with one of her abrupt movements and took the family Bible from the whatnot in a corner of the parlor. Putting the book on the table, and moistening a livid fingertip, she turned the pages rapidly, till she came to one on which she laid her hand like a stony paperweight. "See here," she said, and read out in her level chanting voice:

" *'Thou shalt not suffer a witch to live.'*

"That's in Exodus, that's where it is," she added, leaving the book open as if to confirm the statement.

Bosworth continued to glance anxiously from one to the other of the four people about the table. He was younger than any of them, and had had more contact with the modern world; down in Starkfield, in the bar of the Fielding House, he could hear himself laughing with the rest of the men at such old wives' tales. But it was not for nothing that he had been born under the icy shadow of Lonetop, and had shivered and hungered as a lad through the bitter Hemlock County winters. After his parents died, and he had taken hold of the farm himself, he had got more out of it by using improved methods, and by supplying the increasing throng of summer boarders over Stotesbury way with milk and vegetables. He had been made a Selectman of North Ashmore; for so young a man he had a standing in the county. But the roots of the old life were still in him. He could remember, as a little boy, going twice a year with his mother to that bleak hill farm out beyond Sylvester Brand's, where Mrs. Bosworth's aunt, Cressidora Cheney, had been shut up for years in a cold clean room with iron bars to the windows. When little Orrin first saw Aunt Cressidora she was a small white old woman, whom her sisters use to "make decent" for visitors the day that Orrin and his mother were expected. The child wondered why there were bars on the window. "Like a canary bird," he said to his mother. The phrase made Mrs. Bosworth reflect. "I do believe they keep Aunt Cressidora too lonesome," she said; and the next time she went up the mountain with the little boy he carried to his great-aunt a canary in a little wooden cage. It was a great excitement; he knew it would make her happy.

The old woman's motionless face lit up when she saw the bird, and her eyes began to glitter. "It belongs to me," she said instantly, stretching her soft bony hand over the cage.

"Of course it does, Aunt Cressy," said Mrs. Bosworth, her eyes filling.

But the bird, startled by the shadow of the old woman's hand, began to flutter and beat its wings distractedly. At the sight, Aunt Cressidora's calm face suddenly became a coil of twitching features. "You she-devil, you!" she cried in a high squealing voice; and thrusting her hand into the cage she dragged out the terrified bird and wrung its neck. She was plucking the hot body, and squealing "she-devil, she-devil!" as they drew little Orrin from the room. On the way down the mountain his mother wept a great deal, and said: "You must never tell anybody that poor Auntie's crazy, or the men would come and take her down to the asylum at Starkfield, and the shame of it would kill us all. Now promise." The child promised.

He remembered the scene now, with its deep fringe of mystery, secrecy and rumor. It seemed related to a great many other things below the surface of his thoughts, things which stole up anew, making him feel that all the old people he had known, and who "believed in these things," might after all be right. Hadn't a witch been burned at North Ashmore? Didn't the summer folk still drive over in jolly buckboard loads to see the meeting-house where the trial had been held, the pond where they had ducked her and she had floated? . . . Deacon Hibben believed; Bosworth was sure of it. If he didn't, why did people from all over the place come to him when their animals had queer sicknesses, or when there was a child in the family that had to be kept shut up because it fell down flat and foamed? Yes, in spite of his religion, Deacon Hibben *knew*. . . .

And Brand? Well, it came to Bosworth in a flash: that North Ashmore woman who was burned had the name of Brand. The same stock, no doubt; there had been Brands in Hemlock County ever since the white men had come there. And Orrin, when he was a child, remembered hearing his parents say that Sylvester Brand hadn't ever oughter married his own cousin, because of the blood. Yet the couple had had two healthy girls, and when Mrs. Brand pined away and died nobody suggested that anything had been wrong with her mind. And Vanessa and Ora were the handsomest girls anywhere round. Brand knew it, and scrimped and saved all he could to send Ora, the eldest, down to Starkfield to learn bookkeeping. "When she's married I'll send you," he used to say to little Venny, who was his favorite. But Ora never married. She was away three years, during which Venny ran wild on the slopes of Lonetop; and when Ora came back she sickened and died—poor girl! Since then Brand had grown more savage and morose. He was a hard-working farmer, but there wasn't much to be got out of those barren Bearcliff acres. He was said to have taken to drink since his wife's death; now and then men ran across him in the "dives" of Stotesbury. But not often. And between times he labored hard on his stony acres and did his best for his daughters. In the neglected graveyard of Cold Corners there was a slanting headstone marked with his wife's name; near it, a year since, he had laid his eldest daughter. And sometimes, at dusk, in the autumn, the village people saw him walk slowly by, turn in between the graves, and stand looking down on the two stones. But he never brought a flower there, or planted a bush; nor Venny either. She was too wild and ignorant. . . .

Mrs. Rutledge repeated: "That's in Exodus."

The three visitors remained silent, turning about their hats in reluctant hands. Rutledge faced them, still with that empty pellucid gaze which frightened Bosworth. What was he seeing?

"Ain't any of you folks got the grit—?" his wife burst out again, half hysterically.

Deacon Hibben held up his hand. "That's no way, Mrs. Rutledge. This ain't a question of having grit. What we want first of all is . . . proof . . ."

"That's so," said Bosworth, with an explosion of relief, as if the words had lifted something black and crouching from his breast. Involuntarily the eyes of both men had turned to Brand. He stood there smiling grimly, but did not speak.

"Ain't it so, Brand?" the Deacon prompted him.

"Proof that spooks walk?" the other sneered.

"Well—I presume you want this business settled too?"

The old farmer squared his shoulders. "Yes—I do. But I ain't a sperritualist. How the hell are you going to settle it?"

Deacon Hibben hesitated; then he said, in a low incisive tone: "I don't see but one way—Mrs. Rutledge's."

There was a silence.

"What?" Brand sneered again. "Spying?"

The Deacon's voice sank lower. "If the poor girl *does* walk . . . her that's your child . . . wouldn't you be the first to want her laid quiet? We all know there've been such cases . . . mysterious visitations. . . . Can any one of us here deny it?"

"I seen 'em," Mrs. Rutledge interjected.

There was another heavy pause. Suddenly Brand fixed his gaze on Rutledge. "See here, Saul Rutledge, you've got to clear up this damned calumny, or I'll know why. You say my dead girl comes to you." He labored with his breath, and then jerked out: "When? You tell me that, and I'll be there."

Rutledge's head drooped a little, and his eyes wandered to the window. "Round about sunset, mostly."

"You know beforehand?"

Rutledge made a sign of assent.

"Well, then—tomorrow, will it be?"

Rutledge made the same sign.

Brand turned to the door. "I'll be there." That was all he said. He strode out between them without another glance or word. Deacon Hibben looked at Mrs. Rutledge. "We'll be there too," he said, as if she had asked him; but she had not spoken, and Bosworth saw that her thin body was trembling all over. He was glad when he and Hibben were out again in the snow.

III

They thought that Brand wanted to be left to himself, and to give him time to unhitch his horse they made a pretense of hanging about in the doorway while Bosworth searched his pockets for a pipe he had no mind to light.

But Brand turned back to them as they lingered. "You'll meet me down by Lamer's pond tomorrow?" he suggested. "I want witnesses. Round about sunset."

They nodded their acquiescence, and he got into his sleigh, gave the horse a cut across the flanks, and drove off under the snow-smothered hemlocks. The other two men went to the shed.

"What do you make of this business, Deacon?" Bosworth asked, to break the silence.

The Deacon shook his head. "The man's a sick man—that's sure. Something's sucking the life clean out of him."

But already, in the biting outer air, Bosworth was getting himself under better control. "Looks to me like a bad case of the ague, as you said."

"Well—ague of the mind, then. It's his brain that's sick."

Bosworth shrugged. "He ain't the first in Hemlock County."

"That's so," the Deacon agreed. "It's a worm in the brain, solitude is."

"Well, we'll know this time tomorrow, maybe," said Bosworth. He scrambled into his sleigh, and was driving off in his turn when he heard his companion calling after him. The Deacon explained that his horse had cast a shoe; would Bosworth drive him down to the forge near North Ashmore, if it wasn't too much out of his way? He didn't want the mare slipping about on the freezing snow, and he could probably get the blacksmith to drive him back and shoe her in Rutledge's shed. Bosworth made room for him under the bearskin, and the two men drove off, pursued by a puzzled whinny from the Deacon's old mare.

The road they took was not the one that Bosworth would have followed to reach his own home. But he did not mind that. The shortest way to the forge passed close by Lamer's pond, and Bosworth, since he was in for the business, was not sorry to look the ground over. They drove on in silence.

The snow had ceased, and a green sunset was spreading upward into the crystal sky. A stinging wind barbed with ice flakes caught them in the face on the open ridges, but when they dropped down into the hollow by Lamer's pond the air was as soundless and empty as an unswung bell. They jogged along slowly, each thinking his own thoughts.

"That's the house . . . that tumble-down shack over there, I suppose?" the Deacon said, as the road drew near the edge of the frozen pond.

"Yes: that's the house. A queer hermit fellow built it years ago, my father used to tell me. Since then I don't believe it's ever been used but by the gypsies."

Bosworth had reined in his horse, and sat looking through pine trunks purpled by the sunset at the crumbling structure. Twilight already lay under the trees, though day lingered in the open. Between two sharply-patterned pine boughs he saw the evening star, like a white boat in a sea of green.

182

His gaze dropped from that fathomless sky and followed the blue-white undulations of the snow. It gave him a curious agitated feeling to think that here, in this icy solitude, in the tumble-down house he had so often passed without heeding it, a dark mystery, too deep for thought, was being enacted. Down that very slope, coming from the graveyard at Cold Corners, the being they called "Ora" must pass toward the pond. His heart began to beat stiflingly. Suddenly he gave an exclamation: "Look!"

He had jumped out of the cutter and was stumbling up the bank toward the slope of snow. On it, turned in the direction of the house by the pond, he had detected a woman's footprints; two; then three; then more. The Deacon scrambled out after him, and they stood and stared.

"God—barefoot!" Hibben gasped. "Then it *is* . . . the dead. . . ."

Bosworth said nothing. But he knew that no live woman would travel with naked feet across that freezing wilderness. Here, then, was the proof the Deacon had asked for—they held it. What should they do with it?

"Supposing we was to drive up nearer—round the turn of the pond, till we get close to the house," the Deacon proposed in a colorless voice. "Mebbe then. . . ."

Postponement was a relief. They got into the sleigh and drove on. Two or three hundred yards farther the road, a mere lane under steep bushy banks, turned sharply to the right, following the bend of the pond. As they rounded the turn they saw Brand's cutter ahead of them. It was empty, the horse tied to a treetrunk. The two men looked at each other again. This was not Brand's nearest way home.

Evidently he had been actuated by the same impulse which had made them rein in their horse by the pondside, and then hasten on to the deserted hovel. Had he too discovered those spectral footprints? Perhaps it was for that very reason that he had left his cutter and vanished in the direction of the house. Bosworth found himself shivering all over under his bearskin. "I wish to God the dark wasn't coming on," he muttered. He tethered his own horse near Brand's, and without a word he and the Deacon ploughed through the snow, in the track of Brand's huge feet. They had only a few yards to walk to overtake him. He did not hear them following him, and when Bosworth spoke his name, and he stopped short and turned, his heavy face was dim and confused, like a darker blot on the dusk. He looked at them dully, but without surprise.

"I wanted to see the place," he merely said.

The Deacon cleared his throat. "Just take a look . . . yes . . . we thought so. . . . But I guess there won't be anything to *see*. . . ." He attempted a chuckle.

The other did not seem to hear him, but labored on ahead through the pines. The three men came out together in the cleared space before the house. As they emerged from beneath the trees they seemed to have left night behind. The evening star shed a luster on the speckless snow, and Brand, in that lucid circle, stopped with a jerk, and pointed to the same light footprints turned toward the house—the track of a woman in the snow. He stood still, his face working. "Bare feet. . . ." he said.

The Deacon piped up in a quavering voice: "The feet of the dead."

Brand remained motionless. "The feet of the dead," he echoed.

Deacon Hibben laid a frightened hand on his arm. "Come away now, Brand; for the love of God come away."

The father hung there, gazing down at those light tracks on the snow— light as fox or squirrel trails they seemed, on the white immensity. Bosworth thought to himself: "The living couldn't walk so light—not even Ora Brand couldn't have, when she lived. . . ." The cold seemed to have entered into his very marrow. His teeth were chattering.

Brand swung about on them abruptly. "*Now!*" he said, moving on as if to an assault, his head bowed forward on his bull neck.

"Now—now? Not in there?" gasped the Deacon. "What's the use? It was tomorrow he said—" He shook like a leaf.

"It's now," said Brand. He went up to the door of the crazy house, pushed it inward, and meeting with an unexpected resistance, thrust his heavy shoulder against the panel. The door collapsed like a playing card, and Brand stumbled after it into the darkness of the hut. The others, after a moment's hesitation, followed.

Bosworth was never quite sure in what order the events that succeeded took place. Coming in out of the snow dazzle, he seemed to be plunging into total blackness. He groped his way across the threshold, caught a sharp splinter of the fallen door in his palm, seemed to see something white and wraithlike surge up out of the darkest corner of the hut, and then heard a revolver shot at his elbow, and a cry—

Brand had turned back, and was staggering past him out into the lingering daylight. The sunset, suddenly flushing through the trees, crimsoned his face like blood. He held a revolver in his hand and looked about him in his stupid way.

184

"They *do* walk, then," he said and began to laugh. He bent his head to examine his weapon. "Better here than in the churchyard. They shan't dig her up *now*," he shouted out. The two men caught him by the arms, and Bosworth got the revolver away from him.

IV

The next day Bosworth's sister Loretta, who kept house for him, asked him, when he came in for his midday dinner, if he had heard the news.

Bosworth had been sawing wood all the morning, and in spite of the cold and the driving snow, which had begun again in the night, he was covered with an icy sweat, like a man getting over a fever.

"What news?"

"Venny Brand's down sick with pneumonia. The Deacon's been there, I guess she's dying."

Bosworth looked at her with listless eyes. She seemed far off from him, miles away. "Venny Brand?" he echoed.

"You never liked her, Orrin."

"She's a child. I never knew much about her."

"Well," repeated his sister, with the guileless relish of the unimaginative for bad news, "I guess she's dying." After a pause she added: "It'll kill Sylvester Brand, all alone up there."

Bosworth got up and said: "I've got to see to poulticing the gray's fetlock." He walked out into the steadily falling snow.

Venny Brand was buried three days later. The Deacon read the service; Bosworth was one of the pallbearers. The whole countryside turned out, for the snow had stopped falling, and at any season a funeral offered an opportunity for an outing that was not to be missed. Besides, Venny Brand was young and handsome—at least some people thought her handsome, though she was so swarthy—and her dying like that, so suddenly, had the fascination of tragedy.

"They say her lungs filled right up. . . . Seems she'd had bronchial troubles before . . . I always said both them girls was frail. . . . Look at Ora, how she took and wasted away! And it's colder'n all outdoors up there to Brand's. . . . Their mother, too, *she* pined away just the same. They don't ever make old bones on the mother's side of the family. . . . There's that young Bedlow over there; they say Venny was engaged to him. . . .

Oh, Mrs. Rutledge, excuse *me.* . . . Step right into the pew; there's a seat for you alongside of grandma. . . ."

Mrs. Rutledge was advancing with deliberate step down the narrow aisle of the bleak wooden church. She had on her best bonnet, a monumental structure which no one had seen out of her trunk since old Mrs. Silsee's funeral, three years before. All the women remembered it. Under its perpendicular pile her narrow face, swaying on the long thin neck, seemed whiter than ever; but her air of fretfulness had been composed into a suitable expression of mournful immobility.

"Looks as if the stonemason had carved her to put atop of Venny's grave," Bosworth thought as she glided past him; and then shivered at his own sepulchral fancy. When she bent over her hymn book her lowered lids reminded him again of marble eyeballs; the bony hands clasping the book were bloodless. Bosworth had never seen such hands since he had seen old Aunt Cressidora Cheney strangle the canary bird because it fluttered.

The service was over, the coffin of Venny Brand had been lowered into her sister's grave, and the neighbors were slowly dispersing. Bosworth, as pallbearer, felt obliged to linger and say a word to the stricken father. He waited till Brand had turned from the grave with the Deacon at his side. The three men stood together for a moment; but not one of them spoke. Brand's face was the closed door of a vault, barred with wrinkles like bands of iron.

Finally the Deacon took his hand and said: "The Lord gave—"

Brand nodded and turned away toward the shed where the horses were hitched. Bosworth followed him. "Let me drive along home with you," he suggested.

Brand did not so much as turn his head. "Home? What home?" he said; and the other fell back.

Loretta Bosworth was talking with the other women while the men unblanketed their horses and backed the cutters out into the heavy snow. As Bosworth waited for her, a few feet off, he saw Mrs. Rutledge's tall bonnet lording it above the group. Andy Pond, the Rutledge farm hand, was backing out the sleigh.

"Saul ain't here today, Mrs. Rutledge, is he?" one of the village elders piped, turning a benevolent old tortoise head about on a loose neck, and blinking up into Mrs. Rutledge's marble face.

Bosworth heard her measure out her answer in slow incisive words. "No. Mr. Rutledge he ain't here. He would 'a' come for certain, but his aunt Minorca Cummins is being buried down to Stotesbury this very day and he had to go down there. Don't it sometimes seem zif we was all walking right in the Shadow of Death?"

As she walked toward the cutter, in which Andy Pond was already seated, the Deacon went up to her with visible hesitation. Involuntarily Bosworth also moved nearer. He heard the Deacon say: "I'm glad to hear that Saul is able to be up and around."

She turned her small head on her rigid neck, and lifted the lids of marble.

"Yes, I guess he'll sleep quieter now. And *her* too, maybe, now she don't lay there alone any longer," she added in a low voice, with a sudden twist of her chin toward the fresh black stain in the graveyard snow. She got into the cutter, and said in a clear tone to Andy Pond: "'S long as we're down here I don't know but what I'll just call round and get a box of soap at Hiram Pringle's."

The Fury of Flowers and Worms

ANNE SEXTON

Let the flowers make a journey
on Monday so that I can see
ten daisies in a blue vase
with perhaps one red ant
crawling to the gold center.
A bit of the field on my table,
close to the worms
who struggle blindly,
moving deep into their slime,
moving deep into God's abdomen,
moving like oil through water,
sliding through the good brown.

The daisies grow wild
like popcorn.
They are God's promise to the field.
How happy I am, daisies, to love you.
How happy you are to be loved
and found magical, like a secret
from the sluggish field.
If all the world picked daisies
wars would end, the common cold would stop,
unemployment would end, the monetary market
would hold steady and no money would float.

Listen world,
if you'd just take the time to pick
the white fingers, the penny heart,
all would be well.
They are so unexpected.
They are as good as salt.
If someone had brought them
to van Gogh's room daily
his ear would have stayed on.
I would like to think that no one would die anymore
if we all believed in daisies
but the worms know better, don't they?
They slide into the ear of a corpse
and listen to his great sigh.

The Sleeping Giant

a hill in Hamden, Connecticut

DONALD HALL

The whole day long, under the walking sun
That poised an eye on me from its high floor,
Holding my toy beside the clapboard house
I looked for him, the summer I was four.

I was afraid the waking arm would break
From the loose earth and rub against his eyes
A fist of trees, and the whole country tremble
In the exultant labor of his rise;

Then he with giant steps in the small streets
Would stagger, cutting off the sky, to seize
The roofs from house and home because we had
Covered his shape with dirt and planted trees;

And then kneel down and rip with fingernails
A trench to pour the enemy Atlantic
Into our basin, and the water rush,
With the streets full and all the voices frantic.

That was the summer I expected him.
Later the high and watchful sun instead
Walked low behind the house, and school began,
And winter pulled a sheet over his head.

Thomas Chambers, *The Connecticut Valley*

The River of Rivers
in Connecticut

WALLACE STEVENS

There is a great river this side of Stygia,
Before one comes to the first black cataracts
And trees that lack the intelligence of trees.

In that river, far this side of Stygia,
The mere flowing of the water is a gayety,
Flashing and flashing in the sun. On its banks,

No shadow walks. The river is fateful,
Like the last one. But there is no ferryman.
He could not bend against its propelling force.

It is not to be seen beneath the appearances
That tell of it. The steeple at Farmington
Stands glistening and Haddam shines and sways.

It is the third commonness with light and air,
A curriculum, a vigor, a local abstraction . . .
Call it, once more, a river, an unnamed flowing,

Space-filled, reflecting the seasons, the folk-lore
Of each of the senses; call it, again and again,
The river that flows nowhere, like a sea.

The Undiminished Hero

The idea of the hero has been reinterpreted throughout the ages. In ancient Greek tragedy the hero was a person of considerable importance, beset by fate, but unwilling to accept it. With all his dignity he refused to bow to the destiny the gods had decreed; yet he knew full well that he would end a loser. Believing in himself, he would cry out against his lot and try by various means to go his own way. This determination, this pride, was usually the source of some shortcoming that would eventually bring about his undoing. Thus the ancient Greek was noble in his hopelessness.

So, too, the American Puritans, caught in the toils of the Calvinistic doctrine, found themselves in a hopeless dilemma. If God had predestined people to sin, what could they do to avoid their fate? If they tried to make the best of things for themselves, they might be thrust further into sin. It took great courage for a Puritan to face life; he was in the truest sense a hero.

The New England Puritans were even more heroic because they had to face the wilderness with only their own resources to rely on, and yet they had set themselves the seemingly impossible task of reforming the entire world. When the absolute position on salvation became less harsh, the hopeless struggle against predestination diminished. The changing views of the individual's place in the universe also tended to lessen the struggle. If an individual was capable of ruling his destiny, then to what extent could he be a tragic hero? He certainly was not pitted against hopeless odds. How then could he aspire to high, heroic purposes?

If, on the other hand, people formed a part of a mechanical world, as scientific discoveries suggested, would the hopelessness of their struggle raise them to heroic heights? Or is the best answer that whenever a person stakes his life or well-being on high purposes, he becomes a hero? In the struggle against wrong, in the fight to realize oneself, in the championing of causes, whether lost or not, may a person become a hero? And what of those who do not rise to life's challenges or are beaten down? Is there a heroic element in them? Then, too, there is the term *anti-hero*—the person who is removed from the gallantry and courage of the contest—is the anti-hero in any way heroic? Last of all, there is the idealized person who appears so noble, so resplendent, so invincible in his superiority. Is that person a true hero?

In reading the selections in this section, part of the pleasure is to see to what extent the measure of heroism is suggested. One will refine his or her own sense of values in the process.

All in green
went my love riding

e. e. cummings

All in green went my love riding
on a great horse of gold
into the silver dawn.

four lean hounds crouched low and smiling
the merry deer ran before.

Fleeter be they than dappled dreams
the swift sweet deer
the red rare deer.

Four red roebuck at a white water
the cruel bugle sang before.

Horn at hip went my love riding
riding the echo down
into the silver dawn.

four lean hounds crouched low and smiling
the level meadows ran before.

Softer be they than slippered sleep
the lean lithe deer
the fleet flown deer.

Four fleet does at a gold valley
the famished arrow sang before.

The Undiminished Hero

Bow at belt went my love riding
riding the mountain down
into the silver dawn.

four lean hounds crouched low and smiling
the sheer peaks ran before.

Paler be they than daunting death
the sleek slim deer
the tall tense deer.

Four tall stags at a green mountain
the lucky hunter sang before.

All in green went my love riding
on a great horse of gold
into the silver dawn.

four lean hounds crouched low and smiling
my heart fell dead before.

The Gray Champion

NATHANIEL HAWTHORNE

There was once a time when New England groaned under the actual
pressure of heavier wrongs than those threatened ones which brought on
the Revolution. James II, the bigoted successor of Charles the Voluptuous,
had annulled the charters of all the colonies, and sent a harsh and unprin-
cipled soldier to take away our liberties and endanger our religion. The ad-
ministration of Sir Edmund Andros lacked scarcely a single characteristic of
tyranny: a Governor and Council, holding office from the King, and wholly
independent of the country; laws made and taxes levied without concur-
rence of the people immediate or by their representatives; the rights of
private citizens violated, and the titles of all landed property declared void;
the voice of complaint stifled by restrictions on the press; and, finally, disaf-
fection overawed by the first band of mercenary troops that ever marched
on our free soil. For two years our ancestors were kept in sullen submission
by that filial love which had invariably secured their allegiance to the
mother country, whether its head chanced to be a Parliament, Protector, or
Popish Monarch. Till these evil times, however, such allegiance had been
merely nominal, and the colonists had ruled themselves, enjoying far more
freedom than is even yet the privilege of the native subjects of Great Britain.

At length a rumor reached our shores that the Prince of Orange had
ventured on an enterprise, the success of which would be the triumph of
civil and religious rights and the salvation of New England. It was but a
doubtful whisper: it might be false, or the attempt might fail; and, in either
case, the man that stirred against King James would lose his head. Still the
intelligence produced a marked effect. The people smiled mysteriously in
the streets, and threw bold glances at their oppressors; while far and wide
there was a subdued and silent agitation, as if the slightest signal would
rouse the whole land from its sluggish despondency. Aware of their danger,
the rulers resolved to avert it by an imposing display of strength, and
perhaps to confirm their despotism by yet harsher measures. One afternoon

in April, 1689, Sir Edmund Andros and his favorite councillors, being warm with wine, assembled the red-coats of the Governor's Guard, and made their appearance in the streets of Boston. The sun was near setting when the march commenced.

The roll of the drum at that unquiet crisis seemed to go through the streets, less as the martial music of the soldiers, than as a muster-call to the inhabitants themselves. A multitude, by various avenues, assembled in King Street, which was destined to be the scene, nearly a century afterwards, of another encounter between the troops of Britain, and a people struggling against her tyranny. Though more than sixty years had elapsed since the pilgrims came, this crowd of their descendants still showed the strong and sombre features of their character perhaps more strikingly in such a stern emergency than on happier occasions. There were the sober garb, the general severity of mien, the gloomy but undismayed expression, the scriptural forms of speech, and the confidence in Heaven's blessing on a righteous cause, which would have marked a band of the original Puritans, when threatened by some peril of the wilderness. Indeed, it was not yet time for the old spirit to be extinct; since there were men in the street that day who had worshipped there beneath the trees, before a house was reared to the God for whom they had become exiles. Old soldiers of the Parliament were here, too, smiling grimly at the thought that their aged arms might strike another blow against the house of Stuart. Here, also, were the veterans of King Philip's war, who had burned villages and slaughtered young and old, with pious fierceness, while the godly souls throughout the land were helping them with prayer. Several ministers were scattered among the crowd, which, unlike all other mobs, regarded them with such reverence, as if there were sanctity in their very garments. These holy men exerted their influence to quiet the people, but not to disperse them. Meantime, the purpose of the Governor, in disturbing the peace of the town at a period when the slightest commotion might throw the country into a ferment, was almost the universal subject of inquiry, and variously explained.

"Satan will strike his master-stroke presently," cried some, "because he knoweth that his time is short. All our godly pastors are to be dragged to prison! We shall see them at a Smithfield fire in King Street!"

Hereupon the people of each parish gathered closer round their minister, who looked calmly upwards and assumed a more apostolic dignity, as well befitted a candidate for the highest honor of his profession, the crown of martyrdom. It was actually fancied, at that period, that New England might have a John Rogers of her own to take the place of that worthy in the Primer.

"The Pope of Rome has given orders for a new St. Bartholomew!" cried others. "We are to be massacred, man and male child!"

Neither was this rumor wholly discredited, although the wiser class believed the Governor's object somewhat less atrocious. His predecessor under the old charter, Bradstreet, a venerable companion of the first settlers, was known to be in town. There were grounds for conjecturing, that Sir Edmund Andros intended at once to strike terror by a parade of military force, and to confound the opposite faction by possessing himself of their chief.

"Stand firm for the old charter, Governor!" shouted the crowd, seizing upon the idea. "The good old Governor Bradstreet!"

While this cry was at the loudest, the people were surprised by the well-known figure of Governor Bradstreet himself, a patriarch of nearly ninety, who appeared on the elevated steps of a door, and, with characteristic mildness, besought them to submit to the constituted authorities.

"My children," concluded this venerable person, "do nothing rashly. Cry not aloud, but pray for the welfare of New England, and expect patiently what the Lord will do in this matter!"

The event was soon to be decided. All this time, the roll of the drum had been approaching through Cornhill, louder and deeper, till with reverberations from house to house, and the regular tramp of martial footsteps, it burst into the street. A double rank of soldiers made their appearance, occupying the whole breadth of the passage, with shouldered matchlocks, and matches burning, so as to present a row of fires in the dusk. Their steady march was like the progress of a machine, that would roll irresistibly over everything in its way. Next, moving slowly, with a confused clatter of hoofs on the pavement, rode a party of mounted gentlemen, the central figure being Sir Edmund Andros, elderly, but erect and soldier-like. Those around him were his favorite councillors, and the bitterest foes of New England. At his right hand rode Edward Randolph, our arch-enemy, that "blasted wretch," as Cotton Mather calls him, who achieved the downfall of our ancient government, and was followed with a sensible curse, through life and to his grave. On the other side was Bullivant, scattering jests and mockery as he rode along. Dudley came behind, with a downcast look, dreading, as well he might, to meet the indignant gaze of the people, who beheld him, their only countryman by birth, among the oppressors of his native land.

The captain of a frigate in the harbor, and two or three civil officers under the Crown, were also there. But the figure which most attracted the public eye, and stirred up the deepest feeling, was the Episcopal clergyman of King's Chapel, riding haughtily among the magistrates in his priestly vestments, the fitting representatives of prelacy and persecution, the union of church and state, and all those abominations which had driven the Puritans to the wilderness. Another guard of soldiers, in double rank, brought up the rear.

The whole scene was a picture of the condition of New England, and its moral, the deformity of any government that does not grow out of the nature of things and the character of the people. On one side the religious multitude, with their sad visages and dark attire, and on the other, the group of despotic rulers, with the high churchman in the midst, and here and there a crucifix at their bosoms, all magnificently clad, flushed with wine, proud of unjust authority, and scoffing at the universal groan. And the mercenary soldiers, waiting but the word to deluge the street with blood, showed the only means by which obedience could be secured.

"O Lord of Hosts," cried a voice among the crowd, "provide a Champion for thy people!"

This ejaculation was loudly uttered, and served as a herald's cry, to introduce a remarkable personage. The crowd had rolled back, and were now huddled together nearly at the extremity of the street, while the soldiers had advanced no more than a third of its length. The intervening space was empty—a paved solitude, between lofty edifices, which threw almost a twilight shadow over it. Suddenly, there was seen the figure of an ancient man, who seemed to have emerged from among the people, and was walking by himself along the centre of the street, to confront the armed band. He wore the old Puritan dress, a dark cloak and a steeple-crowned hat, in the fashion of at least fifty years before, with a heavy sword upon his thigh, but a staff in his hand to assist the tremulous gait of age.

When at some distance from the multitude, the old man turned slowly around, displaying a face of antique majesty, rendered doubly venerable by the hoary beard that descended on his breast. He made a gesture at once of encouragement and warning, then turned again, and resumed his way.

"Who is this gray patriarch?" asked the young men of their sires.

"Who is this venerable brother?" asked the old men among themselves.

But none could make reply. The fathers of the people, those of fourscore years and upwards, were disturbed, deeming it strange that they should forget one of such evident authority, whom they must have known in their early days, the associate of Winthrop, and all the old councillors, giving laws; and making prayers, and leading them against the savage. The elderly men ought to have remembered him, too, with locks as gray in their youth, as their own were now. And the young! How could he have passed so utterly from their memories—that hoary sire, the relic of long-departed times, whose awful benediction had surely been bestowed on their uncovered heads, in childhood?

"Whence did he come? What is his purpose? Who can this old man be?" whispered the wondering crowd.

Meanwhile, the venerable stranger, staff in hand, was pursuing his solitary walk along the centre of the street. As he drew near the advancing soldiers, and as the roll of their drum came full upon his ears, the old man raised himself to a loftier mien, while the decrepitude of age seemed to fall from his shoulders, leaving him in gray but unbroken dignity. Now, he marched onward with a warrior's step, keeping time to the military music. Thus the aged form advanced on one side, and the whole parade of soldiers and magistrates on the other, till, when scarcely twenty yards remained between, the old man grasped his staff by the middle, and held it before him like a leader's truncheon.

"Stand!" cried he.

The eye, the face, and attitude of command; the solemn, yet warlike peal of that voice, fit either to rule a host in the battle-field or be raised to God in prayer, were irresistible. At the old man's word and outstretched arm, the roll of the drum was hushed at once, and the advancing line stood still. A tremulous enthusiasm seized upon the multitude. That stately form, combining the leader and the saint, so gray, so dimly seen, in such an ancient garb, could only belong to some old champion of the righteous cause, whom the oppressor's drum had summoned from his grave. They raised a shout of awe and exultation, and looked for the deliverance of New England.

The Governor, and the gentlemen of his party, perceiving themselves brought to an unexpected stand, rode hastily forward, as if they would have pressed their snorting and affrighted horses right against the hoary apparition. He, however, blenched not a step, but glancing his severe eye round the group, which half encompassed him, at last bent it sternly on Sir Edmund Andros. One would have thought that the dark old man was chief ruler there, and that the Governor and Council, with soldiers at their back, representing the whole power and authority of the Crown, had no alternative but obedience.

"What does this old fellow here?" cried Edward Randolph, fiercely. "On, Sir Edmund! Bid the soldiers forward, and give the dotard the same choice that you give all his countrymen—to stand aside or be trampled on!"

"Nay, nay, let us show respect to the good grandsire," said Bullivant, laughing. "See you not, he is some old round-headed dignitary, who hath lain asleep these thirty years, and knows nothing of the change of times? Doubtless, he thinks to put us down with a proclamation in Old Noll's name!"

"Are you mad, old man?" demanded Sir Edmund Andros, in loud and harsh tones. "How dare you stay the march of King James's Governor?"

"I have stayed the march of a King himself, ere now," replied the gray figure, with stern composure. "I am here, Sir Governor, because the cry of an oppressed people hath disturbed me in my secret place; and beseeching this favor earnestly of the Lord, it was vouchsafed me to appear once again on earth, in the good old cause of his saints. And what speak ye of James? There is no longer a Popish tyrant on the throne of England, and by tomorrow noon, his name shall be a byword in this very street, where ye would make it a word of terror. Back, though wast a Governor, back! With this night thy power is ended—tomorrow, the prison!—back, lest I foretell the scaffold!"

The people had been drawing nearer and nearer, and drinking in the words of their champion, who spoke in accents long disused, like one unaccustomed to converse, except with the dead of many years ago. But his voice stirred their souls. They confronted the soldiers, not wholly without arms, and ready to convert the very stones of the street into deadly weapons. Sir Edmund Andros looked at the old man; then he cast his hard and cruel eye over the multitude, and beheld them burning with that lurid wrath, so difficult to kindle or to quench; and again he fixed his gaze on the aged form, which stood obscurely in an open space, where neither friend nor foe had thrust himself. What were his thoughts, he uttered no word which might discover. But whether the oppressor were overawed by the Gray Champion's look, or perceived his peril in the threatening attitude of the people, it is certain that he gave back, and ordered his soldiers to commence a slow and guarded retreat. Before another sunset, the Governor, and all that rode so proudly with him, were prisoners, and long ere it was known that James had abdicated, King William was proclaimed throughout New England.

But where was the Gray Champion? Some reported that, when the troops had gone from King Street, and the people were thronging tumultuously in their rear, Bradstreet, the aged Governor, was seen to embrace a form more aged than his own. Others soberly affirmed, that while they marvelled at the venerable grandeur of his aspect, the old man had faded from their eyes, melting slowly into the hues of twilight, till, where he stood, there was an empty space. But all agreed that the hoary shape was gone. The men of that generation watched for his reappearance, in sunshine and in twilight, but never saw him more, nor knew when his funeral passed, nor where his gravestone was.

And who was the Gray Champion? Perhaps his name might be found in the records of that stern Court of Justice, which passed a sentence, too mighty for the age, but glorious in all after-times, for its humbling lesson to the monarch and its high example to the subject. I have heard, that whenever the descendants of the Puritans are to show the spirit of their sires, the old man appears again. When eighty years had passed, he walked once more in King Street. Five years later, in the twilight of an April morning, he stood on the green, beside the meeting-house, at Lexington, where now the obelisk of granite, with a slab of slate inlaid, commemorates the first fallen of the Revolution. And when our fathers were toiling at the breastwork on Bunker's Hill, all through that night the old warrior walked his rounds. Long, long may it be, ere he comes again! His hour is one of darkness, and adversity, and peril. But should domestic tyranny oppress us, or the invader's step pollute our soil, still may the Gray Champion come, for he is the type of New England's hereditary spirit; and his shadowy march, on the eve of danger, must ever be the pledge, that New England's sons will vindicate their ancestry.

The Vanishing Red

ROBERT FROST

He is said to have been the last Red Man
In Acton. And the Miller is said to have laughed—
If you like to call such a sound a laugh.
But he gave no one else a laugher's license.
For he turned suddenly grave as if to say,
'Whose business,—if I take it on myself,
Whose business—but why talk round the barn?—
When it's just that I hold with getting a thing done with'
You can't get back and see it as he saw it.
It's too long a story to go into now.
You'd have to have been there and lived it.
Then you wouldn't have looked on it as just a matter
Of who began it between the two races.

Some guttural exclamation of surprise
The Red Man gave in poking about the mill
Over the great big thumping shuffling millstone
Disgusted the Miller physically as coming
From one who had no right to be heard from.
'Come, John,' he said, 'you want to see the wheel-pit?'

He took him down below a cramping rafter,
And showed him, through a manhole in the floor,
The water in desperate straits like frantic fish,
Salmon and sturgeon, lashing with their tails.

Then he shut down the trap door with a ring in it
That jangled even above the general noise,
And came upstairs alone—and gave that laugh,
And said something to a man with a meal-sack
That the man with the meal-sack didn't catch—then.
Oh, yes, he showed John the wheel-pit all right.

FROM *A Plea for Captain John Brown*

HENRY DAVID THOREAU

I hear many condemn these men because they were so few. When were the good and the brave ever in a majority? Would you have had him wait till that time came?—till you and I came over to him? The very fact that he had no rabble or troop of hirelings about him would alone distinguish him from ordinary heroes. His company was small indeed, because few could be found worthy to pass muster. Each one who there laid down his life for the poor and oppressed, was a picked man, called out of many thousands, if not millions; apparently a man of principle, of rare courage and devoted humanity, ready to sacrifice his life at any moment for the benefit of his fellow man. It may be doubted if there were as many more their equals in these respects in all the country—I speak of his followers only—for their leader, no doubt, scoured the land far and wide, seeking to swell his troop. These alone were ready to step between the oppressor and the oppressed. Surely, they were the very best men you could select to be hung. That was the greatest compliment which this country could pay them. They were ripe for her gallows. She has tried a long time, she has hung a good many, but never found the right one before.

When I think of him, and his six sons, and his son in law,—not to enumerate the others,—enlisted for this fight; proceeding coolly, reverently, humanely to work, for months if not years, sleeping and waking upon it, summering and wintering the thought, without expecting any reward but a good conscience, while almost all America stood ranked on the other side, I say again that it affects me as a sublime spectacle. If he had had any journal advocating *"his cause,"* any organ as the phrase is, monotonously and wearisomely playing the same old tune, and then passing round the hat, it would have been fatal to his efficiency. If he had acted in any way so as to be let alone by the government, he might have been suspected. It was the fact that the tyrant must give place to him, or he to the tyrant, that distinguished him from all the reformers of the day that I know.

It was his peculiar doctrine that a man has a perfect right to interfere by force with the slaveholder, in order to rescue the slave. I agree with him. They who are continually shocked by slavery have some right to be shocked by the violent death of the slaveholder, but no others. Such will be more shocked by his life than by his death. I shall not be forward to think him mistaken in his method who quickest succeeds to liberate the slave. I speak for the slave when I say, that I prefer the philanthropy of Captain Brown to that philanthropy which neither shoots me nor liberates me. At any rate, I do not think it is quite sane for one to spend his whole life in talking or writing about this matter, unless he is continuously inspired, and I have not done so. A man may have other affairs to attend to. I do not wish to kill nor to be killed, but I can foresee circumstances in which both these things would be by me unavoidable. We preserve the so-called "peace" of our community by deeds of petty violence every day. Look at the policeman's billy and hand cuffs! Look at the jail! Look at the gallows! Look at the chaplain of the regiment! We are hoping only to live safely on the outskirts of *this* provisional army. So we defend ourselves and our hen roosts, and maintain slavery. I know that the mass of my countrymen think that the only righteous use that can be made of Sharps' rifles and revolvers is to fight duels with them, when we are insulted by other nations, or to hunt Indians, or shoot fugitive slaves with them, or the like. I think that for once the Sharps' rifles and the revolvers were employed in a righteous cause. The tools were in the hands of one who could use them.

The same indignation that is said to have cleared the temple once will clear it again. The question is not about the weapon, but the spirit in which you use it. No man has appeared in America as yet who loved his fellow man so well, and treated him so tenderly. He lived for him. He took up his life and he laid it down for him. What sort of violence is that which is encouraged, not by soldiers but by peaceable citizens, not so much by lay-men as by ministers of the gospel, not so much by the fighting sects as by the Quakers, and not so much by Quaker men as by Quaker women?

This event advertises me that there is such a fact as death—the possibility of a man's dying. It seems as if no man had ever died in America before, for in order to die you must first have lived. I dont believe in the hearses and palls and funerals that they have had. There was no death in the case, because there had been no life; they merely rotted or sloughed off, pretty much as they had rotted or sloughed along. No temple's vail was rent, only a hole dug somewhere. Let the dead bury their dead. The best of them fairly ran down like a clock. Franklin—Washington—they were let off without dying; they were merely missing one day. I hear a good many pretend that they are going to die;—or that they have died for aught that I know. Nonsense! I'll defy them to do it. They haven't got life enough in them. They'll deliquesce like fungi, and keep a hundred eulogists mopping the spot where they left off. Only half a dozen or so have died since the world began. Do you think that you are going to die, sir? No! there's no hope for you. You haven't got your lesson yet. You've got to stay after school. We make a needless ado about capital punishment—taking lives, when there is no life to take. *Memento mori!* We don't understand that sublime sentence which some worthy got sculptured on his gravestone once. We've interpreted it in a grovelling and snivelling sense; we've wholly forgotten how to die.

But be sure you do die, nevertheless. Do your work, and finish it. If you know how to begin, you will know when to end.

These men, in teaching us how to die, have at the same time taught us how to live. If this man's acts and words do not create a revival, it will be the severest possible satire on the acts and words that do. It is the best news that America has ever heard. It has already quickened the feeble pulse of the North, and infused more and more generous blood into her veins and heart, than any number of years of what is called commercial and political prosperity could. How many a man who was lately contemplating suicide has now something to live for!

One writer says that Brown's peculiar monomania made him to be "dreaded by the Missourians as a supernatural being." Sure enough, a hero in the midst of us cowards is always so dreaded. He is just that thing. He shows himself superior to nature. He has a spark of divinity in him.

"Unless above himself he can
Erect himself, how poor a thing is man!"

Newspaper editors argue also that it is a proof of his *insanity* that he thought he was appointed to do this work which he did—that he did not suspect himself for a moment! They talk as if it were impossible that a man could be "divinely appointed" in these days to do any work whatever; as if vows and religion were out of date as connected with any man's daily work,—as if the agent to abolish Slavery could only be somebody appointed by the President, or by some political party. They talk as if a man's death were a failure, and his continued life, be it of whatever character, were a success.

When I reflect to what a cause this man devoted himself, and how religiously, and then reflect to what cause his judges and all who condemn him so angrily and fluently devote themselves, I see that they are as far apart as the heavens and earth are asunder.

The amount of it is, our *"leading men"* are a harmless kind of folk, and they know *well enough* that *they* were not divinely appointed, but elected by the votes of their party.

Who is it whose safety requires that Captain Brown be hung? Is it indispensable to any Northern man? Is there no resource but to cast these men also to the Minotaur? If you do not wish it say so distinctly. While these things are being done, beauty stands veiled and music is a screeching lie. Think of him—of his rare qualities! such a man as it takes ages to make, and ages to understand; no mock hero, nor the representative of any party. A man such as the sun may not rise upon again in this benighted land. To whose making went the costliest material, the finest adamant; sent to be the redeemer of those in captivity. And the only use to which you can put him is to hang him at the end of a rope! You who pretend to care for Christ crucified, consider what you are about to do to him who offered himself to be the savior of four millions of men.

Any man knows when he is justified, and all the wits in the world cannot enlighten him on that point. The murderer always knows that he is justly punished; but when a government takes the life of a man without the consent of his conscience, it is an audacious government, and is taking a step towards its own dissolution. Is it not possible that an individual may be right and a government wrong? Are laws to be enforced simply because they were made? or declared by any number of men to be good, if they are *not* good? Is there any necessity for a man's being a tool to perform a deed of which his better nature disapproves? Is it the intention of law-makers that *good* men shall be hung ever? Are judges to interpret the law according to the letter, and not the spirit? What right have *you* to enter into a compact with yourself that you *will* do thus or so, against the light within you? Is it for *you* to *make up* your mind—to form any resolution whatever—and not accept the convictions that are forced upon you, and which ever pass your understanding? I do not believe in lawyers, in that mode of attacking or defending a man, because you descend to meet the judge on his own ground, and, in cases of the highest importance, it is of no consequence whether a man breaks a human law or not. Let lawyers decide trivial cases. Business men may arrange that among themselves. If they were the interpreters of the everlasting laws which rightfully bind man, that would be another thing. A counterfeiting law-factory, standing half in a slave land and half in a free! What kind of laws for free men can you expect from that?

I am here to plead his cause with you. I plead not for his life, but for his character—his immortal life; and so it becomes your cause wholly, and is not his in the least. Some eighteen hundred years ago Christ was crucified; this morning, perchance, Captain Brown was hung. These are the two ends of a chain which is not without its links. He is not Old Brown any longer; he is an Angel of Light.

I see now that it was necessary that the bravest and humanest man in all the country should be hung. Perhaps he saw it himself. I *almost fear* that I may yet hear of his deliverance, doubting if a prolonged life, if *any* life, can do as much good as his death.

"Misguided"! "Garrulous"! "Insane"! "Vindictive"! So ye write in your easy chairs, and thus he wounded responds from the floor of the Armory, clear as a cloudless sky, true as the voice of nature is: "No man sent me here; it was my own prompting and that of my Maker. I acknowledge no master in human form."

And in what a sweet and noble strain he proceeds, addressing his captors, who stand over him: "I think, my friends, you are guilty of a great wrong against God and humanity, and it would be perfectly right for any one to interfere with you so far as to free those you wilfully and wickedly hold in bondage."

And referring to his movement: "It is, in my opinion, the greatest service a man can render to God."

"I pity the poor in bondage that have none to help them; that is why I am here; not to gratify any personal animosity, revenge, or vindictive spirit. It is my sympathy with the oppressed and the wronged, that are as good as you, and as precious in the sight of God."

You don't know your testament when you see it.

"I want you to understand that I respect the rights of the poorest and weakest of colored people, oppressed by the slave power, just as much as I do those of the most wealthy and powerful."

"I wish to say, furthermore, that you had better, all you people at the South, prepare yourselves for a settlement of that question, that must come up for settlement sooner than you are prepared for it. The sooner you are prepared the better. You may dispose of me very easily. I am nearly dis-

210

posed of now; but this question is still to be settled—this negro question, I mean; the end of that is not yet."

I foresee the time when the painter will paint that scene, no longer going to Rome for a subject; the poet will sing it; the historian record it; and, with the Landing of the Pilgrims and the Declaration of Independence, it will be the ornament of some future national gallery, when at least the present form of Slavery shall be no more here. We shall then be at liberty to weep for Captain Brown. Then, and not till then, we will take our revenge.

Martha Carrier, *1669–1692*

CONSTANCE CARRIER

Mid-August now,
your death-day's anniversary.
Three centuries afterward, your memory walks
a countryside you never knew, a land
the family, drifting southward, settled in—
no different from that Massachusetts town
save that the sea's not near.
Use my eyes. Look:
here is the river, there the hill they built on,
and in the burying ground a stone to Thomas,
telling of his great age, his equal strength,
the children, yours and his. No word of you.

Your body rotted on another hill.

In Corwin's house at Salem, I climbed the stairs
you climbed, stood where they questioned you
in that square chamber in a long-past May—
the court, the girls, the onlookers, the guards;
the screams of accusation, and your voice
rising above: *The Devil is a liar!*
It is a shameful thing that you should mind these folk!

Once Andover had warned your family out
(shiftless or quarrelsome, or both, who knows?), this neighbor
walked with a wry neck, that one's cows went dry:
things feared enough came true for those you hated,
your words the words recalled.

So, as the times grew darker, your fame grew
("that rampant hag, that arrant Queen of Hell"),
yet, careless or thick-skinned, you stayed defiant.
You in your early thirties, eighteen years
wed, short of temper and harsh-tongued,
blood-sister of another named as witch,
part of a clan already devil-tainted—
could you not curb your anger, calm your speech,
give spite less food to feed on?

But shrewishness was all you had for weapon,
honed on those years of rough hardscrabble living:
reason enough to be resentful, quick
to take and quick to offer insult, to be ranged
with the maleficent in that bleak season
when devils moved among us, fleshed like men,
to bribe and covenant.

You were no Mary Easty, gentle even
in her petitioning:
> *They say myself and others have made a league*
> *with the Devil: we cannot confess. I know*
> *and the Lord He knows they believe me. . . .*

Yet when you heard your sons, tied neck to heels,
gasp their incriminations with their blood;
the child their sister innocently agree;
the girls, showing the marks you left upon their bodies,
clamor to list your crimes—what gave you strength
still to deny?
> Those who confessed went free.

No help from those whom torture made betray you.
And Thomas: did he, like his namesake, doubt?—
that strange man, twice your age, with forty years
of silence left to face his nightmares in.

The Undiminished Hero

They say you died well. Quickly, does that mean,
or finally drained of protest, or given somehow
a new brief dignity as you climbed the scaffold?

No matter. Praise alone is due that dying.
Pity is lost on iron, the stone of Mars,
rough to the touch, and graceless, gathering
and holding heat—say, anger; glowing with it,
till, tempered, it translates itself to steel.

The Lesson

SAM C. BROWN, JR.

It seemed at the time as though it was all Harry's fault—that's my cousin, Harry—but in retrospect I have to admit that I was almost, if perhaps not quite, as much to blame as he was. I tended to blame him partly because he was older than I—nearly nineteen, while I was sixteen and a half—but also partly, I realize now, because I needed a scapegoat so as to keep my good intentions from seeming to pave the wrong road. But hell-bent they were, and I with them; and just because it was Harry's idea does not eradicate the keen pleasure I took in first following Harry, and then acting as his accomplice.

Poaching lobsters was what we were up to—I say "poaching" now, as I did then, not merely because it was technically that, but because it sounds more innocuous than "stealing" or "robbing." But robbery it was, in fact—larceny of the highest order—for we were depriving a man not merely of the fruits of his labor, but of the source of his entire income. A good analogy would be the theft or destruction of row after row of a wheat farmer's crop, irreplaceable until the next year's harvest. The enormity of our crime didn't occur to me, of course, at the time. I was a summer visitor who was exposed at home mostly to professional men, people like my lawyer father, whose sources of income were pretty much all in their heads. You can rob a lawyer of every bit of material worth he owns, and he can still practice law in a borrowed suit; but a lobsterman with consistently empty traps cannot earn his living.

But as I say, none of this was evident to Harry and me that summer; we were just caught up in the excitement of the theft, on open water (why, right in plain sight!), of those little creatures whose meat we found so succulent when boiled the next afternoon in our rocky grotto on the shore. Our fathers, who were brothers, had regularly brought their children to the Maine coast for a vacation which always included several lobster feeds. Ever since our folks had introduced us to the dish when we were ex-toddlers, we had both loved fresh lobster, boiled in salt water under seaweed, dunked in melted butter, and eaten on a barnacled rock above the swirling tide.

This summer, Harry's family had sent us up to their shore cottage a week before they came up for their August vacation, and we were to "open the place" and keep constructively busy in a "safe" environent. The week before, Harry had been picked up by the police along with several friends on charges, later dropped, of distrubing the peace, and he and his parents were ready for a temporary separation. My parents were receptive to their suggestion that I accompany Harry, principally, I think, because they did not much approve of the girl I was dating at the time, a moist-eyed, giggly gazelle I had taken quite a shine to. There was nothing at all wrong with her, but to parents I guess a teenager's girlfriend is generally either idiotic or slatternly, or both. And so we were sent to Maine as a way of keeping us off the streets. Ironically, we would probably have been into less real trouble in suburban Boston.

Our first day there together had been easy enough to kill, opening padlocked doors and shuttered windows, sweeping out minimal living space, de-mousing our sleeping quarters, and getting in a supply of food. But our adolescent interest in constructive projects was typically limited, though our energy was typically not; and after two nights of filling the silence with jokes about our school chums and arrogantly smoking cigarettes openly in the house (even Harry had not yet dared do so in front of his parents), we were bored.

"Hey, Mark." Harry that morning was sprawled indolently over a chair leaned up against the sunlit kitchen window. "Let's do something."

"Sure." I fumbled for a cigarette. "Feel like a swim or something?"

"Naw. 's too cold." Harry fingered a shade pull and looked out the window toward our rude boathouse. "We might get the dory out."

"Okay." I peered out the door toward the bay in the direction Harry was looking. Blinding bits of sunlight were bursting like continuous shrapnel from the surface of the water. It hurt to look. A bit to the left of this fiery display was a reef, an island really, partially exposed even at high tide, surrounded by a great many lobster buoys, tiny bobbing specks that trailed in kite-tail fashion off toward the eastern point of the mainland. Something larger bobbed evenly near the reef. "Hey, Harry," I said, "there's a lobster boat."

"Lobster!" Harry sat up. "Hey, that's for us." He got out of the chair expectantly. "Whaddya say, lobster feed tonight?"

"Good idea." I dragged on my cigarette, still looking out at the lobster boat with its tiny single helmsman, chugging now to a new buoy off the reef. The boat slowed, its stern heaving sluggishly, and the lobsterman hooked a buoy and began to haul in the line. "We'll have to drive over to Evans' Wharf to the lobster pound. Got any money?"

"Yeah. Some." Harry, too, watched as the distant lobsterman gracefully pulleyed the heavy trap to the gunwale, flipped open its lid, and began to toss back into the sea the many undersized lobsters which customarily were caught in it. Harry was silent for a moment. "You still want to work on the dory?" he asked.

"Sure. Nothin' else to do. But let's go get some lobsters first. And butter. And hey!" I squashed out my cigarette with slight nervous agitation. "Maybe we could get some beer!"

"Yeah." Harry obviously wasn't listening very closely. We both loved beer, but had never been able to get any except when our parents, mellowed by a vacation cocktail, had allowed us each a can. I was thinking now that we might drive around until we found an out-of-the-way grocery store where Harry's deep voice and mature height might pass for those of a twenty-one-year-old. Surely Harry would be interested. "Some beer, eh, Harry?"

"Wait a minute." He screwed up his eyes, peering at the distant boat. "Why don't we save our dough? *We* could do that."

"We could do what? Save dough on beer? How?"

"No, *we* could do *that*—" he gestured—"in the dory." He turned to me. "Pull some traps. He does it alone. There's two of us. *We* could do *that*."

"Pull traps?" I paused, reflective. "But we don't have *any*, Harry—?"

"Yeah, but *he* does."

"You mean, steal his lobsters?" I felt let down. "Aw, we can buy 'em."

"Look at him. He throws out most of all of 'em anyway. We wouldn't take the big ones. No problem. Hey, Mark?" Harry's eyes flickered. "Let's get at that dory."

I was not convinced. Theft did not particularly appeal to my moral sense, and I wasn't sure I'd know how to haul a trap. But those reasons could not be expressed publicly, of course; so I said, "I don't know, Harry. Suppose we get caught?"

"Caught? With what evidence? Anyone comes by, we just toss 'em back in the bay. And what lobsterman that you know of ever takes his boat out at night?"

"You mean we'll go out and pull traps in the dark?" I asked.

"Sure," Harry said. "Aw, we'll be able to see okay out on the open water. And there won't be any chance of being caught by a nosy lobster boat at *night*."

That pretty well did it. I was still uneasy about the idea of theft, but Harry had obliterated any argument I could, at that age and under those circumstances, effectively present. I almost (but not quite) wished that Mom and Dad were around so that I could protest that it would be impossible to pull it off without their knowledge. But what the hell, I thought; it sounded pretty darn exciting.

That afternoon, we lugged out the family dory, strenuously shoved it down the ramp into the water, marked the obvious leaks, hauled the boat out and caulked it, and lowered it in again to let it swell. It wouldn't really be tight for a couple of days and until we'd caulked it again, but it was not an old boat and would certainly serve us that night. Then, sweaty and happily absorbed in our project, we drove off to seek beer.

After we'd driven for about five miles, we saw a little grocery store on the left. MORRILL'S STORE, a sign said, and another sign proclaimed COLD BEER TO GO. We pulled in, got out of the car, and went into the store. I was jittery, so I let Harry lead the way.

A middle-aged man with wire-rimmed glasses jutted up behind the counter. "H'lo, fellas," he said. "What can I get you?"

Harry tried to look casual as he surveyed the glass-doored refrigeration compartment behind the counter with its army of assorted beers, ales, and soft drinks. "Hmm," he said. "Guess I'll take two six-packs of, uh, Miller's."

The man turned and procured the beer without a blink. He put it on the counter. "Anything else, fellas?" he asked brightly.

"No, thanks," Harry said, and paid for the beer. We walked out quickly, waiting until we were in the car again to cackle delightedly at each other. "You hot ticket!" I said. "Tut-tut," said Harry, "all in a day's work." We chuckled for several minutes. I felt exuberant; my last trace of uneasiness had disappeared. We were men! And we were going on a lobstering adventure!

We ate a regular supper that evening, figuring that we'd have our lobster feed the next afternoon after our midnight excursion. The time passed slowly until after dark; we had a can of beer each and played some cards, but were really too nervous to do anything well. We each lost a hand of gin rummy through pure carelessness, discarding the wrong cards, and ultimately we lost interest.

Finally, after looking out the windows for hours (forty-five minutes, perhaps), Harry decreed that it was dark enough to set out. We put on our jackets, climbed into the boat, and began to row stealthily out through the slightly choppy water. There was no moon; not a vessel was in sight on the bay. The perfect crime!

"Here's one." Harry was at the oars. "I'll back up to it. You grab it." The black water swirled around the stern as Harry maneuvered the boat toward the small bobbing buoy. The breeze gusted a bit, whipping cold droplets of water from the wet oars across my face. I shivered. Off to my left, a few lights glimmered on the point beyond our house; straight ahead was the faintly visible reef, and far beyond was the dark horizon. The buoy was far colder and heavier than I had imagined it would be, but I got it into the boat all right. I wondered if it was the beer that was making me a little shaky.

Harry shipped the oars. "Lemme give you a hand." Together we pulled the slimy potwarp up over the transom. The darned thing was bigger around than it looked lying in coils on the shore near Frank's Lobster Pound, and the slime made it hard to grip. But, with a few grunts and an occasional loss of balance, we got the line all the way up—and there came the trap: it emerged darkly, with a rush of water, and banged against the boat.

"Hey! Not so loud!" Harry said. I fumbled, and the trap slipped back a foot or so and submerged with a swish. "Sorry!" I whispered hoarsely. "Couldn't help it." "Well don't let it *slip*, for God's sake!" Harry's breath was hissing through his teeth now. It was hard work. We pulled together and got it lodged precariously over the gunwale, where it teetered and drained noisily.

Suddenly we heard a noise like a wet towel being snapped loudly several times—FWADASAPAPAP—and we practically lost the trap again. "What the hell was *that?*" I gasped. Then it dawned on us that it was a lobster, flapping his tail as he always does out of water in a vain attempt to propel himself back into the sea. We both broke into hoarsely voiceless laughter. "Damn lobster!" Harry said. From then on it was easier. We emptied the lobsters into the boat (they all seemed undersized to us) and let the trap gently—"Watch it now!" back into the water, smiling even as we panted, and occasionally imitating both the lobster's flapping noise and our own earlier fright, "*Fwadasapapap!*" and wheezed laughter. We were having a ball!

We worked for perhaps twenty-five minutes, pulling three traps, before we had what we thought would be an ample feed for the two of us: about eight rather small lobsters. To ease our consciences, we did leave two or three larger lobsters in the last two traps. "It's kinda funny," Harry remarked as he swished the lobsters around in the bilge, "there's so few of 'em in any one trap." I pulled on the oars. "Well, Har," I offered, "you don't get rich lobstering." We didn't say much else till we got to shore.

The next afternoon we built a fire in the shadow of a large overhanging rock near the high-water mark not far from the house. The horizon was misty, but the sun was out and our beer was cold and plentiful, and we felt pretty good. "Darn fine catch, captain!" Harry said as he cracked open his third claw. Butter dribbled randomly down my chin and the breeze ruffled my hair and T-shirt. Behind us, the fire cracked and smoked. I smiled broadly and took a quick pull at my beer. "You bet," I said.

"Hey, Harry, there he is again." Across the dancing sunlit ripples, we could see the lobsterman hauling his traps near the reef-island. Harry sloshed a chunk of lobster up and down in the can of melted butter and wiped his chin. "Seems to me I recognize that white buoy with the blue band," he said, and threw me a grin. "How 'bout you?"

"Can't recall. Does it go *fwadasapapap?*" We both roared. The lobsterman, we noticed, wasn't throwing out any undersized lobsters from these traps. "Guess we saved him some trouble." "Anything to help a fellow lobsterman," Harry said. We roared again, our laughter becoming the tear-producing giggles that leave one weak in the stomach and euphoric. Only in adolescence can this kind of gentle sadism be so amusing; I wonder, in retrospect, what had gotten into us.

The success and pleasure produced by our initial poaching experiment buoyed us for an inevitable second night of crime, and the confidence inspired by that success led to a third. Before we knew it, we had poached four nights running, becoming bolder each time, ultimately taking only the biggest lobsters and actually throwing the undersized ones back into the bay. This move was perhaps the unwisest of all, at least as far as escaping detection was concerned, for it left each trap completely empty at eleven p.m. and hence likely to be nearly empty when the owner pulled them next morning. Like all amateur criminals, especially those whose intent is far less malicious than the damage done, we did not give sufficient attention to the details which can lead to detection. We also failed to give enough credit to our unidentified victim, the lobsterman. He turned out to be far more wise, and we far more stupid, than we had imagined.

On the fifth night of poaching, Harry and I set out at about ten thirty, a little later than usual, after having a couple of beers each in the house. We were positively heady, not so much from the liquor as from an inflated sense of our own powers. We had hauled heavy traps, eaten free lobster, and drunk illegal brew for nearly five days straight without a hitch, and we were, I fear, more than a little wild-eyed and arrogant. The world, so to speak, was our lobster. And so we donned our light jackets and pushed off into the unusually still water of this particular night without even lowering our voices. Harry made an obscene noise from the stern seat, and I laughed so hard that I nearly dropped one oar into the water. Harry grabbed it with a great clatter, and we whooped a bit as the dory lurched awkwardly.

We were in the midst of hauling our third trap—giggling and joking about the heavy slime on the potwarp—when Harry suddenly became still and said, "Shsh!"

I stopped giggling and put one hand on the dripping gunwale. "What?" I whispered.

"Motor." I looked up and listened. From not too far off at all came a putt-putt-putt-putt. The lobster boat!

"Where is it?" I whispered.

"Can't see," Harry replied, tensing. "No lights?"

"Quick! Drop the trap!"

"No, don't drop it! Too loud! Lower it!"

We eased the trap into the water and hurriedly cast the line and buoy after it. "Let's get out of here," Harry said, and quickly put the oars in the water and began to row.

The putt-putt of the approaching vessel grew louder and clearer. No doubt about it, it was a lobster boat. But why no lights? I froze in the stern seat, my eyes darting around trying to see through the heavy moonless night. Suddenly the reef exploded in light. To the right of it, a powerful searchlight threw its beam onto the reef, then began knifing in other directions. *My God*, I thought. *The lobsters!*

In our haste we had completely forgotten that several lobsters lay partly submerged in the bilge of the dory. Absolute evidence! We'd be killed!

"Throw 'em out!" he whispered frantically, pulling at the oars as fast as he could without making a racket.

"Too many," I said. "Cover 'em!" I yanked off my jacket and bid Harry do likewise. He shook his head vigorously and kept rowing. I managed to get all the lobsters under my jacket (which became immediately soaked in bilgewater) just before the searchlight struck us. Straightening up from a crouch, I saw Harry's nervous face and awkwardly positioned body piercingly illuminated against an invisible background. Harry froze.

The searchlight bobbed a bit and pushed ahead until it was nearly upon us. The putt-putt died to a low rumble, and some smaller lights went on, revealing the dim outlines of a high prow, a long hull, and a stiff little cabin. The searchlight clicked off, and over its dying lens came a voice.

"Evenin', boys." Pause.

"H-hi," Harry stammered.

A flashlight clicked on and played on the two of us and the dory. The waves lapped at the hulls of both boats and seemed, impossibly, to drown the sound of the engine's muffled burbling. Harry moved the oars a bit in the water and tried to look relaxed.

"Out f'r a row, boys?" Pause.

"Yeah," Harry said. He gestured toward the shore. "We—we're in there. Our house." The flashlight beam caught his face and he turned his eyes toward me. "We kind of like to row. Good dory."

"Yes 'tis, boys," the faceless voice replied evenly, almost softly. The flashlight beam moved to me, then to the floor of the dory.

"You always leave your jacket in the bilge, son?"

I shivered. A small breeze rippled my T-shirt. "Warm night," I said weakly. It was warm, but not so warm as to make one discard a jacket carelessly in the bilge. He would catch us. I knew he would!

The pale beam of light slid around the edges of my jacket as it partly floated, partly lay over the lobsters. I held my breath; Harry and I stared in terror at it. What if one of the lobsters should crawl out? What if—

FWADASAPAPAP.

The jacket flapped; the flashlight clicked off. An enormous silence followed. I could hear nothing but the pounding in my ears.

FWADASAPAPAPapap.

"Boys." Pause.

"Boys, you row right over here." The voice had a new note of quiet but powerful urgency. Harry swallowed hard and backed the dory clumsily up to the side of the lobster boat.

I looked up from the stern and saw the gradually visible face of the lobsterman. He wore a small dark yachting cap pulled low over a large, sharp nose and hollow cheeks. His neck seemed too thick for the thin face; but his eyes quickly distracted me from the rest of him. He had the quietest, most unfathomable eyes I had ever seen. They could have been intensely angry

223

or thoroughly benign; I could not tell. But they scared me to death.

"Boys," he said. "Someone's been pullin' my traps." He leaned over the gunwale and I noticed a slight tremor in his hands and face. "I make a livin' on them traps. If they're empty, I got nothin'."

He paused for a moment, staring very deeply at Harry, who was transfixed, frozen to the oars. The lobsterman straightened up slightly and reached into his boat. When he leaned over again, one hand held a plank of wood, and the other a shotgun.

I was about to yell out, but the lobsterman began to talk in his quietly urgent way before I had a chance. I checked myself. "Boys," he said, "I want you to see what'll happen if I ketch them poachuhs." With a sudden thrust he chucked the plank over the dory. My eyes followed it to where it splashed heavily into the water just beyond our gunwale. Before I could turn my gaze again toward the lobster boat, the silence was shattered with a deafening blast that caused me literally to jump off my seat and Harry to drop the oars into the dory with a clatter. There in the foaming water which rocked our boat bobbed the two halves of the former plank.

When I looked back, breathless and with heart pounding furiously, the lobsterman was putting his shotgun back into the boat. He settled himself down with hands on the gunwale again and looked at us, his jaws working.

"I don't shoot folks," he said. "But I don't mind shootin' a boat if I have to." He paused for emphasis and lowered his voice. "Mighty hard swimmin' ashore at night."

In another moment, he had straightened up, taken the helm, and revved up the engine. The lobster boat putt-putted to a deafening staccato, spun heavily away from us, and left the dory on a rising swell which made us lunge to keep our balance. Harry grabbed the oars.

"Holy God," I said. "Holy, holy God."

"Throw 'em out!" Harry fairly shouted. I grabbed my jacket and threw out the lobsters as fast as I could. Harry pulled at the oars and we headed for shore, both of us shaking rather badly.

As I reflected much later on our narrow escape, I realized that the lobsterman would have been perfectly justified in sinking our dory that night instead of merely shattering a plank. This fact has given me an enduring respect for the principle that no man is automatically entitled to the fruits of another's labor. But more important, I think, is the fact that he chose *not* to sink the dory; for he impressed our minds indelibly with a lesson about the efficacy of charity in matters of justice. He was a remarkably wise man.

224

Women

LOUISE BOGAN

Women have no wilderness in them,
They are provident instead,
Content in the tight hot cell of their hearts
To eat dusty bread.

They do not see cattle cropping red winter grass,
They do not hear
Snow water going down under culverts
Shallow and clear.

They wait, when they should turn to journeys,
They stiffen, when they should bend.
They use against themselves that benevolence
To which no man is friend.

They cannot think of so many crops to a field
Or of clean wood cleft by an axe.
Their love is an eager meaninglessness
Too tense, or too lax.

They hear in every whisper that speaks to them
A shout and a cry.
As like as not, when they take life over their door-sills
They should let it go by.

FROM *Woman in the Nineteenth Century*

MARGARET FULLER

And now I have designated in outline, if not in fullness, the stream which is ever flowing from the heights of my thought.

In the earlier tract I was told I did not make my meaning sufficiently clear. In this I have consequently tried to illustrate it in various ways, and may have been guilty of much repetition. Yet as I am anxious to leave no room for doubt, I shall venture to retrace once more the scope of my design in points, as was done in old-fashioned sermons.

Man is a being of twofold relations, to nature beneath and intelligences above him. The earth is his school, if not his birthplace; God his object; life and thought his means of interpreting nature and aspiring to God.

Only a fraction of this purpose is accomplished in the life of any one man. Its entire accomplishment is to be hoped only from the sum of the lives of men, or Man considered as a whole.

As this whole has one soul and one body, any injury or obstruction to a part or to the meanest member affects the whole. Man can never be perfectly happy or virtuous till all men are so.

To address Man wisely, you must not forget that his life is partly animal, subject to the same laws with Nature.

But you cannot address him wisely unless you consider him still more as soul, and appreciate the conditions and destiny of soul.

The growth of Man is twofold, masculine and feminine.

So far as these two methods can be distinguished, they are so as

Energy and Harmony;

Power and Beauty;

Intellect and Love;

or by some such rude classification; for we have not language primitive and pure enough to express such ideas with precision.

These two sides are supposed to be expressed in Man and Woman, that is, as the more and the less, for the faculties have not been given pure to either, but only in preponderance. There are also exceptions in great number, such as men of far more beauty than power, and the reverse. But as a general rule it seems to have been the intention to give a preponderance on the one side that is called masculine, and on the other, one that is called feminine.

There cannot be a doubt that if these two developments were in perfect harmony, they would correspond to and fulfill one another, like hemispheres or the tenor and bass in music.

But there is no perfect harmony in human nature; and the two parts answer one another only now and then; or if there be a persistent consonance, it can only be traced at long intervals, instead of discoursing an obvious melody.

What is the cause of this?

Man in the order of time was developed first; as energy comes before harmony; power before beauty.

Woman was therefore under his care as an elder. He might have been her guardian and teacher.

But as human nature goes not straight forward, but by excessive action and then reaction in an undulated course, he misunderstood and abused his advantages, and became her temporal master instead of her spiritual sire.

On himself came the punishment. He educated Woman more as a servant than a daughter, and found himself a king without a queen.

The children of this unequal union showed unequal natures, and more and more men seemed sons of the handmaid rather than princess.

At last there were so many Ishmaelites that the rest grew frightened and indignant. They laid the blame on Hagar, and drove her forth into the wilderness.

But there were none the fewer Ishmaelites for that.

At last men became a little wiser, and saw that the infant Moses was in every case saved by the pure instincts of Woman's breast. For as too much adversity is better for the moral nature than too much prosperity, Woman in this respect dwindled less than Man, though in other respects still a child in leading-strings.

So Man did her more and more justice, and grew more and more kind.

But yet—his habits and his will corrupted by the past—he did not clearly see that Woman was half himself; that her interests were identical with his; and that by the law of their common being he could never reach his true proportions while she remained in any wise shorn of hers.

And so it has gone on to our day; both ideas developing, but more slowly than they would under a clearer recognition of truth and justice, which would have permitted the sexes their due influence on one another and mutual improvement from more dignified relations.

Wherever there was pure love, the natural influences were for the time restored.

Wherever the poet or artist gave free course to his genius, he saw the truth and expressed it in worthy forms, for these men especially share and need the feminine principle. The divine birds need to be brooded into life and song by mothers.

Wherever religion (I mean the thirst for truth and good, not the love of sect and dogma) had its course, the original design was apprehended in its simplicity, and the dove presaged sweetly from Dodona's oak.

I have aimed to show that no age was left entirely without a witness of the equality of the sexes in function, duty, and hope.

Also that when there was unwillingness or ignorance which prevented this being acted upon, women had not the less power for their want of light and noble freedom. But it was power which hurt alike them and those against whom they made use of the arms of the servile—cunning, blandishment, and unreasonable emotion.

That now the time has come when a clearer vision and better action are possible—when Man and Woman may regard one another as brother and sister, the pillars of one porch, the priests of one worship.

I have believed and intimated that this hope would receive an ampler fruition than ever before in our own land.

And it will do so if this land carry out the principles from which sprang our national life.

I believe that at present women are the best helpers of one another.

Let them think, let them act, till they know what they need.

We only ask of men to remove arbitrary barriers. Some would like to do more. But I believe it needs that Woman show herself in her native dignity to teach them how to aid her; their minds are so encumbered by tradition.

When Lord Edward Fitzgerald traveled with the Indians, his manly heart obliged him at once to take the packs from the squaws and carry them. But we do not read that the red men followed his example, though they are ready enough to carry the pack of the white woman, because she seems to them a superior being.

Let Woman appear in the mild majesty of Ceres, and rudest churls will be willing to learn from her.

You ask: what use will she make of liberty, when she has so long been sustained and restrained?

I answer: in the first place this will not be suddenly given. I read yesterday a debate of this year on the subject of enlarging women's rights over property. It was a leaf from the classbook that is preparing for the needed instruction. The men learned visibly as they spoke. The champions of Woman saw the fallacy of arguments on the opposite side, and were startled by their own convictions. With their wives at home, and the readers of the paper, it was the same. And so the stream flows on; thought urging action, and action leading to the evolution of still better thought.

But were this freedom to come suddenly, I have no fear of the consequences. Individuals might commit excesses, but there is not only in the sex a reverence for decorums and limits inherited and enhanced from generation to generation, which many years of other life could not efface, but a native love in Woman, as Woman, of proportion, of "the simple art of not too much"—a Greek moderation which would create immediately a restraining party, the natural legislators and instructors of the rest, and would gradually establish such rules as are needed to guard without impeding life.

The Graces would lead the choral dance, and teach the rest to regulate their steps to the measure of beauty.

But if you ask me what offices they may fill, I reply—any. I do not care what case you put; let them be sea-captains, if you will. I do not doubt there are women well fitted for such an office, and if so, I should be as glad to see them in it as to welcome the maid of Saragossa or the maid of Missolonghi or the Suliote heroine or Emily Plater.

I think women need especially at this juncture a much greater range of occupation than they have, to rouse their latent powers. A party of travelers lately visited a lonely hut on a mountain. There they found an old woman, who told them she and her husband had lived there forty years. "Why," they said, "did you choose so barren a spot?" She did not know: "*it was the man's notion.*"

And during forty years she had been content to act, without knowing why, upon the "man's notion." I would not have it so.

In families that I know, some little girls like to saw wood, others to use carpenters' tools. Where these tastes are indulged, cheerfulness and good-humor are promoted. Where they are forbidden, because "such things are not proper for girls," they grow sullen and mischievous.

Fourier had observed these wants of women, as no one can fail to do who watches the desires of little girls or knows the ennui that haunts grown women, except where they make to themselves a serene little world by art of some kind. He therefore, in proposing a great variety of employments in manufactures or the care of plants and animals, allows for one third of women as likely to have a taste for masculine pursuits, one third of men for feminine.

Who does not observe the immediate glow and serenity that is diffused over the life of women before restless or fretful by engaging in gardening, building, or the lowest department of art? Here is something that is not routine, something that draws forth life towards the infinite.

I have no doubt, however, that a large proportion of women would give themselves to the same employments as now, because there are circumstances that must lead them. Mothers will delight to make the nest soft and warm. Nature would take care of that; no need to clip the wings of any bird that wants to soar and sing, or finds in itself the strength of pinion for a migratory flight unusual to its kind. The difference would be that all need not be constrained to employments for which *some* are unfit.

I have urged upon the sex self-subsistence in its two forms of self-reliance and self-impulse, because I believe them to be the needed means of the present juncture.

I have urged on Woman independence of Man, not that I do not think the sexes mutually needed by one another, but because in Woman this fact has led to an excessive devotion which has cooled love, degraded marriage, and prevented either sex from being what it should be to itself or the other.

I wish Woman to live *first* for God's sake. Then she will not make an imperfect man her god, and thus sink to idolatry. Then she will not take what is not fit for her from a sense of weakness and poverty. Then if she finds what she needs in Man embodied, she will know how to love and be worthy of being loved.

By being more a soul she will not be less Woman, for nature is perfected through spirit.

Now there is no woman, only an overgrown child.

That her hand may be given with dignity, she must be able to stand alone. I wish to see men and women capable of such relations as are depicted by Landor in his *Pericles and Aspasia*, where grace is the natural garb of strength, and the affections are calm, because deep. The softness is that of a firm tissue, as when

> The gods approve
> The depth, but not the tumult of the soul,
> A fervent, not ungovernable love.

A profound thinker has said, "No married woman can represent the female world, for she belongs to her husband. The idea of Woman must be represented by a virgin."

But that is the very fault of marriage and of the present relation between the sexes, that the woman *does* belong to the man instead of forming a whole with him. Were it otherwise, there would be no such limitation to the thought.

Woman, self-centered, would never be absorbed by any relation; it would be only an experience to her as to man. It is a vulgar error that love, *a* love, to Woman is her whole existence, she also is born for Truth and Love in their universal energy. Would she but assume her inheritance, Mary would not be the only virgin mother. Not Manzoni alone would celebrate in his wife the virgin mind with the maternal wisdom and conjugal affections. The soul is ever young, ever virgin.

And will not she soon appear? The woman who shall vindicate their birthright for all women; who shall teach them what to claim, and how to use what they obtain? Shall not her name be for her era Victoria, for her country and life Virginia? Yet predictions are rash; she herself must teach us to give her the fitting name.

An idea not unknown to ancient times has of late been revived, that in the metamorphoses of life the soul assumes the form first of Man, then of Woman, and takes the chances and reaps the benefits of either lot. Why then, say some, lay such emphasis on the rights or needs of Woman? What she wins not as Woman will come to her as Man.

That makes no difference. It is not Woman, but the law of right, the law of growth that speaks in us and demands the perfection of each being in its kind—apple as apple, Woman as Woman. Without adopting your theory, I know that I, a daughter, live through the life of Man; but what concerns me now is that my life be a beautiful, powerful, in a word, a complete life in its kind. Had I but one more moment to live I must wish the same.

Suppose at the end of your cycle, your great world-year, all will be completed whether I exert myself or not (and the supposition is *false*—but suppose it true), am I to be indifferent about it? Not so! I must beat my own pulse true in the heart of the world; for *that* is virtue, excellence, health.

Thou, Lord of Day, didst leave us tonight so calmly glorious, not dismayed that cold winter is coming, not postponing thy beneficence to the fruitful summer! Thou didst smile on thy day's work when it was done, and adorn thy down-going as thy up-rising, for thou art loyal, and it is thy nature to give life, if thou canst, and shine at all events!

I stand in the sunny noon of life. Objects no longer glitter in the dews of morning, neither are yet softened by the shadows of evening. Every spot is seen, every chasm revealed. Climbing the dusty hill, some fair effigies that once stood for symbols of human destiny have been broken; those I still have with me show defects in this broad light. Yet enough is left, even by experience, to point distinctly to the glories of that destiny; faint but not to be mistaken streaks of the future day. I can say with the bard,

> Though many have suffered shipwreck, still beat noble hearts.

Always the soul says to us all, cherish your best hopes as a faith, and abide by them in action. Such shall be the effectual fervent means to their fulfillment:

> For the Power to whom we bow
> Has given its pledge that, if not now,
> They of pure and steadfast mind,
> By faith exalted, truth refined,
> *Shall* hear all music loud and clear,
> Whose first notes they ventured here.
> Then fear not thou to wind the horn,
> Though elf and gnome thy courage scorn;
> Ask for the castle's King and Queen;
> Though rabble rout may rush between,
> Beat thee senseless to the ground,
> In the dark beset thee round;
> Persist to ask, and it will come;
> Seek not for rest in humbler home;
> So shalt thou see, what few have seen,
> The palace home of King and Queen.

A Church Mouse

MARY E. WILKINS FREEMAN

"I never heard of a woman's bein' saxton."

"I dun' know what difference that makes; I don't see why they shouldn't have women saxtons as well as men saxtons, for my part, nor nobody else neither. They'd keep dusted 'nough sight cleaner. I've seen the dust layin' on my pew thick enough to write my name in a good many times, an' ain't said nothin' about it. An' I ain't going' to say nothin' now again Joe Sowen, now he's dead an' gone. He did jest as well as most men do. Men git in a good many places where they don't belong, an' where they set as awkward as a cow on a hen-roost, jest because they push in ahead of women. I ain't blamin' 'em; I s'pose if I could push in I should, jest the same way. But there ain't no reason that I can see, nor nobody else neither, why a woman shouldn't be saxton."

Hetty Fifield stood in the rowen hay-field before Caleb Gale. He was a deacon, the chairman of the selectmen, and the rich and influential man of the village. One looking at him would not have guessed it. There was nothing imposing about his lumbering figure in his calico shirt and baggy trousers. However, his large face, red and moist with perspiration, scanned the distant horizon with a stiff and reserved air; he did not look at Hetty.

"How'd you go to work to ring the bell?" said he. "It would have to be tolled, too, if anybody died."

"I'd jest as lief ring that little meetin'-house bell as to stan' out here an' jingle a cow-bell," said Hetty; "an' as for tollin', I'd jest as soon toll the bell for Methusaleh, if he was livin' here! I'd laugh if I ain't got strength 'nough for that."

"It takes a kind of a knack."

"If I ain't got as much knack as old Joe Sowen ever had, I'll give up the ship."

"You couldn't tend the fires."

"Couldn't tend the fires—when I've cut an' carried in all the wood I've

Childe Hassam, *Church at Old Lyme, Connecticut*

burned for forty year! Couldn't keep the fires a-goin' in them two little wood-stoves!"

"It's consider'ble work to sweep the meetin'-house."

"I guess I've done 'bout as much work as to sweep that little meetin'-house, I ruther guess I have."

"There's one thing you ain't thought of."

"What's that?"

"Where'd you live? All old Sowen got for bein' saxton was twenty dollar a year, an' we couldn't pay a woman so much as that. You wouldn't have enough to pay for your livin' anywheres."

"Where am I goin' to live whether I'm saxton or not?"

Caleb Gale was silent.

There was a wind blowing, the rowen hay drifted round Hetty like a brown-green sea touched with ripples of blue and gold by the asters and golden-rod. She stood in the midst of it like a May-weed that had gathered a slender toughness through the long summer; her brown cotton gown clung about her like a wilting leaf, outlining her harsh little form. She was as sallow as a squaw, and she had pretty black eyes; they were bright, although she was old. She kept them fixed upon Caleb. Suddenly she raised herself upon her toes; the wind caught her dress and made it blow out; her eyes flashed. "I'll tell you where I'm goin' to live," said she. *"I'm goin' to live in the meetin'-house."*

Caleb looked at her. *"Goin' to live in the meetin'-house!"*

"Yes, I be."

"Live in the meetin'-house!"

"I'd like to know why not."

"Why—you couldn't—live in the meetin'-house. You're crazy."

Caleb flung out the rake which he was holding, and drew it in full of rowen. Hetty moved around in front of him, he raked imperturbably; she moved again right in the path of the rake, then he stopped. "There ain't no sense in such talk."

"All I want is jest the east corner of the back gall'ry, where the chimbly goes up. I'll set up my cookin'-stove there, an' my bed, an' I'll curtain it off with my sunflower quilt, to keep off the wind."

"A cookin'-stove an' a bed in the meetin'-house!"

"Mis' Grout she give me that cookin'-stove, an' that bed I've allers slept on, before she died. She give 'em to me before Mary Anne Thomas, an' I moved 'em out. They air settin' out in the yard now, an' if it rains that stove an' that bed will be spoilt. It looks some like rain now. I guess you'd better give me the meetin'-house key right off."

"You don't think you can move that cookin'-stove an' that bed into the meetin'-house—I ain't goin' to stop to hear such talk."

"My worsted-work, all my mottoes I've done, an' my wool flowers, air out there in the yard."

Caleb raked. Hetty kept standing herself about until he was forced to stop, or gather her in with the rowen hay. He looked straight at her, and scowled; the perspiration trickled down his cheeks. "If I go up to the house can Mis' Gale git me the key to the meetin'-house?" said Hetty.

"No, she can't."

"Be you goin' up before long?"

"No, I ain't." Suddenly Caleb's voice changed: it had been full of stubborn vexation, now it was blandly argumentative. "Don't you see it ain't no use talkin' such nonsense, Hetty? You'd better go right along, an' make up your mind it ain't to be thought of."

"Where be I goin' to-night, then?"

"To-night?"

"Yes; where be I a-goin'?"

"Ain't you got any place to go to?"

"Where do you s'pose I've got any place? Them folks air movin' into Mis' Grout's house, an' they as good as told me to clear out. I ain't got no folks to take me in. I dun' know where I'm goin'; mebbe I can go to your house?"

Caleb gave a start. "We've got company to home," said he, hastily. "I'm 'fraid Mis' Gale wouldn't think it was convenient."

Hetty laughed. "Most everybody in the town has got company," said she.

Caleb dug his rake into the ground as if if were a hoe, then he leaned on it, and stared at the horizon. There was a fringe of yellow birches on the edge of the hay-field; beyond them was a low range of misty blue hills. "You ain't got no place to go to, then?"

"I dun' know of any. There ain't no poor-house here, an' I ain't got no folks."

Caleb stood like a statue. Some crows flew cawing over the field. Hetty waited. "I s'pose that key is where Mis' Gale can find it?" she said, finally.

Caleb turned and threw out his rake with a jerk. "She knows where 'tis; it's hangin' up behind the settin'-room door. I s'pose you can stay there to-night, as long as you ain't got no other place. We shall have to see what can be done."

Hetty scuttled off across the field. "You mustn't take no stove nor bed into the meetin'-house," Caleb called after her; "we can't have that, nohow."

Hetty went on as if she did not hear.

The golden-rod at the sides of the road was turning brown; the asters were in their prime, blue and white ones; here and there were rows of thistles with white tops. The dust was thick; Hetty, when she emerged from Caleb's house, trotted along in a cloud of it. She did not look to the right or left, she kept her small eager face fixed straight ahead, and moved forward like some little animal with the purpose to which it was born strong within it.

Presently she came to a large cottage-house on the right of the road; there she stopped. The front yard was full of furniture, tables and chairs standing among the dahlias and clumps of marigolds. Hetty leaned over the fence at one corner of the yard, and inspected a little knot of household goods set aside from the others. There were a small cooking-stove, a hair trunk, a yellow bedstead stacked up against the fence, and a pile of bedding. Some children in the yard stood in a group and eyed Hetty. A woman appeared in the door—she was small, there was a black smutch on her face, which was haggard with fatigue, and she scowled in the sun as she looked over at Hetty. "Well, got a place to stay in?" said she, in an unexpectedly deep voice.

"Yes, I guess so," replied Hetty.

"I dun' know how in the world I can have you. All the beds will be full—I expect his mother some to-night, an' I'm dreadful stirred up any-how."

"Everybody's havin' company; I never see anything like it." Hetty's voice was inscrutable. The other woman looked sharply at her.

"You've got a place, ain't you?" she asked, doubtfully.

"Yes, I have."

At the left of this house, quite back from the road, was a little unpainted cottage, hardly more than a hut. There was smoke coming out of the chimney, and a tall youth lounged in the door. Hetty, with the woman and children staring after her, struck out across the field in the little foot-path towards the cottage. "I wonder if she's goin' to stay there?" the woman muttered, meditating.

The youth did not see Hetty until she was quite near him, then he aroused suddenly as if from sleep, and tried to slink off around the cottage. But Hetty called after him. "Sammy," she cried, "Sammy, come back here, I want you!"

"What d'ye want?"

"Come back here!"

The youth lounged back sulkily, and a tall woman came to the door. She bent out of it anxiously to hear Hetty.

"I want you to come an' help me move my stove an' things," said Hetty.

"Where to?"

"Into the meetin'-house."

"The meetin'-house?"

"Yes, the meetin'-house."

The woman in the door had sodden hands; behind her arose the steam of a wash-tub. She and the youth stared at Hetty, but surprise was too strong an emotion for them to grasp firmly.

"I want Sammy to come right over an' help me," said Hetty.

"He ain't strong enough to move a stove," said the woman.

"Ain't strong enough!"

"He's apt to git lame."

"Most folks are. Guess I've got lame. Come right along, Sammy!"

"He ain't able to lift much."

"I s'pose he's able to be lifted, ain't he?"

"I dun' know what you mean."

"The stove don't weigh nothin'," said Hetty; "I could carry it myself if I could get hold of it. Come, Sammy!"

Hetty turned down the path, and the youth moved a little way after her, as if perforce. Then he stopped, and cast an appealing glance back at his mother. Her face was distressed. "Oh, Sammy, I'm afraid you'll git sick," said she.

"No, he ain't goin' to git sick," said Hetty. "Come, Sammy." And Sammy followed her down the path.

It was four o'clock then. At dusk Hetty had her gay sunflower quilt curtaining off the chimney-corner of the church gallery; her stove and little bedstead were set up, and she had entered upon a life which endured successfully for three months. All that time a storm brewed; then it broke; but Hetty sailed in her own course for the three months.

It was on a Saturday that she took up her habitation in the meeting-house. The next morning, when the boy who had been supplying the dead sexton's place came and shook the door, Hetty was prompt on the other side. "Deacon Gale said for you to let me in so I could ring the bell," called the boy.

"Go away," responded Hetty. "I'm goin' to ring the bell; I'm saxton."

Hetty rang the bell with vigor, but she made a wild, irregular jangle at first; at the last it was better. The village people said to each other that a new hand was ringing. Only a few knew that Hetty was in the meeting-house. When the congregation had assembled, and saw that gaudy tent pitched in the house of the Lord, and the resolute little pilgrim at the door of it, there was a commotion. The farmers and their wives were stirred out of their Sabbath decorum. After the service was over, Hetty, sitting in a pew corner of the gallery, her little face dark and watchful against the flaming background of her quilt, saw the people below gathering in groups, whispering, and looking at her.

Presently the minister, Caleb Gale, and the other deacon came up the gallery stairs. Hetty sat stiffly erect. Caleb Gale went up to the sunflower quilt, slipped it aside, and looked in. He turned to Hetty with a frown. To-day his dignity was supported by important witnesses. "Did you bring that stove an' bedstead here?"

Hetty nodded.

"What made you do such a thing?"

"What was I goin' to do if I didn't? How's a woman as old as me goin' to sleep in a pew, an' go without a cup of tea?"

The men looked at each other. They withdrew to another corner of the gallery and conferred in low tones; then they went down-stairs and out of the church. Hetty smiled when she heard the door shut. When one is hard pressed, one, however simple, gets wisdom as to vantage-points. Hetty comprehended hers perfectly. She was the propounder of a problem; as long as it was unguessed, she was sure of her foothold as propounder. This little village in which she had lived all her life had removed the shelter from her head; she being penniless, it was beholden to provide her another; she asked it what. When the old woman with whom she had lived died, the town promptly seized the estate for taxes—none had been paid for years. Hetty had not laid up a cent; indeed, for the most of the time she had received no wages. There had been no money in the house; all she had gotten for her labor for a sickly, impecunious old woman was a frugal board. When the old woman died, Hetty gathered in the few household articles for which she had stipulated, and made no complaint. She walked out of the house when the new tenants came in; all she asked was, "What are you going to do with me?" This little settlement of narrow-minded, prosperous farmers, however hard a task charity might be to them, could not turn an old woman out into the fields and highways to seek for food as they would a Jersey cow. They had their Puritan consciences, and her note of distress would sound louder in their ears than the Jersey's bell echoing down the valley in the stillest night. But the question as to Hetty Fifield's disposal was a hard one to answer. There was no almshouse in the village, and no private family was willing to take her in. Hetty was strong and capable; although she was old, she could well have paid for her food and shelter by her labor; but this could not secure her an entrance even among this hard-working and thrifty people, who would ordinarily grasp quickly enough at service without wage in dollars and cents. Hetty had somehow gotten for herself an unfortunate name in the village. She was held in the light of a long-thorned brier among the beanpoles, or a fierce little animal with claws and teeth bared. People were afraid to take her into their families; she had the reputation of always taking her own way, and never heeding the voice of authority. "I'd take her in an' have her give me a lift with the work," said one sickly farmer's wife; "but, near's I can find out, I couldn't never be sure that I'd get molasses in the beans, nor saleratus in my sour-milk cakes, if she took a notion not to put it in. I don't dare to risk it."

Stories were about concerning Hetty's authority over the old woman with whom she had lived. "Old Mis' Grout never dared to say her soul was her own," people said. Then Hetty's sharp, sarcastic sayings were repeated; the justice of them made them sting. People did not want a tongue like that in their homes.

Hetty as a church sexton was directly opposed to all their ideas of church decorum and propriety in general; her pitching her tent in the Lord's house was almost sacrilege; but what could they do? Hetty jangled the Sabbath bells for the three months; once she tolled the bell for an old man, and it seemed by the sound of the bell as if his long, calm years had swung by in a weak delirium; but people bore it. She swept and dusted the little meeting-house; and she garnished the walls with her treasures of worsted-work. The neatness and the garniture went far to quiet the dissatisfaction of the people. They had a crude taste. Hetty's skill in fancy-work was quite celebrated. Her wool flowers were much talked of, and young girls tried to copy them. So these wreathes and clusters of red and blue and yellow wool roses and lilies hung as acceptably between the meeting-house windows as pictures of saints in a cathedral.

Hetty hung a worsted motto over the pulpit; on it she set her chiefest treasure of art, a white wax cross with an ivy vine trailing over it, all covered with silver frost-work. Hetty always surveyed this cross with a species of awe; she felt the irresponsibility and amazement of a genius at his own work.

When she set it on the pulpit, no queen casting her rich robes and her jewels upon a shrine could have surpassed her in generous enthusiasm. "I guess when they see that they won't say no more," she said.

But the people, although they shared Hetty's admiration for the cross, were doubtful. They, looking at it, had a double vision of a little wax Virgin upon an altar. They wondered if it savored of popery. But the cross remained, and the minister was mindful not to jostle it in his gestures.

It was three months from the time Hetty took up her abode in the church, and a week before Christmas, when the problem was solved. Hetty herself precipitated the solution. She prepared a boiled dish in the meeting-house, upon a Saturday, and the next day the odors of turnip and cabbage were strong in the senses of the worshippers. They sniffed and looked at one another. This superseding the legitimate savor of the sanctuary, the fragrance of peppermint lozenges and wintergreen, the breath of Sunday clothes, by the homely week-day odors of kitchen vegetables, was too much for the sensibilities of the people. They looked indignantly around at Hetty, sitting before her sunflower hanging, comfortable from her good dinner of the day before, radiant with the consciousness of a great plateful of cold vegetables in her tent for her Sabbath dinner.

Poor Hetty had not many comfortable dinners. The selectmen doled out a small weekly sum to her, which she took with dignity as being her hire; then she had a mild forage in the neighbors' cellars and kitchens, of poor apples and stale bread and pie, paying for it in teaching her art of worsted-work to the daughters. Her Saturday's dinner had been a banquet to her: she had actually bought a piece of pork to boil with the vegetables; somebody had given her a nice little cabbage and some turnips, without a thought of the limitations of her housekeeping. Hetty herself had not a thought. She made the fires as usual that Sunday morning; the meeting-house was very clean, there was not a speck of dust anywhere, the wax cross on the pulpit glistened in a sunbeam slanting through the house. Hetty, sitting in the gallery, thought innocently how nice it looked.

After the meeting, Caleb Gale approached the other deacon. "Somethin's got to be done," said he. And the other deacon nodded. He had not smelt the cabbage until his wife nudged him and mentioned it; neither had Caleb Gale.

In the afternoon of the next Thursday, Caleb and the other two selectmen waited upon Hetty in her tabernacle. They stumped up the gallery stairs, and Hetty emerged from behind the quilt and stood looking at them scared and defiant. The three men nodded stiffly; there was a pause; Caleb Gale motioned meaningly to one of the others, who shook his head; finally he himself had to speak. "I'm 'fraid you find it pretty cold here, don't you, Hetty?" said he.

"No, thank ye; it's very comfortable," replied Hetty, polite and wary.

"It ain't very convenient for you to do your cookin' here, I guess."

"It's jest as convenient as I want. I don't find no fault."

"I guess it's rayther lonesome here nights, ain't it?"

"I'd 'nough sight ruther be alone than have comp'ny, any day."

"It ain't fit for an old woman like you to be livin' alone here this way."

"Well, I dun' know of anything that's any fitter; mebbe you do."

Caleb looked appealingly at his companions; they stood stiff and irresponsive. Hetty's eyes were sharp and watchful upon them all.

"Well, Hetty," said Caleb, "we've found a nice, comfortable place for you, an' I guess you'd better pack up your things, an' I'll carry you right over there." Caleb stepped back a little closer to the other men. Hetty, small and trembling and helpless before them, looked vicious. She was like a little animal driven from its cover, for whom there is nothing left but desperate warfare and death.

"Where to?" asked Hetty. Her voice shrilled up into a squeak.

Caleb hesitated. He looked again at the other selectmen. There was a solemn, far-away expression upon their faces. "Well," said he, "Mis' Radway wants to git somebody, an'—"

"You ain't goin' to take me to that woman's!"

"You'd be real comfortable—"

"I ain't goin'."

"Now, why not, I'd like to know?"

242

"I don't like Susan Radway, hain't never liked her, an' I ain't goin' to live with her."

"Mis' Radway's a good Christian woman. You hadn't ought to speak that way about her."

"You know what Susan Radway is, jest as well's I do; an' everybody else does too. I ain't goin' a step an' you might jest as well make up your mind to it."

Then Hetty seated herself in the corner of the pew nearest her tent, and folded her hands in her lap. She looked over at the pulpit as if she were listening to preaching. She panted, and her eyes glittered, but she had an immovable air.

"Now, Hetty, you've got sense enough to know you can't stay here," said Caleb. "You'd better put on your bonnet, an' come right along before dark. You'll have a nice ride."

Hetty made no response.

The three men stood looking at her. "Come, Hetty," said Caleb, feebly; and another selectman spoke. "Yes, you'd better come," he said, in a mild voice.

Hetty continued to stare at the pulpit.

The three men withdrew a little and conferred. They did not know how to act. This was a new emergency in their simple, even lives. They were not constables; these three steady, sober old men did not want to drag an old woman by main force out of the meeting-house, and thrust her into Caleb Gale's buggy as if it were a police wagon.

Finally Caleb brightened. "I'll go over an' git mother," said he. He started with a brisk air, and went down the gallery stairs; the others followed. They took up their stand in the meeting-house yard, and Caleb got into his buggy and gathered up the reins. The wind blew cold over the hill. "Hadn't you better go inside and wait out of the wind?" said Caleb.

"I guess we'll wait out here," replied one; and the other nodded.

"Well, I sha'n't be gone long," said Caleb. "Mother'll know how to manage her." He drove carefully down the hill; his buggy wings rattled in the wind. The other men pulled up their coat collars, and met the blast stubbornly.

"Pretty ticklish piece of business to tackle," said one, in a low grunt.

"That's so," assented the other. Then they were silent, and waited for Caleb. Once in a while they stamped their feet and slapped their mittened hands. They did not hear Hetty slip the bolt and turn the key of the meet-ing-house door, nor see her peeping at them from a gallery window.

Caleb returned in twenty minutes; he had not far to go. His wife, stout and handsome and full of vigor, sat beside him in the buggy. Her face was red with the cold wind; her thick cashmere shawl was pinned tightly over her broad bosom. "Has she come down yet?" she called out, in an imperi-ous way.

The two selectmen shook their heads. Caleb kept the horse quiet while his wife got heavily and briskly out of the buggy. She went up the meeting-house steps, and reached out confidently to open the door. Then she drew back and looked around. "Why," said she, "the door's locked; she's locked the door. I call this pretty work!"

She turned again quite fiercely, and began beating on the door. "Hetty!" she called; "Hetty, Hetty Fifield! Let me in! What have you locked this door for?"

She stopped and turned to her husband.

"Don't you s'pose the barn key would unlock it?" she asked.

"I don't b'lieve 'twould."

"Well, you'd better go home and fetch it."

Caleb again drove down the hill, and the other men searched their pockets for keys. One had the key of his corn-house, and produced it hope-fully; but it would not unlock the meeting-house door.

A crowd seldom gathered in the little village for anything short of a fire; but to-day in a short time quite a number of people stood on the meeting-house hill, and more kept coming. When Caleb Gale returned with the barn key his daughter, a tall, pretty young girl, sat beside him, her little face alert and smiling in her red hood. The other selectmen's wives toiled eagerly up the hill, with a young daughter of one of them speeding on ahead. Then the two young girls stood close to each other and watched the pro-ceedings. Key after key was tried; men brought all the large keys they could find, running importantly up the hill, but none would unlock the meeting-house door. After Caleb had tried the last available key, stooping and screw-ing it anxiously, he turned around. "There ain't no use in it, any way," said he; "most likely the door's bolted."

"You don't mean there's a bolt on that door?" cried his wife.

"Yes, there is."

"Then you might jest as well have tore 'round for hen's feathers as keys. Of course she's bolted it if she's got any wit, an' I guess she's got most as much as some of you men that have been bringin' keys. Try the windows."

But the windows were fast. Hetty had made her sacred castle impregnable except to violence. Either the door would have to be forced or a window broken to gain an entrance.

The people conferred with one another. Some were for retreating, and leaving Hetty in peaceful possession until time drove her to capitulate. "She'll open it to-morrow," they said. Others were for extreme measures, and their impetuosity gave them the lead. The project of forcing the door was urged; one man started for a crow-bar.

"They are a parcel of fools to do such a thing," said Caleb Gale's wife to another woman. "Spoil that good door! They'd better leave the poor thing alone till to-morrow. I dun' know what's goin' to be done with her when they git in. I ain't goin' to have father draggin' her over to Mis' Radway's by the hair of her head."

"That's jest what I say," returned the other woman.

Mrs. Gale went up to Caleb and nudged him. "Don't you let them break that door down, father," said she.

"Well, well, we'll see," Caleb replied. He moved away a little; his wife's voice had been drowned out lately by a masculine clamor, and he took advantage of it.

All the people talked at once; the wind was keen, and all their garments fluttered; the two young girls had their arms around each other under their shawls; the man with the crow-bar came stalking up the hill.

"Don't you let them break down that door, father," said Mrs. Gale.

"Well, well," grunted Caleb.

Regardless of remonstrances, the man set the crow-bar against the door; suddenly there was a cry, "There she is!" Everybody looked up. There was Hetty looking out of a gallery window.

Everybody was still. Hetty began to speak. Her dark old face, peering out of the window, looked ghastly; the wind blew her poor gray locks over it. She extended her little wrinkled hands. "Jest let me say one word," said she; "jest one word." Her voice shook. All her coolness was gone. The magnitude of her last act of defiance had caused it to react upon herself like an overloaded gun.

"Say all you want to, Hetty, an' don't be afraid," Mrs. Gale called out.

"I jest want to say a word," repeated Hetty. "Can't I stay here, nohow? It don't seem as if I could go to Mis' Radway's. I ain't nothin' again' her. I s'pose she's a good woman, but she's used to havin' her own way, and I've been livin' all my life with them that was, an' I've had to fight to keep a footin' on the earth, an' now I'm gittin' too old for't. If I can jest stay here in the meetin'-house, I won't ask for nothin' any better. I sha'n't need much to keep me, I wa'n't never a hefty eater; an' I'll keep the meetin'-house jest as clean as I know how. An' I'll make some more of them wool flowers. I'll make a wreath to go the whole length of the gallery, if I can git wool 'nough. Won't you let me stay? I ain't complainin', but I've always had a dretful hard time; seems as if now I might take a little comfort the last of it, if I could stay here. I can't go to Mis' Radway's nohow." Hetty covered her face with her hands; her words ended in a weak wail.

Mrs. Gale's voice rang out clear and strong and irrepressible. "Of course you can stay in the meetin'-house," said she; "I should laugh if you couldn't. Don't you worry another mite about it. You sha'n't go one step to Mis' Radway's; you couldn't live a day with her. You can stay jest where you are; you've kept the meetin'-house enough sight cleaner than I've ever seen it. Don't you worry another mite, Hetty."

Mrs. Gale stood majestically, and looked defiantly around; tears were in her eyes. Another woman edged up to her. "Why couldn't she have that little room side of the pulpit, where the minister hangs his hat?" she whispered. "He could hang it somewhere else."

"Course she could," responded Mrs. Gale, with alacrity, "jest as well as not. The minister can have a hook in the entry for his hat. She can have her stove an' her bed in there, an' be jest as comfortable as can be. I should laugh if she couldn't. Don't you worry, Hetty."

The crowd gradually dispersed, sending out stragglers down the hill until it was all gone. Mrs. Gale waited until the last, sitting in the buggy in state. When her husband gathered up the reins, she called back to Hetty: "Don't you worry one mite more about it, Hetty. I'm comin' up to see you in the mornin'!"

It was almost dusk when Caleb drove down the hill; he was the last of the besiegers, and the feeble garrison was left triumphant.

The next day but one was Christmas, the next night Christmas Eve. On Christmas Eve Hetty had reached what to her was the flood-tide of peace and prosperity. Established in that small, lofty room, with her bed and her stove, with gifts of a rocking-chair and table, and a goodly store of food, with no one to molest or disturb her, she had nothing to wish for on earth. All her small desires were satisfied. No happy girl could have a merrier Christmas than this old woman with her little measure full of gifts. That

Christmas Eve Hetty lay down under the sunflower quilt, and all her old hardships looked dim in the distance, like far-away hills, while her new joys came out like stars.

She was a light sleeper; the next morning she was up early. She opened the meeting-house door and stood looking out. The smoke from the village chimneys had not yet begun to rise blue and rosy in the clear frosty air. There was no snow, but over all the hill there was a silver rime of frost; the bare branches of the trees glistened. Hetty stood looking. "Why, it's Christmas mornin'," she said, suddenly. Christmas had never been a gala-day to this old woman. Christmas had not been kept at all in this New England village when she was young. She was led to think of it now only in connection with the dinner Mrs. Gale had promised to bring her to-day.

Mrs. Gale had told her she should have some of her Christmas dinner, some turkey and plum-pudding. She called it to mind now with a thrill of delight. Her face grew momentarily more radiant. There was a certain beauty in it. A finer morning light than that which lit up the wintry earth seemed to shine over the furrows of her old face. "I'm goin' to have turkey an' plum-puddin' today," said she; "it's Christmas." Suddenly she started, and went into the meeting-house, straight up the gallery stairs. There in a clear space hung the bell-rope. Hetty grasped it. Never before had a Christmas bell been rung in this village; Hetty had probably never heard of Christmas bells. She was prompted by pure artless enthusiasm and grateful happiness. Her old arms pulled on the rope with a will, the bell sounded peal on peal. Down in the village, curtains rolled up, letting in the morning light, happy faces looked out of the windows. Hetty had awakened the whole village to Christmas Day.

Mr. Flood's Party

EDWIN ARLINGTON ROBINSON

Old Eben Flood, climbing alone one night
Over the hill between the town below
And the forsaken upland hermitage
That held as much as he should ever know
On earth again of home, paused warily.
The road was his with not a native near;
And Eben, having leisure, said aloud,
For no man else in Tilbury Town to hear:

"Well, Mr. Flood, we have the harvest moon
Again, and we may not have many more;
The bird is on the wing, the poet says,
And you and I have said it here before.
Drink to the bird." He raised up to the light
The jug that he had gone so far to fill,
And answered huskily: "Well, Mr. Flood,
Since you propose it, I believe I will."

Alone, as if enduring to the end
A valiant armor of scarred hopes outworn,
He stood there in the middle of the road
Like Roland's ghost winding a silent horn.
Below him, in the town among the trees,
Where friends of other days had honored him,
A phantom salutation of the dead
Rang thinly till old Eben's eyes were dim.

Then, as a mother lays her sleeping child
Down tenderly, fearing it may awake,
He set the jug down slowly at his feet
With trembling care, knowing that most things break,
And only when assured that on firm earth
It stood, as the uncertain lives of men
Assuredly did not, he paced away,
And with his hand extended paused again:

"Well, Mr. Flood, we have not met like this
In a long time; and many a change has come
To both of us, I fear, since last it was
We had a drop together. Welcome home!"
Convivially returning with himself,
Again he raised the jug up to the light;
And with an acquiescent quaver said:
"Well, Mr. Flood, if you insist, I might.

"Only a very little, Mr. Flood—
For auld lang syne. No more, sir; that will do."
So, for the time, apparently it did,
And Eben evidently thought so too,
For soon amid the silver loneliness
Of night he lifted up his voice and sang,
Secure, with only two moons listening,
Until the whole harmonious landscape rang—

"For auld lang syne." The weary throat gave out;
The last word wavered, and the song was done.
He raised again the jug regretfully
And shook his head, and was again alone.
There was not much that was ahead of him,
And there was nothing in the town below—
Where strangers would have shut the many doors
That many friends had opened long ago.

The Writer

RICHARD WILBUR

In her room at the prow of the house
Where light breaks, and the windows are tossed with linden,
My daughter is writing a story.

I pause in the stairwell, hearing
From her shut door a commotion of typewriter-keys
Like a chain hauled over a gunwale.

Young as she is, the stuff
Of her life is a great cargo, and some of it heavy:
I wish her a lucky passage.

But now it is she who pauses,
As if to reject my thought and its easy figure.
A stillness greatens, in which

The whole house seems to be thinking,
And then she is at it again with a bunched clamor
Of strokes, and again is silent.

I remember the dazed starling
Which was trapped in that very room, two years ago;
How we stole in, lifted a sash

And retreated, not to affright it;
And how for a helpless hour, through the crack of the door,
We watched the sleek, wild, dark

And iridescent creature
Batter against the brilliance, drop like a glove
To the hard floor, or the desk-top,

And wait then, humped and bloody,
For the wits to try it again; and how our spirits
Rose when, suddenly sure,

It lifted off from a chair-back,
Beating a smooth course for the right window
And clearing the sill of the world.

It is always a matter, my darling,
Of life or death, as I had forgotten. I wish
What I wished you before, but harder.

Marsden Hartley, *Mt. Katahdin*

Man and Daughter in the Cold

JOHN UPDIKE

"Look at that girl ski!" The exclamation arose at Ethan's side as if, in the disconnecting cold, a rib of his had cried out; but it was his friend, friend and fellow-teacher, an inferior teacher but superior skier, Matt Langley, admiring Becky, Ethan's own daughter. It took an effort, in this air like slices of transparent metal interposed everywhere, to make these connections and to relate the young girl, her round face red with windburn as she skimmed down the run-out slope, to himself. She was his daughter, age thirteen. Ethan had twin sons, two years younger, and his attention had always been focussed on their skiing, on the irksome comedy of their double needs—the four boots to lace, the four mittens to find—and then their cute yet grim competition as now one and now the other gained the edge in the expertise of geländesprungs and slalom form. On their trips north into the mountains, Becky had come along for the ride. "Look how solid she is," Matt went on. "She doesn't cheat on it like your boys—those feet are absolutely together." The girl, grinning as if she could hear herself praised, wiggle-waggled to a flashy stop that sprayed snow over the men's ski tips.

"Where's Mommy?" she asked.

Ethan answered, "She went with the boys into the lodge. They couldn't take it." Their sinewy little male bodies had no insulation; weeping and shivering, they had begged to go in after a single T-bar run.

"What sissies," Becky said.

Matt said, "This wind is wicked. And it's picking up. You should have been here at nine; Lord, it was lovely. All that fresh powder, and not a stir of wind."

Becky told him, "Dumb Tommy couldn't find his mittens, we spent an *hour* looking, and then Daddy got the Jeep stuck." Ethan, alerted now for signs of the wonderful in his daughter, was struck by the strange fact that she was making conversation. Unafraid, she was talking to Matt without her father's intercession.

"Mr. Langley was saying how nicely you were skiing."

"You're Olympic material, Becky."

The girl perhaps blushed; but her cheeks could get no redder. Her eyes, which, were she a child, she would have instantly averted, remained a second on Matt's face, as if to estimate how much he meant it. "It's easy down here," Becky said. "It's babyish."

Ethan asked, "Do you want to go up to the top?" He was freezing standing still, and the gondola would be sheltered from the wind.

Her eyes shifted to his, with another unconsciously thoughtful hesitation. "Sure. If you want to."

"Come along, Matt?"

"Thanks, no. It's too rough for me; I've had enough runs. This is the trouble with January—once it stops snowing, the wind comes up. I'll keep Elaine company in the lodge." Matt himself had no wife, no children. At thirty-eight, he was as free as his students, as light on his skis and as full of brave know-how. "In case of frostbite," he shouted after them, "rub snow on it."

Becky effortlessly skated ahead to the lift shed. The encumbered motion of walking on skis, not natural to him, made Ethan feel asthmatic: a fish out of water. He touched his parka pocket, to check that the inhalator was there. As a child he had imagined death as something attacking from outside, but now he saw that it was carried within; we nurse it for years, and it grows. The clock on the lodge wall said a quarter to noon. The giant thermometer read two degrees above zero. The racks outside were dense as hedges with idle skis. Crowds, any sensation of crowding or delay, quickened his asthma; as therapy he imagined the emptiness, the blue freedom, at the top of the mountain. The clatter of machinery inside the shed was comforting, and enough teen-age boys were boarding gondolas to make the ascent seem normal and safe. Ethan's breathing eased. Becky proficiently handed her poles to the loader points up; her father was always caught by surprise, and often as not fumbled the little maneuver of letting his skis be taken from him. Until, five years ago, he had become an assistant professor at a New Hampshire college an hour to the south, he had never skied; he had lived in those Middle Atlantic cities where snow, its moment of virgin beauty by, is only an encumbering nuisance, a threat of suffocation. Whereas his children had grown up on skis.

Alone with his daughter in the rumbling isolation of the gondola, he wanted to explore her, and found her strange—strange in her uninquisitive child's silence, her accustomed poise in this ascending egg of metal. A dark figure with spreading legs veered out of control beneath them, fell forward, and vanished. Ethan cried out, astonished, scandalized; he imagined the man had buried himself alive. Becky was barely amused, and looked away before the dark spots struggling in the drift were lost from sight. As if she might know, Ethan asked, "Who was that?"

"Some kid." Kids, her tone suggested, were in plentiful supply; one could be spared.

He offered to dramatize the adventure ahead of them: "Do you think we'll freeze at the top?"

"Not exactly."

"What do you think it'll be like?"

"Miserable."

"Why are we doing this, do you think?"

"Because we paid the money for the all-day lift ticket."

"Becky, you think you're pretty smart, don't you?"

"Not really."

The gondola rumbled and lurched into the shed at the top; an attendant opened the door, and there was a howling mixed of wind and of boys whooping to keep warm. He was roughly handed two pairs of skis, and the handler, muffled to the eyes with a scarf, stared as if amazed that Ethan was so old. All the others struggling into skis in the lee of the shed were adolescent boys. Students: after fifteen years of teaching, Ethan tended to flinch from youth—its harsh noises, its cheerful rapacity, its cruel onward flow as one class replaced another, ate a year of his life, and was replaced by another.

Away from the shelter of the shed, the wind was a high monotonous pitch of pain. His cheeks instantly ached, and the hinges linking the elements of his face seemed exposed. His septum tingled like glass—the rim of a glass being rubbed by a moist finger to produce a note. Drifts ribbed the trail, obscuring Becky's ski tracks seconds after she made them, and at each push through the heaped snow his scope of breathing narrowed. By the time he reached the first steep section, the left half of his back hurt as it did only in the panic of a full asthmatic attack, and his skis, ignored, too heavy to manage, spread and swept him toward a snowbank at the side of the trail. He was bent far forward but kept his balance; the snow kissed his face lightly, instantly, all over; he straightened up, refreshed by the shock, thankful not to have lost a ski. Down the slope Becky had halted and was staring upward at him, worried. A huge blowing feather, a partition of snow, came between them. The cold, unprecedented in his experience, shone through his clothes like furious light, and as he rummaged through his parka for the inhalator he seemed to be searching glass shelves backed by a black wall. He found it, its icy plastic the touch of life, a clumsy key to his insides. Gasping, he exhaled, put it into his mouth, and inhaled; the isoproterenol spray, chilled into drops, opened his lungs enough for him to call to his daughter, "Keep moving! I'll catch up!"

Solid on her skis, she swung down among the moguls and wind-bared ice, and became small, and again waited. The moderate slope seemed a cliff; if he fell and sprained anything, he would freeze. His entire body would become locked tight against air and light and thought. His legs trembled; his breath moved in and out of a narrow slot beneath the pain in his back. The cold and blowing snow all around him constituted an immense crowding, but there was no way out of this white cave but to slide downward toward the dark spot that was his daughter. He had forgotten all his lessons. Leaning backward in an infant's tense snowplow, he floundered through alternating powder and ice.

"You O.K., Daddy?" Her stare was wide, its fright underlined by a pale patch on her cheek.

He used the inhalator again and gave himself breath to tell her, "I'm fine. Let's get down."

In this way, in steps of her leading and waiting, they worked down the mountain, out of the worst wind, into the lower trail that ran between birches and hemlocks. The cold had the quality not of absence but of force: an inverted burning. The last time Becky stopped and waited, the colorless crescent on her scarlet cheek disturbed him, reminded him of some injunction, but he could find in his brain, whittled to a dim determination to persist, only the advice to keep going, toward shelter and warmth. She told him, at a division of trails, "This is the easier way."

"Let's go the quicker way," he said, and in this last descent recovered the rhythm—knees together, shoulders facing the valley, weight forward as if in the moment of release from a diving board—not a resistance but a joyous acceptance of falling. They reached the base lodge, and with unfeeling hands removed their skis. Pushing into the cafeteria, Ethan saw in the momentary mirror of the door window that his face was a spectre's; chin, nose, and eyebrows had retained the snow from the near-fall near the top. "Becky, look," he said, turning in the crowded warmth and clatter inside the door. "I'm a monster."

"I know, your face was absolutely white, I didn't know whether to tell you or not. I thought it might scare you."

He touched the pale patch on her cheek. "Feel anything?"

"No."

"Damn. I should have rubbed snow on it."

Matt and Elaine and the twins, flushed and stripped of their parkas, had eaten lunch; shouting and laughing with a strange guilty shrillness, they said that there had been repeated loudspeaker announcements not to go up to the top without face masks, because of frostbite. They had expected Ethan and Becky to come back down on the gondola, as others had, after tasting the top. "It never occurred to us," Ethan said. He took the blame upon himself by adding, "I wanted to see the girl ski."

Their common adventure, and the guilt of his having given her frostbite, bound Becky and Ethan together in complicity for the rest of the day. They arrived home as sun was leaving even the tips of the hills; Elaine had invited Matt to supper, and while the windows of the house burned golden Ethan shovelled out the Jeep. The house was a typical New Hampshire farmhouse, less than two miles from the college, on the side of a hill, overlooking what had been a pasture, with the usual capacious porch running around three sides, cluttered with cordwood and last summer's lawn furniture. The woodsy sheltered scent of these porches, the sense of rural waste space, never failed to please Ethan, who had been raised in a Newark half-house, then a West Side apartment, and just before college a row house in Baltimore, with his grandparents. The wind had been left behind in the mountains. The air was as still as the stars. Shovelling the light dry snow became a lazy dance. But when he bent suddenly, his knees creaked, and his breathing shortened so that he paused. A sudden rectangle of light was flung from the shadows of the porch. Becky came out into the cold with him. She was carrying a lawn rake.

He asked her, "Should you be out again? How's your frostbite?" Though she was a distance away, there was no need, in the immaculate air, to raise his voice.

"It's O.K. It kind of tingles. And under my chin. Mommy made me put on a scarf."

"What's the lawn rake for?"

"It's a way you can make a path. It really works."

"O.K., you make a path to the garage and after I get my breath I'll see if I can get the Jeep back in."

"Are you having asthma?"

"A little."

"We were reading about it in biology. Dad, see, it's kind of a tree inside you, and every branch has a little ring of muscle around it, and they tighten." From her gestures in the dark she was demonstrating, with mittens on.

What she described, of course, was classic unalloyed asthma, whereas his was shading into emphysema, which could only worsen. But he liked being lectured to—preferred it, indeed, to lecturing—and as the minutes of companionable silence with his daughter passed he took inward notes on the bright quick impressions flowing over him like a continuous voice. The silent cold. The stars. Orion behind an elm. Minute scintillae in the snow at his feet. His daughter's strange black bulk against the white; the solid grace that had stolen upon her. The conspiracy of love. His father and he shovelling the car free from a sudden unwelcome storm in Newark, instantly gray with soot, the undercurrent of desperation, his father a salesman and must get to Camden. Got to get to Camden, boy, get to Camden or bust. Dead of a heart attack at forty-seven. Ethan tossed a shovelful into the air so the scintillae flashed in the steady golden chord from the house windows. Elaine and Matt sitting flushed at the lodge table, parkas off, in deshabille, as if sitting up in bed. Matt's way of turning a half circle on the top of a mogul, light as a diver. The cancerous unwieldiness of Ethan's own skis. His jealousy of his students, the many-headed immortality of their annual renewal. The flawless tall cruelty of the stars. Orion intertwined with the silhouetted elm. A black tree inside him. His daughter, busily sweeping with the rake, childish yet lithe, so curiously demonstrating this preference for his company. Feminine of her to forgive him her frostbite. Perhaps, flattered on skis, felt the cold her element. Her womanhood soon enough to be smothered in warmth. A plow a mile away painstakingly scraped. He was missing the point of the lecture. The point was unstated: an absence. He was looking upon his daughter as a woman but without lust. The music around him was being produced, in the zero air, like a finger on crystal, by this hollowness, this generosity of negation. Without lust, without jealousy. Space seemed love, bestowed to be free in, and coldness the price. He felt joined to the great dead whose words it was his duty to teach.

The Jeep came up unprotestingly from the fluffy snow. It looked happy to be penned in the garage with Elaine's station wagon, and the skis, and the oiled chain saw, and the power mower dreamlessly waiting for spring. Ethan was happy, precariously so, so that rather than break he uttered a sound: "Becky?"

"Yeah?"

"You want to know what else Mr. Langley said?"

"What?" They trudged toward the porch, up the path the gentle rake had cleared.

"He said you ski better than the boys."

"I bet," she said, and raced to the porch, and in the precipitate way, evasive and female and pleased, that she flung herself to the top step he glimpsed something generic and joyous, a pageant that would leave him behind.

Solo on the Drums

ANN PETRY

The orchestra had a week's engagement at the Randlert Theater at Broadway and Forty-second Street. His name was picked out in lights on the marquee. The name of the orchestra and then his name underneath by itself.

There had been a time when he would have been excited by it. And stopped to let his mind and his eyes linger over it lovingly. Kid Jones. The name—his name—up there in lights that danced and winked in the brassy sunlight. And at night his name glittered up there on the marquee as though it had been sprinkled with diamonds. The people who pushed their way through the crowded street looked up at it and recognized it and smiled.

He used to eat it up. But not today. Not after what had happened this morning. He just looked at the sign with his name on it. There it was. Then he noticed that the sun had come out, and he shrugged and went on inside the theater to put on one of the cream-colored suits and get his music together.

After he had finished changing his clothes, he glanced in the long mirror in his dressing room. He hadn't changed any. Same face. No fatter and no thinner. No gray hair. Nothing. He frowned. Because he felt that the things that were eating him up inside ought to show. But they didn't.

When it was time to go out on the stage, he took his place behind the drums, not talking, just sitting there. The orchestra started playing softly. He made a mental note of the fact that the boys were working together as smoothly as though each one had been oiled.

The long gray curtains parted. One moment they were closed. And then they were open. Silently. Almost like magic. The high-powered spots flooded the stage with light. He could see specks of dust gliding down the wide beams of light. Under the bands of light the great space out front was all shadow. Faces slowly emerged out of it—disembodied heads and shoulders that slanted up and back, almost to the roof.

260

He hit the drums lightly. Regularly. A soft, barely discernible rhythm. A background. A repeated emphasis for the horns and the piano. The man with the trumpet stood up and the first notes came out sweet and clear and high.

Kid Jones kept up the drum accompaniment. Slow. Careful. Soft. And he felt his left eyebrow lift itself and start to twitch as the man played the trumpet. It happened whenever he heard the trumpet. The notes crept up, higher, higher, higher. So high that his stomach sucked in against itself. Then a little lower and stronger. A sound sustained. The rhythm of it beating against his ears until he was filled with it and sighing with it.

He wanted to cover his ears with his hands because he kept hearing a voice that whispered the same thing over and over again. The voice was trapped somewhere under the roof—caught and held there by the trumpet. "I'm leaving I'm leaving I'm leaving."

The sound took him straight back to the rain, the rain that had come with the morning. He could see the beginning of the day—raw and cold. He was at home. But he was warm because he was close to her, holding her in his arms. The rain and the wind cried softly outside the window.

And now—well, he felt as though he were floating up and up and up on that long blue note of the trumpet. He half closed his eyes and rode up on it. It had stopped being music. It was that whispering voice, making him shiver. Hating it and not being able to do anything about it. "I'm leaving it's the guy who plays the piano I'm in love with him and I'm leaving now today." Rain in the streets. Heat gone. Food gone. Everything gone because a woman's gone. It's everything you ever wanted, he thought. It's everything you never got. Everything you ever had, everything you ever lost. It's all there in the trumpet—pain and hate and trouble and peace and quiet and love.

The last note stayed up in the ceiling. Hanging on and on. The man with the trumpet had stopped playing but Kid Jones could still hear that last note. In his ears. In his mind.

The spotlight shifted and landed on Kid Jones—the man behind the drums. The long beam of white light struck the top of his head and turned him into a pattern of light and shadow. Because of the cream-colored suit and shirt, his body seemed to be encased in light. But there was a shadow over his face so that his features blended and disappeared. His hairline receded so far back that he looked like a man with a face that never ended. A man with a high, long face and dark, dark skin.

261

The Undiminished Hero

He caressed the drums with the brushes in his hands. They responded with a whisper of sound. The rhythm came over but it had to be listened for. It stayed that way for a long time. Low, insidious, repeated. Then he made the big bass drum growl and pick up the same rhythm.

The Marquis of Brund, pianist with the band, turned to the piano. The drums and the piano talked the same rhythm. The piano high. A little more insistent than the drums. The Marquis was turned sideways on the piano bench. His left foot tapped out the rhythm. His cream-colored suit sharply outlined the bulkiness of his body against the dark gleam of the piano. The drummer and the pianist were silhouetted in two separate brilliant shafts of light. The drums slowly dominated the piano.

The rhythm changed. It was faster. Kid Jones looked out over the crowded theater as he hit the drums. He began to feel as though he were the drums and the drums were he.

The theater throbbed with the excitement of the drums. A man, sitting near the front, shivered and his head jerked to the rhythm. A sailor put his arm around the girl sitting beside him, took his hand and held her face still and pressed his mouth close over hers. Close. Close. Close. Until their faces seemed to melt together. Her hat fell off and neither of them moved. His hand dug deep into her shoulder and still they didn't move.

A kid sneaked in through a side door and slid into an aisle seat. His mouth was wide open and he clutched his cap with both hands, tight and hard against his chest as he listened.

The drummer forgot he was in the theater. There was only him and the drums and they were far away. Long gone. He was holding Lulu, Helen, Susie, Mamie close in his arms. And all of them—all those girls blended into that one girl who was his wife. The one who said, "I'm leaving." She had said it over and over again, this morning, while rain dripped down the windowpanes.

When he hit the drums again it was with the thought that he was fighting with the pinao player. He was choking the Marquis of Brund. He was putting a knife in clean between his ribs. He was slitting his throat with a long straight blade. Take my woman. Take your life.

The drums leaped with the fury that was in him. The men in the band turned their heads toward him—a faint astonishment showed in their faces.

He ignored them. The drums took him away from them, took him back,

262

and back, and back, in time and space. He built up an illusion. He was sending out the news. Grandma died. The foreigner in the litter has an old disease and will not recover. The man from across the big water is sleeping with the chief's daughter. Kill. Kill. Kill. The war goes well with the men with the bad smell and the loud laugh. It goes badly with the chiefs with the round heads and the peacock's walk.

It is cool in the deep track in the forest. Cool and quiet. The trees talk softly. They speak of the dance tonight. The young girl from across the lake will be there. Her waist is slender and her thighs are rounded. Then the words he wanted to forget were all around Kid Jones again. "I'm leaving I'm leaving I'm leaving."

He couldn't help himself. He stopped hitting the drums and stared at the Marquis of Brund—a long malevolent look, filled with hate.

There was a restless, uneasy movement in the theater. He remembered where he was. He started playing again. The horn played a phrase. Soft and short. The drums answered. The horn said the same thing all over again. The drums repeated it. The next time it was more intricate. The phrase was turned around, it went back and forth and up and down. And the drums said it over, exactly the same.

He knew a moment of panic. This was where he had to solo again and he wasn't sure he could do it. He touched the drums lightly. They quivered and answered him.

And then it was almost as though the drums were talking about his own life. The woman in Chicago who hated him. The girl with the round, soft body who had been his wife and who had walked out on him, this morning, in the rain. The old woman who was his mother, the same woman who lived in Chicago, and who hated him because he looked like his father, his father who had seduced her and left her, years ago.

He forgot the theater, forgot everything but the drums. He was welded to the drums, sucked inside them. All of him. His pulse beat. His heart beat. He had become part of the drums. They had become part of him.

He made the big drum rumble and reverberate. He went a little mad on the big drum. Again and again he filled the theater with a sound like thunder. The sound seemed to come not from the drums but from deep inside himself; it was a sound that was being wrenched out of him—a violent, raging, roaring sound. As it issued from him he thought, This is the story of my love, this is the story of my hate, this is all there is left of me. And the sound echoed and reechoed far up under the roof of the theater.

When he finally stopped playing, he was trembling; his body was wet with sweat. He was surprised to see that the drums were sitting there in front of him. He hadn't become part of them. He was still himself. Kid Jones. Master of the drums. Greatest drummer in the world. Selling himself a little piece at a time. Every afternoon. Twice every evening. Only this time he had topped all his other performances. This time, playing like this after what had happened in the morning, he had sold all of himself—not just a little piece.

Someone kicked his foot. "Bow, you ape. Whassamatter with you?"

He bowed from the waist and the spotlight slid away from him, down his pants legs. The light landed on the Marquis of Brund, the piano player. The Marquis' skin glistened like a piece of black seaweed. Then the light was back on Kid Jones.

He felt hot and he thought, I stink of sweat. The talcum he had dabbed on his face after he shaved felt like a constricting layer of cement. A thin layer, but definitely cement. No air could get through to his skin. He reached for his handkerchief and felt the powder and the sweat mix as he mopped his face.

Then he bowed again. And again. Like a—like one of those things you pull the string and it jerks, goes through the motion of dancing. Pull it again and it kicks. Yeah, he thought, you were hot all right. The go-go gals ate you up and you haven't anyplace to go. Since this morning you haven't had anyplace to go. "I'm leaving it's the guy who plays the piano I'm in love with the Marquis of Brund he plays such sweet piano I'm leaving leaving leaving—"

He stared at the Marquis of Brund for a long moment. Then he stood up and bowed again. And again.

Notes About Authors

Henry Beston (1888–1968) was born in Quincy, Massachusetts, but he lived for many years in Nobleboro, Maine, with his wife, the writer, Elizabeth Coatsworth. Nature and history interested him greatly. *The Outermost House* has become a classic among nature books; other works include *American Memory* (history), *The Saint Lawrence River, Northern Farm, White Pine and Blue Water*, and a *State of Maine Reader*, as well as several children's books. In all his writing he showed himself to be a "conscientious and sensitive craftsman."

Louise Bogan (1897–1970) was born in Livermore Falls, Maine, and studied at Boston University. Twice married, she had one daughter and lived in New York during her last several decades. Familiar to readers of *The New Yorker* for many years as its chief poetry editor and critic, Louise Bogan is also an accomplished poet and fiction writer. For her consummate craftsmanship, she is regarded as one of the finest contemporary poets. Her *Collected Poems* received the 1954 Bollingen Prize.

Gerald Warner Brace (1901–1978), although born in Islip, New York, spent much of his life in New England, from his college days at Amherst and Harvard University to his professorships in six New England colleges, including Harvard and Boston University. Among other matters, his novels depict life down Maine and in the academic world: *The World of Carrick's Cove, Winter Solstice*, and *The Department* are well-known, but *The Garretson Chronicles* is justly famous. He lived in Belmont, Massachusetts. His nonfiction is as well written and as wise as his fiction.

Ann Bradstreet (1612–1672) was born in England and married at sixteen to Simon Bradstreet. She came to Ipswich and later to North Andover, Massachusetts, with her husband and her father, who became governor of the Massachusetts Bay Colony. Several editions of her *The Tenth Muse Lately Sprung up in America* have won her recognition, both in her own day and in the present, as a poet of natural and sincere talents.

Sam C. Brown, Jr., who now lives in Saratoga Springs, New York, has

265

spent many summers in camps in Maine. He has found freelance cartooning to his liking and writes occasionally for *Yankee* magazine and *Up Country*.

Constance Carrier (1908–) was born in New Britain, Connecticut, where she continues to live and where she taught Latin for many years in New Britain High School. Her poetry has been widely published in periodicals and has been gathered into two collections: *The Middle Voice*, for which she received the Lamont Poetry Prize in 1954, and *The Angled Road*. She has also completed two translations, *Poems of Propertius* and *Poems of Tibullus*. Her poetry is marked by grace and clarity.

John Cheever (1912–), born in Massachusetts, has won a National Book Award for his novel about a New England family, *The Wapshot Chronicle*. His short stories are also noteworthy; among these, *The World of Apples*, one of his recent collections, shows his sophisticated insight.

Edward Estlin Cummings (1894–1962), although he lived in New York and in other places, was born in Cambridge, Massachusetts, and educated at Harvard (B.A. and M.A.). He was both writer and painter, and he wrote prose and books for children as well as poetry. His works include: *The Enormous Room; CIOPW* (drawings and paintings); *i, six nonlectures; poems*. He avoided punctuation and capitalization in many of his poems, and he tended to be experimental, individualistic and personal in his poetry.

Emily Dickinson (1830–1886) was born in Amherst, Massachusetts, where she lived quietly at home except for such rare, early ventures as her education at Amherst Academy and Mount Holyoke Female Seminary (one year only). She wrote over one thousand brief lyrics of which only six were published during her lifetime. She brought intense insight to the domestic life about her, to the mutation of the seasons, and to the flowers in her garden. The extreme brevity she cherished was matched by her mastery of her craft. Her speculations on the timeless mysteries of love and death are ecstatic and deft. Many editions of her poems appeared after her death; the latest collection is *The Poems of Emily Dickinson*.

Richard Eberhart (1904–) was born in Austin, Minnesota, but much of his life has been spent in teaching and writing in Massachusetts and New Hampshire. He holds a B.A. from Dartmouth, B.A. Litt. and M.A. from Cambridge University, and has studied at Harvard. After his stint in the Navy, he combined teaching and writing with a venture as a businessman. A recipient of many awards, Richard Eberhart has been noted for the honesty, simplicity, and directness of his poetry.

266

Ralph Waldo Emerson (1803–1882) was born in Boston, Massachusetts, and later lived in Concord. A graduate of Harvard College and a student in its Divinity School, he was appointed a Unitarian minister after overcoming a pulmonary disease. He preached and lectured widely and became recognized by the distinguished thinkers of his day. His thought is considered the core of the Transcendental Movement: higher individuality, the spiritual nature of reality, the obedience to instinct, the obligation of optimism and hope, among other views. Such essays as "Self Reliance" and "Friendship" and such poems as "Each and All" and "The Rhodora" mark him as a major writer. His many lectures, essays, and poems appear in *The Complete Works*.

Mary E. Wilkins Freeman (1852–1930) was born in Randolph, Massachusetts, where she spent much of her life until she married in 1902. Her tales are chiefly of New England rural life. She describes local characters and she studies "repressed people in a decaying social system." She is adept at portraying the spirit of these people through dialect. She excelled in writing short stories, although she wrote some novels. *A New England Nun* and *Edgewater People* are two of her short story collections; *Pembroke* and *The Heart's Highway* are two of her novels.

Robert Lee Frost (1874–1963), although born in San Francisco, has always been a New Englander, as his father was. He tried his varied trades in Massachusetts, Vermont, and New Hampshire, and his poems reflect these experiences. He studied at Dartmouth and Harvard and taught and lectured in many colleges. A recipient of Pulitzer prizes as well as many other awards, Frost is considered a major American poet. His poetry, such as *A Witness Tree* and *Aforesaid*, reveals him as a penetrating writer who points out the deeper meanings in the commonplace.

Margaret Fuller (1810–1850) was born at Cambridgeport, Massachusetts, and was educated by her father. Because of her forceful and brilliant mind, she established close ties with thinkers who became known as the Transcendentalists. She exerted a strong influence upon people in Boston's most cultivated circles; from discussions with them emerged her *Woman in the Nineteenth Century*, the first mature consideration of feminism by an American. As a penetrating journalist, Margaret Fuller edited the influential magazine, *The Dial*, voice of the Transcendentalists, reported on America's western life after a visit to Chicago, and worked on the staff of the New York *Tribune* for two years before setting out for Italy. There she married the Marquis Ossoli and became active in the Italian Revolution. When she was returning to the United States with her husband and young son, her boat was shipwrecked off Fire Island and she and her family were drowned. Her other works include *Papers on Literature and Art* and *At Home and Abroad*.

Notes About Authors

Isabella Stewart Gardner (1915–   ), although she is currently listed as a California writer, was born in Newton, Massachusetts, and in her writing, reflects the influence of New England. She studied at the Leighton Rollins School of Acting, East Hampton, New York, and at the Embassy School of Acting, London. She was associate editor, with Karl Shapiro, of *Poetry* magazine. She combines two careers—as professional actress and as an occasional reader for publishers. Among her books of verse are *Birthdays from the Ocean, The Looking Glass*, and *West of Childhood*. Her poems, written with honesty and precision, celebrate and affirm life. She has a "gift for the gestures of language."

Donald Hall (1928–   ), Connecticut born poet, studied at Harvard and Oxford Universities. His *Exiles and Marriages* won the Newdigate Prize (1952). He has taught both at Harvard and at the University of Michigan and is now living in New Hampshire. In his earlier work, he is somewhat traditional in meter and rhythm, but he becomes freer in technique in *A Roof of Tiger Lilies*. His prose works include a realistic evocation of his summers on his grandparent's farm in New Hampshire.

Nathaniel Hawthorne (1804–1864), remained closely associated with his birthplace, Salem, Massachusetts, but he also lived in Concord, Massachusetts, Liverpool, England (as U.S. consul), and Italy. The pervasive effect of Puritanism on New England culture resulting in the decadence that he observed formed the central theme of his stories and novels. With Edgar Allan Poe, Hawthorne developed the short story as a literary genre. He earned his livelihood variously as writer, editor, surveyor of the Port of Salem, and U.S. consul. Important among his collections of short stories and tales are *Twice Told Tales* and *Mosses from an Old Manse;* his novels include *The House of the Seven Gables, The Scarlet Letter*, and *The Marble Faun.*

Maureen Howard (1930–   ), was born in Bridgeport, Connecticut. Although she has not remained in New England (she presently lives in New York), she recognizes the influence of New England on her writing. Graduated from Smith College, she has worked in publishing and in teaching and has served both as a Guggenheim and a Radcliffe Institute Fellow. She has written both fiction and drama, including *Bridgeport Bus, Before My Time*, and *Facts of Life.*

Sarah Orne Jewett (1849–1909), novelist and short story writer, was born in South Berwick, Maine, where she lived much of her life. Her father, a distinguished physician and medical lecturer at Bowdoin College, largely shaped her life, her personality, and her style of writing. She lived intensely in her own time and place, and she observed accurately the people around her: *Deephaven* and *The*

Country of The Pointed Firs reflect her concern for the old, the odd, and the eccentric.

Maxine Kumin (1925–), born in Philadelphia, became a resident of New England through her education at Radcliffe College and her teaching at Tufts University, Newton College of the Sacred Heart, and the University of Massachusetts. Currently she is running a farm in New Hampshire. Her poetry has won many awards, including the Pulitzer Prize, the Eunice Tietjens Memorial Prize, and the William Marion Reedy Award. Among her poetry collections are *The Nightmare Factor* and *Up Country*. A recent novel is *The Designated Heir*. Her writing exhibits precision of language, strength of purpose, and diversity of themes.

Amy Lowell (1874–1925) lived most of her life in her birthplace, Brookline, Massachusetts. Born of a famous family—she was related to James Russell Lowell, distinguished American poet and critic—she was a Brahmin in the fullest sense of that epithet, for she had wealth, culture, and deep intellectual interests. Educated in private schools and through trips abroad, Amy Lowell became associated with the Imagist movement. She possessed an unrivalled talent for expressing sensuous impressions in word pictures with unrhymed cadences. Her work as a critic, biographer, and poet demonstrated the diversity of her talents. Among her writings are *Pictures of the Floating World* and *Legends* (both poetry); *A Critical Fable* (criticism); *John Keats*—a biography esteemed as one of the greatest about the poet.

Robert Lowell (1917–1977), the grandson of James Russell Lowell and relative of Amy Lowell, was born in Boston. Educated at Harvard and at Kenyon College, Robert Lowell taught at Harvard and Boston University and lived in many places, including England, but New England was the chief scene of his pursuit of the meaning of life. Many of his poems are autobiographical. He wrote with an awareness of the impact of words and a sensitivity to variety of form. His collections of poetry include *Lord Weary's Castle* (1946 Pulitzer Prize), *For the Union Dead*, *Life Studies*, *The Dolphins*, and *Day by Day*.

Archibald MacLeish (1892–), born in Illinois, received his LL.B. from Yale, after which he practiced law for a time. He became particularly sensitive to man's relation to society. During his life, he has held many important posts, such as Poetry Consultant to the Library of Congress, assistant Secretary of State, and Boylston Professor of Rhetoric at Harvard. Despite his early expatriation to Europe, and his sojourn in Washington, D.C., New England has been his chief home. He presently resides on a farm near Boston. His poetry has received several Pulitzer Prizes, the Bollingen Prize, and the National Book Award. A writer of drama for the stage, T.V., and radio, as well as of poetry and prose, MacLeish's work includes:

J.B. (awarded the 1958 Pulitzer Prize for drama), *Collected Poems* (1952 Pulitzer Prize), and *Poetry and Experience* (addresses). "A man of passion and compassion, a craftsman of integrity," Archibald MacLeish's writing has left its mark on twentieth-century literature.

David McCord [Thompson Watson] (1897–) graduated from Harvard and for many years was editor of the *Alumni Bulletin*. He has written many volumes of light verse; *Bay Window Ballads, On Occasion, Selected Poems,* and *The Old Bateau*. He is also the author of familiar essays collected in such books as *Oddly Enough, Stirabout,* and *About Boston*. More recently he has published many poems for children culminating in his latest collection, *One at a Time* (1977). He writes with a ready insight into the foibles of mankind.

Herman Melville (1819–1891), born in New York City, was educated by his experiences at sea, his teaching, and such activities as clerking in his brother's store. He not only sailed on both trading and whaling vessels, but he also lived in Tahiti and other islands of the South Seas. *Typee, Omoo,* and *White Jacket*, based upon his adventures, were highly successful and enabled Melville to enter the literary circles of New York and Boston. During his thirteen years of residence near Tanglewood, Massachusetts, nestled in the Berkshires, he met Nathaniel Hawthorne, who was his neighbor. In his own day, *Moby Dick*, now acknowledged his greatest novel, was not popular. His finest short stories, *The Piazza Tales*, were written during his stay in the Berkshires. He wrote one last novel, *Billy Budd,* before devoting his energies to poetry. For nineteen years, Melville worked in almost total obscurity as an outdoor customs inspector in New York. Not until 1920 were his works reassessed. He now is considered an outstanding writer of the sea and a master of realistic narrative as well as a shrewd social critic and philosopher.

William Meredith (1919–) was born in New York City and educated at Princeton. After serving as a teaching fellow at Princeton and a professor at the University of Hawaii, he joined the staff of Connecticut College, New London, where he still teaches. He has also taught at the Bread Loaf Writers' Conference in Vermont. He has won the Yale Series of Younger Poets Award, the Van Wyck Brooks Award, and a National Endowment of the Arts grant. He is Chancellor of the Academy of American Poets. Among his collections are *The Wreck of the Thresher and Other Poems* and *Earth Walk: New and Selected Poems*. In earlier volumes, he used formal patterns; his recent works employ a colloquial style.

James Merrill (1926–) was born in New York City and educated at Amherst College, Massachusetts. He has won many awards among which are the National Book Award and the Bollingen Prize. Currently he resides in Stonington,

Connecticut. *Braving the Elements* and *The Yellow Pages* are recent collections of his poetry. He has written both plays and fiction; *The (Diblos) Notebook* was his latest novel (1965). He uses fixed forms and free verse to write somewhat impersonally of death and birth and rebirth.

William Daniel Mundell (1913–   ) was born in South Newfane, Vermont, where he has lived much of his life. He has served as town selectman, district maintenance foreman for the state highway department, and is skilled in carpentry and stone masonry. A member of The Poetry Society of America, he was also assistant editor of *Poet Lore*. Widely published in major magazines, he has a number of books: *Hill Journey, Plowman's Earth*, and *Mundell Country*. His own photographs illustrate his collections of poetry which reflect insight into the Vermont country and the lives of rural people.

Howard Nemerov (1920–   ) was born in New York City and educated at Harvard. For eighteen years he taught at Bennington College, Vermont, and for a briefer time at Brandeis University, Waltham, Massachusetts. He is currently professor of English at Washington University, St. Louis. He has also served as Consultant in Poetry for the Library of Congress and associate editor of *Furiosa*. Among the many awards he has received are the Golden Rose of the New England Poetry Society, the Brandeis University Creative Arts Award, a Guggenheim Fellowship, and the Academy of American Poets Fellowship. His poetry includes *The Blue Swallows, The Winter Lightning, Gnomes and Occasions*. His fiction includes *The Homecoming Game* (a novel), and *Stories, Fables and Other Diversions* (short stories).

Eugene O'Neill (1888–1953), although born in New York City, lived in New London, Connecticut, and Marblehead and Boston, Massachusetts. He spent his early years traveling about with his actor parents; later he sailed the seas on various adventures. He attended both Princeton and Harvard and began writing as a cub reporter on the New London *Telegraph*. After recovering from tuberculosis, he started writing plays. His first play, *Bound East for Cardiff*, was produced by the Provincetown Theater. His early plays are marked by naturalism, but later works used symbolic expressionism and stream of consciousness techniques. Among his many plays are *Ah, Wilderness, The Iceman Cometh*, and *A Long Day's Journey into Night*. He won three Pulitzer Prizes and the Nobel Prize.

Francis Parkman (1823–1893), member of a prominent Boston family and a graduate of Harvard Law School, was fascinated by frontier life. He suffered poor health throughout his life, but he attempted to strengthen his constitution by journeying to Wyoming and observing frontiersmen and Indians. *The Oregon Trail* was

271

the result. Despite bad eyesight, he completed a series of histories about the French and English struggle for colonial America in such books as *Pioneers of France in the New World* and *Montcalm and Wolfe*. Seeking a cure for a nervous condition, he journeyed to Europe where he developed an interest in horticulture which resulted in *The Book of Roses* and a subsequent appointment as professor of horticulture at Harvard. His lost journals, containing exciting accounts of his explorations of the new frontier, were at last printed in 1948. His works are accurate as history and important as literature.

Ann Petry (1911–), born in Old Saybrook, Connecticut, to professional parents, attended the College of Pharmacy, University of Connecticut, and worked in drugstores in Lyme and Old Saybrook. After her marriage Ann Petry lived in Harlem where she worked on two Harlem newspapers. Meanwhile, at Columbia University she took a course in writing the short story. Her novel, *The Street*, won the 1945 Houghton Mifflin Fellowship Award. Her stories attempt to point up the similarities between Harlem people and all others. Her novels have continued to probe the dramatic and emotional problems of blacks in race conflict and have been given high praise for their artistic merit. *The Narrows* is one of her recent works. At present Ann Petry has returned to Old Saybrook.

Edward Arlington Robinson (1869–1935), was born in Gardiner, Maine, and studied at Harvard. Although he was employed at one time, like Hawthorne, in a customs house in New York City, his subject matter revolves around Tilbury Town, the Gardiner of his birth. In a dry, Yankee manner, he wrote short, incisive portraits of his townspeople. His poems are often dramatic monologues in their technique: *The Children of the Night, The Torrent and the Night Before,* and *The Town Down the River*. After 1910 he was able to give his attention solely to his writing, often at the McDowell Colony in Peterborough, New Hampshire. He also wrote plays—*Van Zorn*, a comedy, and *The Porcupine*, a tragedy. His collection of poetry, *Man against the Sky*, suggests his pessimistic view of life. He had a deep sense of the tragedy of life in a chaotic world. Some of his later work is found in *King Jasper, Collected Sonnets* (1889–1927), and *Collected Poems*.

May Eleanor Sarton (1912–), born in Belgium, arrived in the United States when her father became a professor at Harvard. Her formal education was at Shady Hill School and Cambridge High and Latin. She chose Eva La Gallienne's Civic Repertory Theater as her way to continue her training in the theater. She has worked at many jobs, among them film scriptwriter at the Office of War Information, and lecturer on poetry at Wellesley and several other colleges. The subjects of her poetry are derived from her close study of places—she has lived in Europe; Cambridge, Massachusetts; Nelson, New Hampshire; and presently in York,

Maine. Her poetry includes *A Durable Fire* and *Collected Poems* (1930–1973); her novels include *Kinds of Love* and *As We Are Now;* her autobiographical works include *I Knew a Phoenix, Plant Dreaming Deep,* and *Journal of a Solitude.*

Anne Sexton (1928–1974) was born in Newton, Massachusetts, and educated at Garland Junior College, Boston, and at Radcliffe Institute, Cambridge, Massachusetts. She taught creative writing at Boston University and was appointed Cranshaw Professor of Literature, Colgate University. Besides the Pulitzer Prize for Poetry, she received, among other awards, the Bread Loaf Writers' Conference Robert Frost Fellowship, the Shelley Memorial Award, and a Guggenheim Fellowship. Among her books of poetry are *The Book of Folly, The Death Notebooks,* and *The Awful Rowing Towards God* (published posthumously). She wrote a play, *Mercy Street,* and several children's books. Her poetry explored the private areas of experience with frankness and insight. She used strict forms that varied from poem to poem.

Wallace Stevens (1879–1955) was born in Reading, Pennsylvania, lived a portion of his life in New York City, and then in 1916 moved to Hartford, Connecticut, where he was associated with an insurance company. He studied at Harvard; then, while working as a reporter in New York, won his law degree at New York Law School and was admitted to the bar in 1904. He was awarded the Bollingen Prize in Poetry, the National Book Award in Poetry twice, and the Pulitzer Prize in Poetry. He is considered one of the truly significant contemporary American poets. He wrote more than ten volumes of poetry during his business life; among these are *Ideas of Order, The Man With the Blue Guitar,* and *The Necessary Angel.* His daughter, Holly Stevens, edited the posthumous volumes, *Letters of Wallace Stevens,* and *The Palm at the End of the Mind.*

Edward Taylor (1644–1729), though born in England, came to Boston and graduated from Harvard. He served as pastor and physician in the Massachusetts frontier town of Westfield. Only in 1937, when his poems were first published from a recently discovered manuscript, was he recognized as a poet of high importance. He wrote graceful, sensitive verse in the tradition of such English metaphysical poets as George Herbert and Henry Vaughan, but his point of view about God and man is distinctly that of a Puritan. Papers at Yale University afforded data for a comprehensive edition of his *Poems* in 1960. Some of his sermons and preparatory meditations in verse were edited as *Christographia.*

Henry David Thoreau (1817–1862) was born in Concord, Massachusetts, of French, Scottish, Quaker, and Puritan stock. He had a scientific understanding of nature, but as a Transcendentalist, he wanted more the "wideness of heaven than

273

the limit of the microscope." Educated at Harvard, he taught school for a while, gave lyceum lectures, and worked as a surveyor and pencilmaker. Since he was plagued by tuberculosis, many of his accomplishments were achieved with a struggle. He traveled on several occasions to Cape Cod, Canada, the Great Lakes, and Mississippi. Always the individual, he became a champion of the independence of others. *Walden*, or *Life in the Woods* lucidly expressed his controversial attitude toward modern civilization and his response to its demands. His keen interest in the Abolitionist Movement prompted his finest speeches among which his "Plea for Captain John Brown" is one of the most memorable. Although only *Walden* and *A Week on the Concord and Merrimack Rivers* were published during his lifetime, his volumes of journals became the basis for a number of posthumously published books. As recently as 1958, *Consciousness in Concord,* the text of a lost journal, appeared. His *Collected Poems* (1943) and *Correspondence* (1958) add further testimony to his originality as a thinker and writer.

Newton F. Tolman (1908–   ), native of Nelson, New Hampshire, lives in a large hunting lodge on the highest point of the town, where, on his thousand acre farm, he pursues his varied activities of writing, guiding hunters, tree farming, fishing, playing for country dances, and giving sage advice to summer folk and natives alike. He writes for the *Berkshire Eagle, Yankee* magazine, the *Atlantic* magazine and other periodicals. He has published two books of essays, *North of Monadnock,* and *Our Loons are Always Laughing.* He has written several town histories and a biography, *The Search for General Miles.* He is also an expert on square dancing and has published a collection of Nelson Contra dance music, as well as *Quick Tunes and Good Times,* a book of recollections about dancing. He is noted for his wry humor and shrewd observance of life in the New Hampshire uplands as it was and is today.

John Updike (1932–   ), born in Pennsylvania, was graduated from Harvard and now resides near Georgetown, Massachusetts. The New England scene figures importantly in many of his stories, particularly those about New Yorkers who make the area their residence or summer home. Among his novels are *Rabbit Run, The Centaur,* and *Marry Me;* his short story collections include *The Same Door, Pidgeon Feathers,* and *Museums and Women.*

Edith Wharton [Newbold Jones] (1862–1937), a member of a distinguished New York family, was privately educated abroad. Much traveled, she made Paris, New York, Newport, Rhode Island, and Lenox, Massachusetts, her various homes. From her New England experiences, *Ethan Frome* emerged as her highest accomplishment in a tragic novel. *The Age of Innocence* won a Pulitzer Prize. Mrs. Wharton's short stories also gained wide recognition: *Crucial Instances, Tales of*

Men and Ghosts, and *Xingu and other Short Stories.* She tried in her stories always to consider what the character would make of the situation. She believed that every great novel should be based on "a profound sense of moral values."

E[lwyn] B[rooks] White (1899–   ) was born in Mt. Vernon, New York, and educated at Cornell University. He resided in New York for many years, but for longer his home has been in North Brooklin, Maine, where he wrote his column "One Man's Meat" for *Harper's.* From its earliest days in the 1920's, he has written for *The New Yorker.* A gifted poet and humorist, he is considered by many critics and readers "the finest essayist in the United States." He loves the woods and is most at home when away from city life. His books for children are justly famous: *Stuart Little, Charlotte's Web* and *The Trumpet of the Swan.* His essays have been collected in *The Second Tree from the Corner* and *One Man's Meat,* among other books; *Letters of E. B. White* appeared in 1976; *Essays of E. B. White* in 1977.

John Greenleaf Whittier (1807–1892), born in Massachusetts of Quaker stock, was largely educated through his religion and his reading. At first an editor of a Boston newspaper and later of several county papers, Whittier wrote both prose and poetry. His *Legends of New England in Prose and Verse* illustrate his interest in local historic themes and the romance underlying the everyday life of rural New England. Because he was so strongly humanitarian, he devoted himself to the Abolitionist cause, at one time as a member of the Massachusetts legislature, at another as founder of the Liberty Party, and at another as the editor of *The National Era.* His finest poetry stemmed from his interest in the countryside: *Poems and Lyrics* (containing "Telling the Bees"), and *In War Time and other Poems.* He wrote his greatest poem, *Snow-Bound,* after the Civil War. For a time his work was neglected, but in recent years, scholars have again given high recognition to the best that he has written.

Richard Wilbur [Purdy] (1921–   ), born in New York, attended Amherst College and Harvard where he taught until he joined the staff at Wesleyan University in Connecticut, where he presently teaches. His writing career began with the mature and polished lyrics of *The Beautiful Changes.* Always intellectual, and at times witty, he writes in a classic style. He won the Pulitzer Prize for his volume of *Poems,* 1957. He has also received the Harriet Monroe and Oscar Blumenthal prizes from *Poetry* magazine. His most recent collection is *The Mind Reader.* His translations of Moliere's *Misanthrope* and *Tartuffe* became successful on the New York stage in 1977; he also wrote the lyrics for the comic opera, *Candide.*

(continued from page iv)

Copyright © Richard Eberhart 1976. Reprinted by permission of Oxford University Press, Inc.

DONALD HALL, "The Blueberry Picking." Reprinted by permission of Curtis Brown, Ltd. Copyright © 1960, 1961 by Donald Hall. "The Sleeping Giant." Reprinted by permission of Curtis Brown, Ltd. Copyright © 1955 by Donald Hall. First appeared in *The New Yorker*.

ROBERT LOWELL, "Grandparents," from *Life Studies* by Robert Lowell, Copyright © 1956, 1959 by Robert Lowell. Reprinted with the permission of Farrar, Straus & Giroux, Inc.

GERALD BRACE, "Boats" is reprinted from *Between Wind and Water,* by Gerald Warner Brace, with the permission of W. W. Norton & Company, Inc. Copyright © 1966 by Gerald Warner Brace.

ISABELLA GARDNER, "Summer Remembered." From *The Looking Glass* (Chicago: Chicago University Press, 1961). Used by permission of the author and The University of Chicago Press.

NEWTON TOLMAN, "Nature Calling." From *Our Loons Are Always Laughing* by Newton Tolman. Reprinted by permission of the author.

JAMES MERRILL, "Willowware Cup." From *Braving the Elements* by James Merrill. Copyright © 1969, 1972 by James Merrill. This poem appeared originally in *Harper's Magazine*. Reprinted by permission of Atheneum Publishers.

EMILY DICKINSON, "A Route of Evanescence." From *The Complete Poems of Emily Dickinson,* edited by Thomas H. Johnson (Boston: Little, Brown and Company, Inc., 1935).

ARCHIBALD MACLEISH, "Night Watch in the City of Boston," from *New and Collected Poems 1917–1976* by Archibald MacLeish. Copyright © 1976 by Archibald MacLeish. Reprinted by permission of Houghton Mifflin Company.

E. B. WHITE, "Walden-June 1939." From *One Man's Meat* by E. B. White. Copyright 1939 by E. B. White. Reprinted by permission of Harper & Row, Publishers, Inc.

MAY SARTON, "All Day I Was With Trees" is reprinted from *Collected Poems, 1930–1973,* by May Sarton, with the permission of W. W. Norton & Company, Inc. Copyright © 1974 by May Sarton.

MAXINE KUMIN, "Stones" from *Up Country* by Maxine Kumin. Copyright © 1972 by Maxine Kumin. Reprinted by permission of Harper & Row, Publishers, Inc.

JOHN CHEEVER, "The Summer Farmer," Copyright © 1948 by John Cheever, reprinted by permission of the author.

WILLIAM MUNDELL, "Private Transaction." Reprinted by the permission of The Stephen Greene Press from *Plowman's Earth,* copyright © 1973 by William D. Mundell.

AMY LOWELL, "Meeting-House Hill," from *The Complete Poetical Works of Amy Lowell.* Copyright 1955 by Houghton Mifflin Company. Reprinted by permission of Houghton Mifflin Company.

HENRY BESTON, "Night on the Great Beach," from *The Outermost House* by Henry Beston, copyright 1928, 1949 by Henry Beston. © renewed by Henry Beston, 1956. Reprinted by permission of Holt, Rinehart and Winston, Inc.

WILLIAM MEREDITH, "At the Natural History Museum." From *Hazard the Painter,* by William Meredith. Copyright © 1971, 1973, 1974, 1975 by William Meredith. Reprinted by permission of Alfred A. Knopf, Inc.

HOWARD NEMEROV, "The Mud Turtle," from *The Blue Swallow* (Chicago: University of Chicago Press, 1967). Reprinted by permission of the author.

276

Acknowledgments

EMILY DICKINSON, "A Visitor in Marl." Reprinted by permission of the publishers and the Trustees of Amherst College from *The Poems of Emily Dickinson*, edited by Thomas H. Johnson, Cambridge, Mass.: The Belknap Press of Harvard University Press, Copyright © 1951, 1955 by the President and Fellows of Harvard College; and Copyright 1935 by Martha Dickinson Bianchi. Copyright © 1963 by Mary L. Hampson. By permission of Little, Brown and Co.

ROBERT FROST, "For Once, Then, Something" and "The Vanishing Red." From *The Poetry of Robert Frost* edited by Edward Connery Lathem. Copyright 1916, 1923, © 1969 by Holt, Rinehart and Winston. Copyright 1944, 1951 by Robert Frost. Reprinted by permission of Holt, Rinehart and Winston, Publishers.

EUGENE O'NEILL, "The Rope." Copyright 1919 and renewed 1947 by Eugene O'Neill. Reprinted from *The Plays of Eugene O'Neill*, by Eugene O'Neill, by permission of Random House, Inc.

DAVID MCCORD, "Go Fly A Saucer." Copyright 1953 by David McCord. From *The Old Bateau and Other Poems*, by David McCord, by permission of Little, Brown and Co.

EDITH WHARTON, "Bewitched." Reprinted with the permission of Charles Scribner's Sons from *The Ghost Stories of Edith Wharton* by Edith Wharton. Copyright 1925 The Pictorial Review Company.

ANNE SEXTON, "The Fury of Flowers And Worms," from *The Death Notebooks*. Copyright © 1974 by Anne Sexton. Reprinted by permission of Houghton Mifflin Company.

WALLACE STEVENS, "The River of Rivers in Connecticut." Copyright 1954 by Wallace Stevens. Reprinted from *The Collected Poems of Wallace Stevens*, by Wallace Stevens, by permission of Alfred A. Knopf, Inc.

E.E. CUMMINGS, "All in green went my love riding." Copyright 1923, 1955 by e. e. cummings. Reprinted by permission of Liveright Publishing Co.

CONSTANCE CARRIER, "Martha Carrier, 1669–1692." © Constance Carrier, 1973. Reprinted by permission of The Swallow Press, Inc.

SAM C. BROWN, JR., "The Lesson." Reprinted with permission from *A Treasury of New England Short Stories from Yankee Magazine*, published by Yankee, Inc., Dublin, N.H., 1974.

LOUISE BOGAN, "Women," from *The Blue Estuaries* by Louise Bogan. Copyright 1957, 1958, 1962, 1963, 1964, 1965, 1966, 1967, 1968 by Louise Bogan. Reprinted with the permission of Farrar, Straus & Giroux, Inc.

EDWIN ARLINGTON ROBINSON, "Mr. Flood's Party." Reprinted by permission of Macmillan Publishing Co., Inc. from *Collected Poems*, by Edwin Arlington Robinson. Copyright 1921 by Edwin Arlington Robinson, renewed 1949 by Ruth Nivison.

RICHARD WILBUR, "The Writer." Copyright © 1971 by Richard Wilbur. Reprinted from his volume *The Mind Reader* by permission of Harcourt Brace Jovanovich, Inc.

JOHN UPDIKE, "Man and Daughter in the Cold." Copyright © 1968 by John Updike. Reprinted from *Museums and Women and Other Stories*, by John Updike, by permission of Alfred A. Knopf, Inc.

ANN PETRY, "Solo on Drums" from *Miss Muriel and Other Stories* by Ann Petry. Copyright © 1971 by Ann Petry. Copyright 1945, 1947, 1958, 1963, 1965 by Ann Petry. Reprinted by permission of Houghton Mifflin Company.

PICTURE CREDITS

Page 8: Edward Hopper, *Lighthouse at Two Lights*. ca. 1927. Watercolor on paper. 13 15/16 x 20 inches. Collection of Whitney Museum of American Art, New York. Bequest of Josephine N. Hopper.

Page 24: Winslow Homer, *Gathering Autumn Leaves*. Collection The Cooper Union Museum, New York.

Page 58: John F. Kensett, *Shrewsbury River*. Courtesy of the New-York Historical Society, New York City. From the Robert L. Stuart Collection.

Page 69: *Clipper Ship Dreadnought*. Currier & Ives, lithograph, 1854(?). Courtesy of the New-York Historical Society, New York City.

Page 82: Statue of Sam Adams. Mike Maggaschi/STOCK, Boston.

Page 100: Village of Burke Hollow, Vt. Courtesy of Agency of Development & Community Affairs, Montpelier, Vermont.

Page 114: Winslow Homer, *The North Woods*. Courtesy The Currier Gallery of Art, Manchester, New Hampshire.

Page 122: Bath, New Hampshire. Earth Scenes/ © George F. Godfrey.

Page 127: John F. Kensett, *Beacon Rock, Newport Harbor*. Courtesy of National Gallery of Art, Washington, D.C. 20565.

Page 140: Portland, Maine. Fredrik D. Bodin/STOCK, Boston.

Page 165: A. C. Goodwin, *Mt. Vernon Street, Boston*. Courtesy Museum of Fine Arts, Boston. Bequest of John T. Spaulding.

Page 169: Winslow Homer, *A Winter-Morning—Shovelling Out*. From *Every Saturday*, January 14, 1871.

Page 191: Thomas Chambers, *The Connecticut Valley*. Courtesy National Gallery of Art, Washington, D.C. 20565.

Page 216: Fisherman. Ellis Herwig/STOCK, Boston.

Page 234: Childe Hassam, *Church at Old Lyme, Connecticut*. Courtesy Albright-Knox Art Gallery, Buffalo, N.Y. Albert H. Fracy Fund.

Page 252: Marsden Hartley, *Mt. Katahdin, 1941*. Hirshhorn Museum and Sculpture Garden, Smithsonian Institution.

Index

Index